ACTIVE LEARNING

While many educators acknowledge the challenges of a curriculum shaped by test preparation, implementing meaningful new teaching strategies can be difficult. *Active Learning* presents an examination of innovative, interactive teaching strategies that were successful in engaging urban students who struggled with classroom learning. Drawing on rich ethnographic data, the book proposes participatory action research (PAR) as a viable approach to teaching and learning that supports the development of multiple literacies in writing, reading, research and oral communication. As Wright argues, in connecting learning to authentic purposes and real-world consequences, participatory action research can serve as a model for meaningful urban school reform.

After an introduction to the history and demographics of the working-class West Coast neighborhood in which the described PAR project took place, the book discusses the "pedagogy of praxis" method and the project's successful development of student voice, sociopolitical analysis capacities, leadership skills, empowerment and agency. Topics addressed include an analysis and discussion of the youth-driven PAR process, the reactions of student researchers, and the challenges for adults in maintaining youth–adult partnerships. A thought-provoking response to current educational challenges, *Active Learning* offers both timely implications for educational reform and recommendations to improve school policies and practices.

Dana E. Wright is an Assistant Professor of Education at Connecticut College.

The Teaching/Learning Social Justice Series

Edited by Lee Anne Bell, Barnard College, Columbia University

ACTIVE LEARNING

Social Justice Education and Participatory
Action Research

Dana E. Wright

Routledge
Taylor & Francis Group

NEW YORK AND LONDON

First published 2015
by Routledge
711 Third Avenue, New York, NY 10017

and by Routledge
2 Park Square, Milton Park, Abingdon, Oxon OX14 4RN

Routledge is an imprint of the Taylor & Francis Group, an informa business

© 2015 Taylor & Francis

Library of Congress Cataloging-in-Publication Data
Wright, Dana E.
Active learning : social justice education and participatory action research /
by Dana E. Wright.
   pages cm. – (Teaching/learning social justice series)
   Includes bibliographical references and index.
   1. Active learning. 2. Action research. 3. Social justice–Study and teaching. I. Title.
   LB1027.23.W75 2015   371.3–dc23

ISBN: 978-1-138-82170-5 (hbk)
ISBN: 978-1-138-82171-2 (pbk)
ISBN: 978-1-315-74314-1 (ebk)

Typeset in Bembo
by Wearset Ltd, Boldon, Tyne and Wear

Printed and bound in the United States of America by Publishers Graphics, LLC on sustainably sourced paper.

CONTENTS

SERIES EDITOR INTRODUCTION

The Teaching/Learning Social Justice series explores issues of social justice—diversity, equality, democracy and fairness—in classrooms and communities. "Teaching/learning" connotes the essential connections between theory and practice that books in this series seek to illuminate. Central are the stories and lived experiences of people who strive both to critically analyze and challenge oppressive relationships and institutions, and to imagine and create more just and inclusive alternatives. My hope is that the series will balance critical analysis with images of hope and possibility in ways that are accessible and inspiring to a broad range of educators and activists who believe in the potential for social change through education and who seek stories and examples of practice, as well as honest discussion of the ever-present obstacles to dismantling oppressive ideas and institutions.

Active Learning: Social Justice Education and Participatory Action Research by Dana E. Wright beautifully illustrates the goals of this series through the vivid portrayal of youth engaged in participatory action research in their community in the United States. It makes a compelling case for the power of youth participatory action research (YPAR) as a vehicle for encouraging critical analysis and democratic action led by and grounded in the lives of young people in oppressed communities. We witness the impact of gentrification and marginalization through the eyes of youth living in one community in a West Coast city, a case that could stand in for many communities across the United States confronting similar economic forces and dislocations.

The book follows a group of young people as they learn YPAR methods from adult organizers from two community-based organizations. Using experiential, Freirean methods of critical consciousness-raising, the adults show young people how to utilize YPAR to study issues in their communities. The close description of the experiential training provides a useful manual for preparing young people to participate in YPAR activities. We see students learn interviewing and facilitation skills and then use these skills to conduct focus groups with other youth in their community. We see them learn critical methods for analyzing data and then collaboratively analyze the data they have collected to generate ideas and strategies for change. The rich qualitative description powerfully illustrates the methods through detailed examples of YPAR in action.

The story in this book highlights the capacities and strengths of young people and also delineates the oppressive structures and practices they are up against. The contrast between the capacities exhibited by these young people and their disaffection or lack of success in school is striking, raising challenging questions about why schools are so unable to draw out and cultivate such strengths in their students. Wright shows how some community organizations take up the slack by supporting youth in developing critical skills as researchers and activists and becoming active agents of change. The honest description of challenges for adults who seek to work as supportive allies with young people will be useful to those who seek to use this model in effective and empowering ways. The book is a valuable resource not only for community organizations, but also for teachers and schools who wish to learn about YPAR methods and to see them illustrated in practice.

Most importantly, the book shows in breathtaking detail young people developing their capacities and realizing their power to create change.

> The knowledge that human agency constructs reality is power—a power that has very specific education and development outcomes. Young people possessing critical knowledge of the true workings of their social contexts see themselves as intelligent and capable … For the first time, education is something students do—instead of something being done to them—to address the injustices that limit possibilities for them, their families, and communities.
>
> (Fine & Cammarota, 2008, p. 10)

This inspiring praxis is thrilling to witness.

Lee Anne Bell, Series Editor
October 2014

Reference

Fine, M., & Cammarota, J. (Eds.) (2008). *Revolutionizing education: Youth participatory action research in motion*. New York: Routledge.

ACKNOWLEDGMENTS

This book would not have been possible without the support of many people who contributed to this project in a variety of ways. I am enormously grateful to all of my colleagues, students, mentors, friends and family members who have shared their experiences and observations with me. These conversations have supported my thinking and writing process throughout this book project.

A special thank-you and sincere appreciation to all of the participants in my study: the student researchers, the two instructors and the affiliated organizations and their staff members who supported the young people's participatory action research project.

I would like to thank Lee Ann Bell, Routledge Series Editor for the Teaching/Learning Social Justice series, and Catherine Bernard, Senior Publisher at Routledge, for their incisive suggestions and for their belief in this project.

Profound thanks to those who read chapters of the manuscript at various stages and provided helpful comments: Lionel Howard, Ari Rotramel, Maria Hantzopoulos, Emma Sterrett, Anu Greenlee Cairo, Jen Weiss, Susie Lundy, Vajra Watson, Emily Ozer and Marie Varghese. I am especially grateful to Mark Warren, Jabari Mahiri and Donna San Antonio, who read an early draft of the entire manuscript and offered insightful suggestions. I also want to express my appreciation to my graduate school colleagues, all those involved in the Nia Project and in Youth in Focus, and my colleagues at Connecticut College.

I am immensely thankful to all those—too many to name here—who have supported and enriched this project at various stages through thoughtful discussions, encouragement and their belief in this work to amplify the voices of young people involved in collaborative inquiry projects for community change. Special thanks go to Sonya Childress, Ruth Tobar, Kenny Bailey, Najma

Nazy'at, Jozan Powel, Maria Brenes, Nisrin Elamin Abdelrahman, Octavia Raheem, Jemar Raheem, Linda Lamm, Justin Williams and Aleesha Taylor.

Special appreciation and thanks go to my family. I am deeply grateful to my partner, Bita Shooshani, who has read multiple drafts, provided observations and advice, and supported me through the research and writing process with encouragement, insight, humor, patience, kindness, wisdom and generosity. Your love and support helped make this book possible. I would like to honor and thank my parents, Penny and Howard Wright, for all of their love and invaluable support. Special thanks go to my brother, Emery Wright, for his encouraging and wise words, visionary work and for the ongoing conversations that keep me grounded and inspired. Thank you to the rest of my family: Joy Peters, Lydia Johns, Laurise Baylor-Lownes and all of my family in Washington, DC, Nancy Ann Tyner and all of my family in North Carolina and; Dea Devereaux, Shahin Safaei, Jessica Vafa and Anita Shooshani. I am thankful to my grandparents—Howard Emery Wright, Sr., Ann Wright and Ruth Powel— as well as my Aunt Beverly Wright Jackson, Aunt Adel Butts and Uncle Buddy Butts, Theodore Tyner and all of my ancestors—you will always be sources of inspiration.

1

INTRODUCTION

The current climate of high-stakes testing—and the resulting narrowed curric-ulum aimed primarily at preparing students for federally and state-mandated tests—has disengaged many students and frustrated countless teachers. Current federal and state education reform policies and their accompanying account-ability discourses mandate top-down, market-based, standardized testing pro-grams that define learning in terms of compartmentalized information recalled on tests. As a result, teachers are often held accountable when their students' performance on these high-stakes tests does not meet expectations. In light of these mandates, many teachers reported in a nationwide survey that they feel pressured to resort to teaching in ways that contradict their own views of sound teaching practices, even neglecting important but untested curriculum areas, in order to teach the content and format that will be on the tests (Abrams, Pedulla & Madaus, 2003). Such transmission models (Freire, 1970/2000) have reduced the incorporation of student voice and diminished the strategy of building upon students' prior knowledge and experiences in the classroom curriculum (Carter & Welner, 2013). The result has been fewer opportunities for students to learn in engaging contexts, the compromising of academic skills such as critical think-ing and high levels of student disengagement.

Yet in the midst of this trying policy environment, concerned teachers, researchers and school leaders are seeking teaching approaches that spark stu-dents' interests and promote a range of critical thinking skills. Many teachers and innovative school leaders are beginning to consider the successful teaching and learning practices not only in those pockets of equity and excellence inside schools, but also outside of school walls. Countless observers acknowledge that the same students who struggle to maintain interest and engagement in school are often able to learn new academic skills in non-school settings. Therefore, it is critical to understand the complex dynamics that yield student success outside of formal educational contexts. Particularly in underperforming schools in low-income neighborhoods and large urban districts that face mandates to increase student performance on standardized tests, an increasingly narrowed curriculum focusing on test preparation often differs from topics students are interested in learning about. While many underfunded and underperforming schools have struggled even harder to engage students, nearly all schools face high levels of student disengagement with learning. Indeed, across urban, suburban and rural U.S. schools districts, schools and teachers face difficulties engaging over two-thirds of high school students in classroom learning (Cothran & Ennis, 2000; Klem & Connell, 2004).

Troubling patterns of student disengagement in classroom learning have begun to challenge more traditional notions of teaching in which teachers select the topics for study and then design curriculum units without considering their relevance to students' interests and concerns. Since higher levels of engagement in learning correspond to higher levels of academic success regardless of socioeconomic status (Klem & Connell, 2004), student engagement is a fundamental concern in the pursuit of academic success for all students. While schools struggle to engage students, research finds that student engagement is responsive to teacher's actions (Cothran & Ennis, 2000). Teaching approaches and curricula that generate student interest and investment incorporate student concerns and perspectives, consider student explanations, build student ownership of content and offer tools to engage students as active interpreters of knowledge and their own experiences to construct meanings (Newman & Schwager, 1992). Student engagement is contingent upon student–teacher relationships, the teaching strategies and curriculum executed by the instructor, and the relevance of the learning content to the students (Bundick, Quaglia, Corso & Haywood, 2014). Therefore, in order to engage students it is important to examine the learning content and curriculum that students find to be responsive to their interests as well as to examine effective teaching strategies and methods to build strong student–teacher relationships.

In addition to low student engagement rates, the nationwide graduation rates are noticeably lower for economically disadvantaged students and Black, Latino and Native American students (U.S. Department of Education, 2014). Scholars have reframed the notion of school dropouts by terming them "push-outs" to bring attention to explicit and implicit push-out practices in which public schools, under pressure from federal and state mandates, push out students who would not perform well on state-mandated high school exit exams (Fine & Jaffe-Walter, 2007; Tuck, 2012). Noguera (2014) asserts that "education policy has focused on raising academic standards and increasing accountability but largely ignored the social and economic conditions that impact school environments and learning opportunities for students" (p. 115). In contrast, recent scholarship on the achievement gap—disparities in school achievement between incomes and racial groups—has shifted the focus from the outcomes of unequal educational practices to the inequities in educational inputs and resources between high- and low-income neighborhoods and schools (Boykin & Noguera, 2011; Noguera & Wing, 2006; Rothstein, 2004). Deindustrialization and the flight of capital from racially segregated urban neighborhoods with a high concentration of poverty (Noguera, 2014) have resulted in a marked structural disinvestment in these neighborhoods and their schools. The structural disinvestment in these neighborhoods and schools has led to a range of disparities between high- and low-income neighborhoods and the schools nested within them. Some scholars have termed the achievement gap "the opportunity gap" to illuminate the accumulated disparities in access to educational resources to support learning: high-quality curriculum, personalized attention, quality teachers and educational materials (Carter & Welner, 2013; Darling-Hammond, 2010; Fine, Torre, Burns & Payne, 2007; Milner, 2010).

Despite the attention that has been paid to the reform of education, these reform strategies have not effectively addressed the public education crisis or improved public schools in low-income communities. The consistent failure of public schools in low-income communities is both a civil rights issue and a social justice issue that demands that communities build power to participate in democratic efforts to work towards educational justice and shape their futures (Warren & Mapp, 2011). Demonstrating the growing, emergent field of alliances between public schools and community-based organizations, Warren (2005) finds that successful urban school reform must be linked to community revitalization, political strategies that address the structures of poverty, and urban social change. Warren and Mapp (2011) find that low-income communities across the country composed of educators, young people and parents are establishing new models for collaborative work that addresses inequities in education, work towards educational and social justice, and improve the quality of the education in their communities. Along these lines, Darling-Hammond (2010) asserts that the struggle for equality in education has

> concerned not only access to schooling but access to an empowering form of quality education—one that can enable people to think critically and powerfully, to take control of the course of their own learning, and to determine their own fate—rather than merely to follow dictates prescribed by others.
>
> (p. 28)

The participatory action research (PAR) curriculum and teaching approaches outlined in this book offer a viable, democratic approach to building powerful youth–adult partnerships to participate in community change efforts for an empowering quality education, educational equity and social justice.

Overview of the Central Youth United Participatory Action Research Project

Responding to contemporary educational challenges, this book discusses components of the innovative curriculum and teaching model that successfully engaged students to develop their academic skills through a collaborative inquiry project. Facilitated with students of color in a community-based setting within their working-class, urban neighborhood, this curriculum was designed to impact their surrounding environment concerning topics that students identified as relevant to their lives. The teaching strategy situated learning within a participatory action research (PAR) project with youth, in which young people research a pressing issue and then develop a community action project to address it.

For example, in the case examined in this work, secondary school students created a research question, "What do young people really need in our neighborhood?" Then, with the support of their two instructors, they designed a research project to collect and analyze data to find the answer to this question and present it to community decision-makers. The students found that their neighborhood needed a youth center to house youth development programming, homework clubs and a computer lab. The youth team presented their findings at a community forum attended by over 60 youth advocates and community organizers and organized a Youth Task Force to commit to following up on their recommendations to build a youth center within three to five years.

One factor behind the success of the curriculum is that the curriculum goals—to actively work collectively towards community improvement—aligned with young people's values and visions to help their community and they were enthusiastic about being involved. For example, Victor, one of the members of the PAR team, understood the main purpose of the PAR project: to gather data to illuminate community needs and to use that data as a tool to guide their actions in working towards community change. Victor was motivated to participate because he wanted to gather information to help the youth team change things to improve his neighborhood community. He explained further that he returned to the project every week because he liked helping other young people and helping to improve his neighborhood by collecting and using data for community change. This collaborative inquiry project involved young people in planning as well as receiving and responding to expert feedback. The curriculum further demanded that students expand their strategic thinking capacities to attain goals within authentic contexts that posed complex challenges of a kind that youth typically do not have the support to engage in school settings. The book argues that the key to engagement, particularly for working-class youth, immigrant youth and youth of color, is a process that extends their structural analysis of asymmetrical power relations and the social and economic inequalities in the larger society that are reflected in its institutions, while also meeting young people's needs to contribute to improving their communities.

Researcher Location and Research Commitments

I was drawn to the research site in this study because Youth Voices was the only nonprofit organization nationally that engaged in youth-led PAR projects using a social justice pedagogy and curriculum that provided training, technical assistance and capacity-building support in PAR methods to schools, networks, community organizing groups, alliances, school districts and coalitions. My interests in curriculum theory and design, pedagogy, student engagement, urban education and the contexts of schooling were first sparked during my work as an English Language Arts teacher in two Bronx and Brooklyn public middle schools. As a public school teacher, I thought deeply about ways to design engaging curriculum and assignments that took into account the contexts of schooling that influence both opportunities for engaged learning and pedagogical approaches, which propelled me to enter graduate school to join a community of scholars seeking to improve the field of education. While pursuing my doctorate in education with a concentration in teaching and learning, I pursued questions of how teaching, learning environments and schools could be transformed to better support students. My interest in PAR grew out of my experiences working with the Nia Project, a positive youth development and community-building organization for Black high school and college students in Boston. As I am an African American woman and former public middle school teacher of largely Black and Latino students from working-class neighborhoods in Brooklyn and the Bronx, my research and professional commitments are to improve the learning opportunities and supports to build the knowledge, participation and agency within all students, with a particular focus on students of color, working-class students and students in urban environments. These commitments propelled me into the role of Executive Director for the Nia Project, where I collaborated with adult and youth staff to develop curriculum and youth leadership development programming and co-directed a teen center in Boston's Lower Roxbury/South End. I noticed that most of the young people who did not do well in high school were able to thrive in an asset-based youth development program focused on developing social analysis skills and community change work. Many of the students who had been labeled as "struggling" in schools successfully took on increasing leadership roles and responsibilities both within the organization and through participation in the public sphere, aiming to improve their institutions and environments.

Because I was simultaneously pursuing a doctorate in teaching and learning at the Harvard Graduate School of Education, these experiences and observations as a youth worker sparked my thinking about the curriculum and pedagogy of non-school learning settings that are successful with students who are disengaged in school. I examined asset-based pedagogies and pedagogical approaches, and identified participatory action research with youth as a viable and innovative approach to building critical analysis skills, agency and participation in community change initiatives.

Later in my trajectory as a researcher, these interests led me to search nationally for a youth-led PAR program that was known for its high-quality curriculum and pedagogy as well as its focus on social justice issues, and that operated at the higher tiers of Hart's (1992; 1997) ladder of youth participation (see Table 2.1 in Chapter 2, p. 25). I identified Youth Voices as organization that fit these criteria. Youth Voices explicitly used a social justice framework, used a popular education teaching approach and had almost 15 years of organizational experience operating at the highest tier of the youth participation continuum. I worked for nearly three years as a curriculum developer and trainer in youth-led PAR methods and supported community-based organizations, youth development programs and school districts in conducting PAR projects with young people.

When Youth Voices was contracted to provide curriculum development and instruction in PAR methods for the Central Youth United (CYU) project, I was drawn to select the CYU project for this study. The CYU project was appealing because the PAR project was affiliated with two youth development organizations, a community development center and a community organizing nonprofit organization, and took place in a neighborhood with a well-known history of activism and organizing for social justice. My role in this project was strictly as a researcher and observer of the process and the organizations affiliated with the study. The four organizations affiliated with the study, as well as the student researchers and two project instructors and coordinators, agreed to participate in my study of Central Youth United and its curriculum and pedagogy.

As an active scholar in pursuit of questions about successful curriculum and pedagogy in non-school settings for many years, I was eventually led to the questions guiding this study: What are the features of successful teaching approaches in community-based learning settings that are effective with students who struggle to succeed in schools? What are the benefits and drawbacks of employing PAR projects as an asset-based, participatory approach to teaching and learning? What are the tensions and possibilities that emerge in youth–adult partnerships designed to take collaborative action on social justice imperatives? What are the implications for secondary schools and classroom learning?

Research Methods and the Study Context

This book draws upon ethnographic data that was collected during the seven-month duration of the youth-led PAR project. Data for this study was collected through interviews with student researchers, interviews with adult instructors and other adults affiliated with the PAR project, focus groups, ethnographic observations, and archival data. All interviews were transcribed verbatim.

This book provides a reconceptualization of teaching approaches by considering active learning projects that engage students in working towards creating more just and equitable communities. It examines a participatory action research project with youth that was housed in the Central Community Development Center (CCDC), a community-based nonprofit organization located in Central, an urban, working-class neighborhood in a large West Coast city. Central's residents are predominately African American, Latino and Asian, and many families had recently migrated from the Philippines, Mexico and El Salvador. The goal of the CCDC's PAR project was first to assess the specific needs for community improvement and then to design an action plan to address these needs based on their recommendations. The CCDC formed a coalition with three other community-based nonprofit organizations with the goal of helping to implement the recommendations of the PAR project. One primary instructor facilitated the team of secondary school students through this collaborative inquiry-based project. In addition, the CCDC also hired a secondary instructor, a PAR trainer and consultant who provided training and technical assistance on the youth-led PAR method. Note that several terms are used in the literature to describe participatory action research (PAR) with young people, including youth participatory action research (YPAR) or "youth-driven" or "youth-led" participatory action research (PAR). This book uses these terms interchangeably.

The hands-on curriculum required the student researchers to share their input and participate at each step of the research design to: (1) select a community issue that mattered to them and craft a research question; (2) devise a research plan to learn more about the topic through surveys, focus groups, interviews or observations; (3) collect data; (4) analyze that data to draw findings and recommendations; and (5) present their research results to local decision-makers and work with them to take action to implement their recommendations.

In the pedagogical approach examined in this book, the instructors employed a curriculum designed to involve secondary school students in research project planning and receiving feedback and guidance from adult instructors to set and achieve goals that would have authentic consequences in the real world. More specifically, the curriculum and pedagogical approach studied in this case engaged young researchers in research design, selecting research methods, creating focus group questions, conducting focus groups, analyzing their collected data and drawing conclusions to present at a community forum. After meeting twice weekly, totaling four hours a week over a seven-month period, the project culminated when the PAR team convened a community forum at which the student researchers presented their research findings and recommendations for action steps to community decision-makers. Their audience consisted of over 60 community stakeholders: elected representatives, neighborhood residents, the media, other young people, adults who work in youth-serving nonprofit organizations and government agencies, community organizers, and philanthropists from foundations. The team's multimedia presentation was

filmed and included a formal PowerPoint presentation of their findings and recommendations, poster board displays, a slide show with a hip-hop music soundtrack, and a question-and-answer session with the audience. To answer their
research question, "What do young people really need in our neighborhood?"
the team analyzed their focus group data with children, youth and adults, and
found that the neighborhood needed a youth center where youth could be safe
and supported. Therefore, their recommendations and action plan called for
collaborative work with adults to secure funding and other resources to build a
neighborhood youth center. The youth research team's presentation sparked the
creation of a Youth Task Force composed of youth and adults. The Youth Task
Force used the findings and recommendations from the PAR project for the
youth center's program development and to draft a plan of action to secure a
teen center in the neighborhood slated to open within the following three to
five years.

The story of their research project's unfolding narrates the tale of a group of
largely under-performing and middle-performing students who became incredibly engaged in this project and developed transferable skills in research, writing,
reading, presentations and critical thinking. The facilitated learning project was
seen as relevant for the student researchers because it provided opportunities to
improve their community. Further, the two adult instructors supported these
students in taking on increasing responsibilities to build their leadership skills
and their capacities to become self-advocates. The curriculum design explored
in this book connects literacy development and research skill development to
learning for meaningful purposes with real-world consequences. When young
people are given meaningful responsibilities to work towards solutions to local
problems that directly impact their lives, such teaching approaches can generate
enthusiasm and engagement. This work explores the journey of a group of students who participated in a facilitated learning project that required them to
identify a real-world problem in their community, research the causes of the
problem, develop a plan to address it and collaborate with adults to take action.

Overview of the Book

The book's primary objective is to expand curriculum and pedagogical
approaches in schools to incorporate active learning approaches into curriculum
design and instruction. One benefit of this work is that it is grounded in rich
ethnographic descriptions of the teaching and learning approaches examined in
this case and provides both theoretical guidelines and practical applications for
teachers. This book can provide a resource to educators at a time when both
teachers and responsive school leaders are considering ways in which to draw
on successful teaching approaches beyond school walls and to make more meaningful connections between schools and the communities that surround them.
As teacher education programs become more aware of such innovative

approaches to engagement and the potential learning benefits from making connections between schools and communities, this book offers current and future teachers useful strategies to incorporate into their own teaching practices.

Drawing on rich ethnographic data, including observations, interviews and focus groups, this book argues that participatory action research is a viable approach to teaching and learning that supports the development of multiple literacies in writing, reading, research and oral communication. While most of these students struggled to learn in school, they were able to succeed in developing their academic identities and increasing their writing, research, reading and presentation skills through their involvement in the participatory action research (PAR) project. Features of the curriculum and teaching approaches in the PAR project studied in this case include: (1) learning apprenticeships that built on student researchers' assets, which enabled them to apply their existing knowledge and understandings of their social contexts to learning tasks; (2) project-based learning to conduct inquiry about "real-world" problems that affected young people and engaged community members, who had a stake in the project results; (3) scaffolded instruction in which student researchers engaged in increasingly challenging and complex academic tasks, with the instructor's support of tasks being gradually withdrawn as the students demonstrated proficiency; and (4) creating ownership over learning and extending students' academic identities in order for them to come to view themselves as capable students through engaging student researchers as researchers, readers, writers and problem-solvers.

While the aim of schools is to serve students, countless cycles of failed school reform policies have neglected to consider their voices and interests. Considering student perspectives about their own learning interests will help educators determine innovative teaching approaches that teach the ways that they learn best. Recently, both policymakers and practitioners have rekindled their interest in student voice and in creating collaborative learning projects designed to help improve the wider communities that schools are nested within. The central argument of the book is that PAR with students is a promising teaching strategy that connects learning to authentic purposes and real-world consequences, and provides an engaging and effective approach to teaching and learning that can serve as a model for meaningful urban school reform.

The book's main themes include the importance of meaningful learning purposes, building on students' assets, collaborative learning through applied learning exercises, and developing empowerment and ownership over learning. *Active Learning*'s argument is distinctive in that it broadens the unit of analysis from the individual barriers to student engagement to consider the learning context, the curriculum, student–teacher relationships, and teaching approaches as possible barriers and solutions. This book asserts that students are inspired to engage as readers, presenters and writers when the curriculum is responsive to student interests and concerns, and when the goal of the project is to involve students' participation in solving pressing problems within their school and neighborhood communities. *Active Learning* argues that the struggle for equality in education must focus on securing an engaging and empowering curriculum for all students that can promote critical thinking, student voice, ownership over learning, and agency to shape their own futures. Transformative education reform and effective curriculum design will not be successful without engaging students' interests and concerns.

This book aims to show the possibilities for successful active learning when learning is tied to meaningful purposes and real-world consequences. A growing body of research finds that the use of creative out-of-school pedagogies in school classrooms can support urban students' engagement and success in school (Fisher, 2007; see also Jocson, 2008). Similarly, the field of PAR with youth has made important contributions to our understanding of how this practice works, dilemmas to navigate and lessons learned (Cammarota & Fine, 2008). This work seeks to contribute research on curriculum, teaching and learning, and to present recommendations for policies and practices to strengthen youth work and improve teaching and learning in school classrooms. The book's primary objective is to expand curriculum and pedagogical approaches in schools to incorporate active learning approaches into curriculum design and instruction. The overarching purpose of the book is to show the possibilities of a collaborative, inquiry-based curriculum as a model for educational transformation.

Grounded in rich ethnographic descriptions of the teaching and learning approaches examined in this case, it provides both theoretical guidelines and practical applications for teachers. The purpose of this work is not to show outcomes, but to look carefully at teaching and learning processes in this case to understand how and why they work and to distill pedagogical principles that others can apply in similar or vastly different learning environments.

In this era of high-stakes testing and standardized curriculum in which policies and popular discourse often zero in on students' deficits—what they do not know and cannot do—this book presents a counternarrative that depicts students who are capable of participating in a responsive, engaging curriculum that builds upon their assets and is relevant to their priority concerns. Perhaps current and future teachers can draw upon these innovative and engaging teaching approaches to explore for themselves the benefits of PAR projects as part of new or existing efforts to connect the curriculum and classroom learning to the wider community as an effective inquiry-based approach to learning. My commitments as a researcher and scholar are to amplify the voices and efforts of young people—particularly marginalized young people—and their adult allies who are working together towards community change to strengthen schools and society. My hope is that this project contributes to the larger tapestry of education justice efforts by educators, students, organizers, youth workers, school leaders, policymakers, advocates and researchers whose work reflects a vision of strong communities supporting more equitable, whole and just schools.

Organization of the Book

Following this introduction, this book is organized into a further eight chapters. This introduction provides a framework for the book, describes the program studied and research methods, discusses researcher location and research commitments, and provides an overview of the book structure.

Chapter 2 argues that a participatory action research (PAR) curriculum and process can be used as a successful pedagogical approach, and discusses the features of PAR projects. It defines active learning and discusses PAR projects with youth as operating within the contexts of the youth discourses and adultism. It also discusses PAR as an asset-based pedagogy and the contexts of teaching and learning. This chapter describes the features of PAR projects with young people and potential benefits, and discusses PAR as a pedagogical strategy in the Central Youth United project.

Chapter 3 introduces the eight young people involved in the action research project and the two adult instructors who facilitated it, and also provides profiles of the nonprofit organizations affiliated with the participatory action research project. This chapter details the history and demographics of the Central neighborhood in which the PAR project took place, and provides a context for the five thematic chapters. It discusses the formation of several grassroots community organizing nonprofits during the mid-1990s that were created to fight the displacement resulting from the building boom of luxury condominiums and lofts in Central. Bringing together voices of the young people in the PAR project, voices of community organizers affiliated with the project, and perspectives from city planning materials, this chapter describes a range of perspectives with on gentrification, displacement and neighborhood shifts. The chapter also describes how and why the Central Youth United (CYU) PAR project began and the key actors and organizations involved in creating it. It also provides a descriptive account of the CYU project's trajectory from beginning to end.

Chapter 4 discusses the "pedagogy of praxis" method in the PAR project that connects reflection on local issues with action to address them. This chapter examines young people's motivation for joining the project, revealing that when the project's purpose and goals align with young people's values and visions to improve their community, they become committed and actively participate in the project. Chapter 4 explains young people's motivations for committing to this project: to be a part of something larger than they are as individuals and to work towards benefiting their community. It also analyzes young people's participation and learning in the CYU project. I discuss the PAR process as a teaching approach that provided participatory, structured activities that centered young people's input and analysis to design and plan the PAR project. The chapter also illuminates young people's responses to aspects of the curriculum such as team-building and other positive youth development strategies that intended to build safety and trust. It discusses the adult role in supporting youth voice and leadership through structured opportunities for youth input on key decision points in project design, planning and implementation. Finally, it shows that increasing young people's voice and empowerment are factors in expanding young people's agency and ownership over their learning.

Chapter 5 provides an analysis and discussion of the youth-led PAR process in which learning was situated in the young people's applied learning project and how it influenced their participation as decision-makers, leaders and change agents. In this chapter, I consider the ways in which student researchers participate in a collaborative decision-making process and analyze the factors involved in collective decisions: peer mentorship, group accountability, agency and ownership. The chapter illuminates student researchers' emergent conceptions of decision-making, leadership, shared power and youth-led processes. I examine the collective, relational nature of leadership that emerged in the project. The chapter reveals the development of a sense of accountability to other group members and personal ownership over the process. In this chapter, I describe young people's engagement in teaching approaches that provide structured, interactive activities that center dialogue and students' prior knowledge to scaffold leadership skills in project design, planning and implementation. The chapter reveals some of the structural factors that were present to support a space for relational leadership and the adult role in promoting project ownership. I discuss the relationship between creating a learning environment supportive of relational leadership and the influence this setting had on student researchers' development of a sense of ownership over the project. The chapter demonstrates that this curriculum design also built student researchers' sense of accountability to their community and motivated them to use their action research findings in the service of community improvement.

Chapter 6 explores the ways in which the pedagogical goals for community improvement relate to the project's successful development of student voice, sociopolitical analysis capacities, leadership skills, empowerment and agency. It examines the ways in which the instructors intended to support the students in developing their sociopolitical analysis skills through curriculum activities that connected their personal experiences of sociopolitical inequities to larger sociopolitical forces. In describing the ways in which these activities enabled vulnerability and risk-taking, the chapter discusses the process through which students developed their capacities to analyze sociopolitical forces and contradictions by drawing from their personal experiences.

Chapter 7 describes the student researchers' reaction to the culminating event of the project in which they presented their findings to over 60 community stakeholders at a community forum. It also identifies effective strategies the instructors used in two instances where they successfully intervened to address conflicts between student researchers that negatively impacted the group's abilities to engage in effective teamwork. The chapter then discusses the concepts of "power over" versus "power with" in analyzing the PAR process.

Chapter 8 illustrates some of the challenges adults faced in maintaining youth–adult partnerships to support youth-led learning projects. This chapter presents an analysis of the barriers, tensions and dilemmas in supporting all student researchers' participation. It discusses the dilemmas and challenges for instructors in attempting to share power and project ownership with young people in PAR projects, while still maintaining appropriate intervention and guidance when they fail to meet group expectations and group needs for the group to be functional. The analysis emphasizes the importance of clear boundaries, consistent consequences, direct communication and discussion to address conflicts, and the need for supportive, reflective space within group processes. In describing the tenuous power balances between youth and adults, the chapter examines the delicate, nuanced nature of youth–adult partnerships to support PAR projects. Rather than place the onus solely on the student researchers or solely on the two instructors, it aims to uncover the tensions that exist in youth–adult partnerships that aim to share power with young people. I analyze the systemic issues of project design, planning and assessment, which provided some barriers to full youth participation in maintaining youth–adult partnerships. The chapter provides an analysis of elements of curriculum design and structure that could be addressed to effectively support student-led learning initiatives. The discussion contributes to understanding the emerging trend in practices striving for "youth-driven" and "youth-led" teaching approaches supported by youth–adult partnerships.

Chapter 9 considers the key themes in the book within broader considerations. It underscores the importance of a pedagogy and curriculum that are relevant to students' interests, that promote analytical thinking, applied learning, student ownership and decision-making, and that carry a meaningful purpose. I consider the broader implications of the PAR case explored in the book and the benefits and limitations of PAR as an approach to teaching and learning. The chapter illustrates the lessons learned in this case and how they can be applied more broadly to any educational setting. I then discuss the implications of this case for classroom teaching and consider implications for school policies and practices. The chapter concludes with implications for educational reform and recommendations to improve school policies and practices.

2

PARTICIPATORY ACTION RESEARCH (PAR) WITH YOUTH AS PEDAGOGY

Introduction

This book argues that ensuring that the curriculum is relevant to students' interests and concerns, promotes critical thinking and carries a meaningful purpose may be crucial to increasing student engagement and successful learning in school. It presents an examination of innovative, interactive teaching strategies that were successful in engaging urban students who struggled to learn in more traditional teaching approaches in classrooms. The book contends that a curriculum that is relevant to students' interests, concerns and experiences, and carries a meaningful purpose to positively impact their wider environments, increases student engagement and successful learning. It describes an engaging curriculum that involves students in participatory inquiry projects that probe real-world issues in their local communities, identify possible solutions and, on the basis of their findings and recommendations, take collective action to address these issues. This book connects the conceptual argument for such a teaching approach with an accessible description of the teaching strategies involved and discusses implications for classroom teaching and learning. It examines participatory action research (PAR) with young people to illustrate the possibilities and principles embedded in an innovative approach to teaching and learning.

This chapter discusses PAR as a pedagogical approach and curriculum that builds on critical youth studies, asset-based pedagogies and culturally relevant pedagogy. The chapter also discusses the benefits of this approach to teaching and learning. It first discusses central theoretical foundations in the critical youth studies literature that inform PAR with young people as a pedagogy, and then discusses asset-based pedagogies.

What Is Active Learning?

The PAR project's pedagogy- and curriculum-centered approach to teaching and learning I term *active learning*. Active learning stands in contrast to transmission models of teaching and learning in which students' heads function as empty vessels where facts and information are deposited, to be memorized and later recalled (Freire, 1970/2000). Active learning comprises four components: First, it involves an interactive, participatory teaching strategy that requires egalitarian relationships and builds upon students' prior knowledge and experiences as a part of the curriculum content. Second, active learning empowers students to analyze information, explain their analyses and create knowledge. Third, it invites students to contextualize their knowledge in light of their analysis of power and geographic, sociocultural, political, economic and historical contexts. Fourth, it supports opportunities for students to engage in collaborative action by applying their analysis to authentic situations and participating in democratic practices aiming to improve their local environments and society at large by making them more equitable and socially just.

The Youth Discourses: Systems of Reasoning That Frame Young People

Current social and cultural categories and concepts about youth—the youth discourses—frame how society views young people. The youth discourses are meaningful systems of reasoning that depend on patterns of ideas, terms, categories, metaphors, narratives and frameworks that operate across social sites and appear to be common sense, true and indisputable (Gee, 2014a; Lesko, 2012; Rogers, 2011). Discourses are characterized by the repetitive use of specific language, categories and images, the emotional meanings affixed to them, the narratives that connect these social categories and metaphors, and the moral frameworks within which these narratives function to convey what is seen as good or bad (Lesko, 2012). As a form of social practices and processes and a complex set of relations, discourses can construct, reproduce, represent and assign meaning to the social world—social practices, categories and structures (Gee, 2014a; Fairclough, 2013; Rogers, 2011).

Specific discourses are composed of distinctive ways of speaking, reading, writing, listening, valuing, feeling and believing in accordance with others that shape our actions and interactions and enact particular social identities, which are recognized in multiple, contradictory or disputed ways (Gee, 2014b). Discourses function across many sites, such as organizations, cultures, academic fields and institutions related to law, psychology, medicine, anthropology and education (Gee, 2014b; Lesko, 2012). Because discourses operate across time and virtually everywhere, this contributes to the sense that discourses are natural, probable, expected (Lesko, 2012), and, as such, the youth discourses are invisible as a matter of common sense. Discourse analysis allows us to understand both social identities and social practices (Gee, 2014b) and "reveals those sets of rules and practices through which power is legitimated" (Griffin, 1993, p. 7).

The multiple youth discourses have important policy and practice implications, as they shape researchers', educators', youth workers' and policymakers' assumptions about young people's needs and abilities and our expectations about young people's roles in schools, youth organizations and our society at large (Wyn & White, 1997). Popular and academic discourses about youth can construct, legitimate, reproduce and make possible certain arguments, concepts, institutions and practices while preventing, silencing or eclipsing others (Griffin, 1993).

A central tenet of critical youth studies theory is that the scientific, institutional and popular youth discourses promote the cultural construction of youth as a distinct social category, which is reproduced and institutionalized through asymmetrical power relations between young people and adults. The youth discourses both set in motion and preclude specific social, cultural and institutional practices. For example, Griffin (1993) posits that "the term, 'at risk,' which has medical and psychiatric connotations, is frequently used to forge connections between the clinical discourse, the discourse of criminality and the discourse of education and training" (p. 201). Although young people labeled "at risk" have not actually transgressed any legal or institutional boundaries, Griffin suggests that youth professionals can discuss these "at risk" youth as *likely* to behave or think in a variety of deviant or deficient ways, justifying psychological, clinical, legal or educational corrective interventions even in the absence of any actual wrongdoing. Youth discourses have historically viewed young people as experiencing a universal, fixed, innate period of emotional "storm and stress," and consequently as problems to be fixed and managed instead of as legitimate assets and resources in their own development and in contributing to improving their environments, institutions and communities (Griffin, 1993; Lesko, 2012; Wyn, 2000; Wyn & White, 1997).

Critical youth studies views the concept of youth as a relational concept that principally carries meaning in relation to the concept of adulthood. Culturally constructed binary categories (e.g. male/female, civilized/savage, adult/youth) are relational concepts that exist and are defined in relation to the other and represent asymmetrical power relations between the two categories (Lesko, 2012). That is, conceptions of youth can only exist and have meaning in relation to the conceptions of adulthood. Wyn and White (1997) assert that understanding youth as a relational concept foregrounds power relations between young people and adults. Discourses construct conceptions of youth that imagine them as universally ignorant, dependent and influenced by their peers while adults are imagined as universally knowledgeable, independent and not influenced by their peers. Youth are seen as in transition, moody, rebellious and prone to risk-taking, while adults are viewed as having arrived and as fixed, stable, conformist and prone to making rational, considered decisions (Griffin, 1993; Wyn & White, 1997).

The youth discourses "differentiate youth according to their alignment with desired developmental norms" and so construct and frame some youth as objects that are normalized and in transition to productive adulthood (Lesko & Talburt, 2012, p. 12). In contrast, youth discourses construct other youth who do not align with developmental norms as abnormal, deviant or deficient, and requiring institutional intervention, treatment, monitoring and supervision to ensure successful development into adulthood (Griffin, 1993; Talburt & Lesko, 2012; Wyn & White, 1997). Representations of youth as abnormal or deficient are often reserved for young people who belong to additional non-dominant social categories, particularly along the axes of race, class, gender, sexual orientation and ability. Critical youth studies scholarship traces the inception of the youth concept back to the Industrial Era within industrialized countries, when added leisure time among working-class, young, white, male immigrants posed a perceived threat to the social order, prompting the dual notions to both protect some young people and control other young people (Baizernian & Magnuson, 1996; Fauske, 1996; Gillis, 1993; Griffin, 1993; Heggen, 2000). This historical context created two related popular, scientific and institutional discourses that remain today: the notion that society must protect some young people (more privileged youth) and control other young people (less privileged youth). Within popular representations of youth, these dual notions deem that some young people are a threat to the status quo and others are the hope for the future. Griffin (1993) insists that this deficiency discourse deems that it is individual youth, such as working-class young people or young people of color, and their families or cultures that are expected to change, rather than the structural or ideological dimensions of inequitable institutions or educational systems. Critical youth studies scholarship offers a critique of youth discourses that conceptualize all young people as fitting into universal categories, masking young people's diversity in terms of geography, gender, race, class, sexual orientation, religion, nationality and other markers of social locations. Framing young people through a deficiency discourse that views them as inadequate limits the abilities of adults to support young people.

Scholarship in the field of education has pointed out that it is essential that research about marginalized groups offers a set of alternative data to "engage in, and respond to ... dominant discourses and representations" of marginalized people (Luttrell, 2003, p. 4). In contrast to binary, static, discrete categories of youth and adult, it may be useful for researchers to consider a relational approach to the youth concept, viewing it as socially and culturally constructed in relation to notions of adulthood. Wyn and White (1997) argue that it is important to acknowledge the significant role of institutions and economic and political contexts that impact young people's individual development and experience of growing up. Critical youth studies scholars advocate for a conceptual approach to youth development that views it as a relational social process in which the meaning of becoming adult is mediated by social and institutional factors, and relationships to historical, sociopolitical, economic and geographic contexts (Finn, 2003; Griffin, 1993; Wyn & White, 1997). Baizernian and Magnuson (1996) suggest that an alternative framework to the categorical youth/adult binary can underscore what adults and youth have in common, such as the aspiration to be part of cooperative pursuits, which might allow for youth–adult partnerships that pursue goals worthy of engagement and commitment. It is important for educational researchers to acknowledge young people's agency and their internal meaning-making, including "personal images, ideas, associations and feelings" that individual young people wield that are "both impacted by and resistant to external representations and regulatory social systems" (Luttrell, 2003, p. 5).

Adultism

The concept of adultism aligns with critical youth studies scholarship that finds that dominant youth discourses frame young people as profoundly different from and inferior to adults in terms of needs, interests, and abilities (Wyn & White, 1997). Adultism has been discussed in recent scholarship as an important concept to understand and apply to sociological and psychological frameworks, youth participation practices and empowering educational practices (Ceaser, 2014; Checkoway, 2011; LeFrançois, 2014). Adultism refers to a set of assumptions, attitudes and beliefs that young people are inferior to adults in terms of their abilities, needs, perspectives and concerns, and these notions are embedded in practices, policies, behaviors, social institutions and systems. Adultism often results in the systematic exclusion of young people from decisions that directly impact their lives. At the institutional level, decision-making or policymaking bodies, systems of governance and institutional practices do not often include young people's input or representation even in youth-serving organizations and institutions. At the interpersonal level, adultism can cause individuals to replicate these attitudes and behaviors towards those perceived as younger and holding a lower status. At the individual level, internalizing adultism can cause young people to question their own legitimacy, ability, expertise and agency. One of the consequences of adultism is that young people are often not consulted in the designing, planning or evaluating of curriculum, school policies and school or neighborhood improvement efforts. In both popular and academic discourses, racism, classism, sexism, heterosexism, ableism and xenophobia have gained saliency over the years in discussions of belief systems that result in systemic discrimination. Building upon this legacy, the concept of adultism is becoming more widely recognized in youth development and community organizing practices and in scholarship as a set of beliefs and discriminatory practices worthy of countering as a social justice issue (Adams et al., 2013; Zeldin, 2004).

While it is true that young people learn, develop and grow over time and may have specific needs (as do adults), awareness of dominant conceptions of youth as fundamentally distinct from adults and inferior to them in terms of their needs, views, concerns and abilities can help adults become aware of their assumptions and establish a balanced understanding of young people. Understanding the variety, contradictions and complexities of particular youth needs and areas for growth and improvement in specific contexts as well as seeing their strengths and potential as resources in terms of their creativity, energy, local knowledge, abilities and ideas can enable adults to better work with young people. Such nuanced perspectives can better allow adults to support young people in learning new skills and learning how to attend to their own participation to engage collaboratively in a community of practice. A balanced view of young people can enable adult researchers, policymakers and educators to provide relevant and successful educational approaches that engage young people to advance their full human potential.

Youth, typically grouped together in the United States as 12- to 18-year-olds (Sabo, 2003b), represent a diverse group of people with intersecting identities. As critical youth studies scholars (Griffin, 1993; Lesko, 2012; Wyn & White, 1997) and current scholars and researchers on using PAR with youth (Cahill, Rios-Moore & Threatts, 2008; Cammarota & Fine, 2008; Morrell, 2008) point out, adultist practices doubly impact underrepresented young people who fall into at least one additional marginalized social category, including youth of color, girls, low-income youth, immigrant youth and lesbian, gay, bisexual, transgender and queer/questioning (LGBTQ) youth. The intersections of these social locations are important to recognize in discussions of the ways in which adultism operates and in considering young people's rights and abilities to participate in decisions that impact them.

Our society assumes that young adults at the age of 18 are capable of active participation in a democracy through effective decision-making, such as voting for elected representatives and other forms of civic participation (Gibson, 2001; Hart, 1997). However, some studies find that it is unrealistic to expect that young people will suddenly become capable of responsible democratic participation when they arrive at a certain biological age without previous, gradual engagement in participatory, democratic decision-making and adult-supported leadership responsibilities (Atweh, Christensen & Dornan, 1998; Hart, 1992). Other research suggests that youth-serving organizations may need to actively promote youth input and participation in decisions that impact their lives so that young people may gradually acquire, through practice, the skills to participate as active members of a democracy (Hart, 1992; Wyn, 2001).

Both critical youth studies scholarship and positive youth development studies demonstrate that young people's voices are delegitimized in society and within its institutions. In both schools and in non-school learning settings, young people's input and ideas are rarely considered in the design, planning, implementation and evaluation of their curricula and learning projects. Yet, involving middle school and high school students in designing and directing the trajectory of their learning may lead to greater student participation, motivation and commitment to their learning goals and process. The field of participatory action research projects with young people builds on the theoretical foundations of critical youth studies and on asset-based pedagogies.

The Role of Asset-Based Pedagogies in Building Sociopolitical Consciousness

Deficit approaches to teaching view the cultural practices, languages and literacies of most students of color and working-class students and their communities as deficiencies to be overcome in order for them to learn the dominant cultural practices, language and literacy taught in schools (Paris & Alim, 2014). In contrast, asset-based pedagogies, sometimes called "asset pedagogies" or "resource pedagogies," reposition the cultural practices, languages and literacies of working-class students and their communities, particularly working-class students of color, as resources to examine, honor and build upon (Paris & Alim, 2014). Ladson-Billings (2014) notes that educational research and scholarship that "tells us what works for middle-class, advantaged students typically fails to reveal the social and cultural advantages that make their success possible" (p. 76). However, Ladson-Billings (2014) reminds us that studying what works for those who have been the most disadvantaged by schooling conveys the pedagogical principles and choices that can realize successful learning for all students.

Culturally relevant pedagogy is an asset-based pedagogy that views students' families and communities as resources and assets to learning. Culturally relevant pedagogy describes teaching as a reflective practice that is effective with diverse learners (Brown-Jeffy & Cooper, 2011; T. C. Howard, 2003; Ladson-Billings, 1995; 2014; Milner, 2011). Research has found that the ability of teachers to build cultural competence amplifies student learning and is a crucial aspect of successful teaching in diverse learning settings (Milner, 2011). Culturally relevant pedagogy has also been theorized as culturally responsive pedagogy (Gay, 2010; Sleeter, 2012; Villegas & Lucas, 2002) and as culturally sustaining pedagogy (Paris, 2012; Paris & Alim, 2014). Ladson-Billings (1995; 2014) provides a seminal theoretical framework of culturally relevant pedagogy that embodies three central principles: (1) academic success; (2) cultural competence; and (3) sociopolitical consciousness. Ladson-Billings (1995; 2014) explains that academic success refers to high expectations for all students to achieve intellectual growth in building literacy, numeracy, technological, social and political skills, which are crucial for active participation in a democracy. Cultural competence is developed by using culture as a platform for learning through appreciating and learning about students' own cultures and the cultures of others, and including students' own experiences, history and perspectives (Ladson-Billings, 1995; 2014). The developing of sociopolitical consciousness involves the ability to develop critical perspectives on policies, cultural norms, institutions and practices that create and reproduce social inequalities in order to recognize, study and solve real-world problems that directly impact students and their communities (Ladson-Billings, 1995; 2014). Culturally relevant pedagogy and culturally sustaining pedagogy both rest on the notion of students as subjects to learn from rather than merely as objects of study (Ladson-Billings, 2014). Work that engages participatory action research projects with young people as an approach to pedagogy and curriculum development builds upon theoretical foundations in critical youth studies as well as the scholarship on culturally relevant pedagogy and asset-based pedagogies.

The Contexts of Schooling and Learning

The significant opportunity gap reflects that many urban schools and districts are failing to effectively support youth of color, immigrant youth and low-income youth in succeeding academically. It is commonly understood that educators are struggling to engage students in urban school districts throughout the United States. Research on the history of public schooling in the United States has shown that Industrial Era school systems aimed to prepare the majority of students for compartmentalized, routine, unreflective factory assembly-line work and thus were designed to teach students skills suited to the assembly line (Tyack, 1974). These unreflective assembly-line skills included compliance, compartmentalized thinking and the execution of tasks in isolation. These early-19th-century schools applied the factory model to the organization and structure of schools so that schools were designed to adapt to stratified societies (Tyack, 1974) to produce both assembly-line laborers and the handful of factory managers who supervised them.

Today's workplaces largely reflect the influence of new managerial and organizational models that are more horizontal rather than hierarchical, and responsive to the changing needs in the wider environment (Wheeler, 2000). Rather than using the factory models in which labor was organized into discrete parts that were later assembled, most modern work is organized into teams and requires teamwork to think through and solve complex problems.

Contemporary workplace organizational models call for innovative schooling models that prepare students to collaborate in team meetings to reach consensus and think critically to solve complex problems. To be prepared to succeed in the contemporary job market, students need to be prepared for work and life skills that center on critical thinking and collaborative decision-making. However, in most schools only a handful of students, usually elected members of student government, have the opportunity to contribute to school-wide decisions about policies that impact their daily lives (Gibson, 2001).

When schools and classrooms do not enlist student input or situate learning in students' knowledge and experience, this may contribute to student disengagement.

Current research shows that community-based approaches are proving to be highly effective with the very students who are disengaged from learning in schools (McLaughlin, 2000). There may be successful teaching and learning principles to distill from these community-based approaches that can help schools engage students and ensure that all students achieve in schools. Youth-led PAR is an emergent field that recent research shows is a successful framework and approach to engaging young people enrolled in under-resourced urban districts and neighborhoods (Cammarota & Fine, 2008; Irizarry, 2009; Morrell, 2008; Romero et al., 2008). Darling-Hammond (2010) observes that the struggle for equality in education must center not only on gaining access to a quality education, but also on securing an engaging and empowering curriculum for all students that can promote critical thinking, student voice, ownership over learning, and agency to shape their own futures. Transformative school reform and effective curriculum design will not be successful without engaging students' interests and concerns (Carter & Welner, 2013; Darling-Hammond, 2010; Fine et al., 2007).

This historical moment presents an opportunity for a significant shift in instructional and curricular approaches to teaching and learning in order to increase student engagement and academic success. Certainly, educators and researchers have begun to challenge the current standardized curriculum that promotes the transmission of a vast amount of content in a short time, making the case for a curriculum that promotes critical thinking, holds relevance for students and carries a meaningful purpose. Yet while many educators acknowledge the common issues and challenges presented by a curriculum shaped by test preparation, it is difficult to determine how to implement new teaching approaches because there are few documented examples of these.

What Is Participatory Action Research With Youth?

Scholarship on using PAR with youth is an emergent field that examines PAR projects conducted by student researchers in conjunction with adult support and guidance. Participatory action research is a process that aims to engage people in investigating their own reality in order to change it (Borda, 1979). PAR is a method in which young people participate as decision-makers in leadership roles to research and implement solutions to the issues that directly impact them. The PAR process with youth requires that young people determine the questions to probe, design the research study, employ research methods to collect data, analyze data, draw findings, make recommendations and collaborate with adults to take action on their recommendations. In the youth-led PAR model, young people take the lead in analyzing information that could spark an organizational improvement, institutional transformation, community initiative, organizing campaign or policy change.

In PAR projects, researchers reconceptualize people traditionally viewed as the objects of study to envision them as co-researchers in the process. As a community-based approach to knowledge production, the PAR process enables participants in a research study to be included as insiders with localized knowledge in each step of the research process. For example, Freire (1970/2000) asserts that a participatory research method

> requires the investigators and the people (who would normally be considered objects of that investigation) to act as *co-investigators*. The more active an attitude [people] take in regard to the exploration of their thematics, the more they deepen their critical awareness of reality, and in spelling out those thematics, take possession of that reality.
>
> (p. 131)

Drawing on popular education frameworks (Brydon-Miller et al., 2009; Freire, 1970/2000; Hall, 1991; Torres, 1992), the PAR model lifts up the voices of those who have historically been excluded from decisions about their own lives and education and engages them in problem-solving to strengthen institutions in their surrounding environments. PAR projects with young people strive to relate individual situations to the power asymmetries within the social structures in which individuals are nested (Cahill et al., 2008; Cannella, 2008). The youth-led PAR process engages young people in active organizational decision-making regarding the institutions and systems that directly impact them.

Participatory action research with young people offers new approaches to developing the capacities of youth as decision-makers in program governance, as agents of change and as community resources (Atweh & Burton, 1995; Atweh et al., 1998; Cooper & Cromey, 2000; McIntyre, 2000; Penuel & Freeman, 1997; Spatig et al., 2001). Youth-led PAR projects are often characterized by risk-taking and experimentation. In these projects, one expects to be able to be oneself and to be welcomed and accepted regardless of one's social identity. In the PAR curriculum studied in this case, icebreakers and team-builders allow youth to let their guard down and require that everyone engages in informal and sometimes outlandish or comical activities, which helps the student researchers drop their performance of cool in order to participate. They are tasked with reflecting on their own stories of discrimination and sharing them with the group, which builds genuine connections and empathy.

Current scholarship and research that examines PAR with young people considers how PAR can be used as a pedagogical approach to support learning for young people—particularly those who are economically, socially and politically marginalized—through their investigation of the systemic causes of issues in their environments in order to improve them (Cahill et al., 2008; Cammarota & Fine, 2008; Cannella, 2008; Ginwright, 2008; Guishard et al., 2005). In youth-led PAR projects, young people hold substantial leadership responsibilities and decision-making roles that impact the framing, design, scope and direction of their research projects.

Youth-led PAR provides several benefits in developing youth decision-making and leadership capacities that impact multiple spheres: young people, the research projects, their institutions and their communities (Cammarota & Fine, 2008). Specific benefits to student researchers include the learning of new skills and capacities, extension of their interpersonal skills, increased empowerment and agency, and expansion of their academic identities as researchers, writers and presenters. PAR is a learning strategy that empowers participants by enabling them to gain new insights into and explanations of the world they experience, to learn how to learn and to discover new possibilities for collaborative action (Elden & Levin, 1991). In the youth-led PAR model, young people and adult researchers collaborate to co-produce original theory and then test and improve it through a process of reflection, action and further reflection and adjustment. In the roles of co-learners, local participants and professional researchers supply their own ideas, models and frameworks that explain and ascribe meaning to their social worlds to generate a new explanatory framework and develop shared local theory (Elden & Levin, 1991). Research findings from PAR projects bear increased validity because they are investigated within the actual environments in which any interventions might be implemented and draw on the expertise of those directly impacted by the issues under study.

The broadening of participation patterns can lead to sound frameworks that incorporate the interests of multiple stakeholder groups and promote continual modification and reinvention to strengthen the resulting knowledge and actions (Walton & Gaffney, 1991). Research shows that the PAR process with youth can build youth leadership capacities, build adults' capacities to partner with youth in program planning and design, and build organizational capacities to support youth leadership development (Cammarota & Fine, 2008). PAR projects have the potential to contribute to making schools and community-based institutions more effective and innovative, and to help strengthen local communities by making them more equitable and socially just.

Employing the metaphor of the ladder, Hart (1997) delineates eight rungs, or degrees, of different levels of participation of young people's participation within PAR projects (Table 2.1). The ladder metaphor is useful in initiating discussions about how adults can support levels of youth involvement in accordance to their interests and capacities (Hart, 1992, 1997). This continuum of youth participation can be helpful to aid schools or organizations in evaluating the current levels of youth involvement in their projects to consider the goals, resources and nature of the PAR initiative to determine whether it makes sense to support increased youth participation. In the PAR model with youth,

TABLE 2.1 The Ladder of Youth Participation

---

8. Youth-initiated, shared decisions with adults
7. Youth-initiated and directed
6. Adult-initiated, shared decisions with young people
5. Consulted and informed
4. Assigned but informed
3. Tokenism
2. Decoration
1. Manipulation or deception

Source: Adapted from Hart (1992; 1997).

skill-building training programs and adult support and feedback are employed to support young people's participation, learning, agency and leadership development (Atweh et al., 1998; Cammarota & Fine, 2008; Fine et al., 2003; Guishard et al., 2005). A growing body of research closely examines what PAR strategies with youth look like, how these strategies actually work in practice, and the tensions and problems involved in implementing these strategies (Bautista, Bertrand, Morrell, Scorza & Matthews, 2013; Cammarota and Fine, 2008; Fine, 2012; Irizarry, 2009; Morrell, 2008; Payne, Starks & Gibson, 2009; Stovall & Delgado, 2009).

PAR With Youth as a Teaching and Learning Approach

Participatory action research with young people can be advanced as a participatory approach to teaching and learning that builds on youth as assets, focuses on youth development, advances academic skills and promotes participation and agency. PAR can be a viable approach to developing young people's learning and agency within youth-led collaborative inquiry projects (Atweh & Burton, 1995; Atweh et al., 1998; Cammarota & Fine, 2008). Such adult-supported learning contexts that promote young people's involvement in project decision-making, planning and design entail providing a curriculum and skill-building instruction to student researchers. PAR projects with youth engage young people as full partners with adults in pursuing learning. The PAR process can be exercised as a pedagogical strategy to promote representative, collective decision-making in which young people contribute input in the direction of their learning. Ultimately, the PAR model can be employed as a participatory approach to teaching and learning that builds on youth assets, advances academic skills, engages participation in shaping the curriculum, focuses on youth development and community-building, supports youth–adult partnerships and promotes participation and agency.

Current scholarship and research on PAR with youth considers how it can be used as a teaching and learning approach for young people, particularly for those who are socioeconomically marginalized (Cammarota & Fine, 2008; Cammarota & Romero, 2009; Ginwright, 2008; Rodríguez & Brown, 2009). PAR as a pedagogy involves young people investigating the conditions in their own environments that directly affect them in order for them to participate in community action projects to improve these conditions (Cahill et al., 2008; Fals-Borda & Rahman, 1991; Tuck et al., 2008). The PAR model with youth necessitates that youth researchers design and plan each step of the research process: selecting the research topic, designing the study, collecting data, analyzing data, presenting their findings to stakeholders, and developing and implementing an action phase based on their research recommendations (Atweh et al., 1998; Fine et al., 2003; McIntyre, 2000). It is a slow process for young people to gain skills, discover their own expertise, generate a new framework and build their agency to effect change through the PAR model. Conceptualizing PAR as a pedagogical approach that engages student researchers and taps into their expertise about the nature of their community's conditions aligns with PAR principles that those closest to the problem studied have the most expertise about how to solve it and are potential resources in solving community problems.

PAR as a Pedagogical Approach in the Central Youth United Project

In the case of Central Youth United (CYU), young people were highly engaged in the PAR project through structured, interactive workshops. In these workshops, two adult project instructors posed questions to elicit student researchers' knowledge and experience about current issues in their neighborhood. These two instructors also facilitated group discussions and exercises that promoted student input on key decision points in the research process. Through this process, student researchers moved from being novice researchers who were unfamiliar with how to design a research project to becoming researchers who collect and analyze data, draw findings, create a research report to present in the public sphere and create and implement a research-based action plan. The interactive curriculum and experiential learning process was fundamental to the intentional pedagogical strategies the two instructors employed to scaffold their learning and build agency within student researchers. Agency is the ability to exert influence and power in a given situation and construct expanded identities of oneself as a change-maker and leader (Mitra, 2004), as well as the ability to hold challenging responsibilities, set and achieve goals and perform actions aimed at making a difference in one's local environments and institutions, or in the wider society (Eccles & Gootman, 2002; Larson & Angus, 2011; Mahoney, Larson & Eccles, 2004). The PAR curriculum and pedagogy also involved a team-building component that ran throughout the program's curriculum and instruction.

3

THE CONTEXT OF CENTRAL YOUTH UNITED AND PARTICIPANT PROFILES

Introduction

This chapter provides a descriptive overview of the Central Youth United (CYU) project. The purpose of the chapter is to give a brief background of the CYU project and present a descriptive account of its trajectory from beginning to end as the context for the following five thematic chapters. First, the chapter provides a profile of the Central neighborhood. Second, it provides the historical context and background of the project, describing how and why CYU began and the key actors and organizations involved in creating it. Third, the chapter presents an account of the phases of the CYU project. Fourth, it presents profiles of each of the CYU project participants, both the two instructors and the eight student researchers. Finally, the chapter provides a profile of the nonprofit organizations affiliated with the project.

Profile of the Central Neighborhood

The Central neighborhood is located in a West Coast city. Since the 1840s, the neighborhood has mostly housed people from low-income, immigrant families working in the service industry. In the 1920s and 1930s, many single Filipino men immigrated to Central and found work primarily as day laborers and dish-washers, or had relocated to Central after serving as factory workers in canneries, as attendants on ships or as agricultural laborers, forming a migrant labor community (Espiritu, 2003; Salomon, 2003). By the 1970s, Central had a population of 10,000 Filipinos. The building boom of the 1950s and 1960s and expanded subway transportation to the area in the 1970s brought in white-collar workers to work in nearby banks and corporate businesses (Salomon, 2003).

This expansion resulted in new high-rise developments, led to large-scale evictions, destroyed over 4,000 low-income homes and many small, community businesses, and displaced thousands, changing the landscape and demographics (Salomon, 2003). According to local city planning department documents, by 2000 approximately 31% of Central residents were Asian, 20% were African American, 12% were Latino and 37% were White.

According to the U.S. census data at the time of the study, half (51%) of Central households earned less than $15,000 a year. These vast economic disparities exist between Central neighborhood households as well. Many wealthy executives relocated to Central from Silicon Valley during what is commonly referred to as the "dot com boom," an economic boom covering roughly 1995–2000 that resulted from a sharp rise in the stock market due to the rapid growth of internet-based companies in the business sector. During this economic boom, local city planners and real estate developers created new luxury condominiums and lofts, which these wealthy executives moved into, becoming Central residents.

According to the Greater Central Area Multiple Listing Service, which lists real estate prices in Central, condos and lofts are currently selling at an average of approximately $1.5 million for a two-bedroom unit, the range being $900,000–$3.5 million. In stark contrast, the U.S. census reports that 40% of Central households earn less than $10,000 a year. These new residents occupying this luxury housing are overwhelmingly wealthy, White, American-born, monolingual English speakers without children who held at least a college degree and are not originally from the neighborhood. The census reports that nearly two-thirds (63%) of Central residents are people of color, one-third speak limited or no English and 44% were born outside of the United States. The census also reports that 82% of Central residents do not hold a college degree and one-fourth of residents do not hold a high school diploma. Towering above government-subsidized and low-income housing, many million-dollar-per-unit condominiums are located only a few blocks away from the Central Youth United meetings at the Central Community Development Center.

Since 1996, 1,000 new "live/work" lofts have been constructed in Central, and 1,500 were under construction or approved for construction at the time of writing. During the rapid development of the Central neighborhood, many working poor families were displaced. According to the U.S. census, there are 13,500 people living in the neighborhood, and Central's population grew by 80% from 1990 to 2000 (compared to the rest of the city's growth rate of 11% during that decade). During this period of displacement in the mid-1990s, several grassroots community organizing and community-based nonprofit organizations formed in order to fight displacement resulting from gentrification in Central.

The Central Anti-Displacement Coalition began organizing residents to fight to enforce and maintain the zoning regulations for the neighborhood that protected homes and small businesses. Many small businesses were being pushed out by developers who won approval from the city for their luxury condo construction projects despite strict industrial zoning regulations for businesses. Developers interested in generating lucrative profits from luxury lofts violated industrial zoning regulations in Central by claiming that the lofts were "live/work" spaces intended for low-income artists. A local city planning department document profiles the Central neighborhood and describes the history of gentrification in Central from the perspective of urban development:

> [Central] became internationally recognized as a mecca for people with new ideas in the field of technology. These people needed somewhere to live. Developers, keenly aware of this influx of young people with discretionary income, began to promote live/work as a perfect solution. Industrial land in [Central] was the cheapest land in proximity to the Multimedia Gulch. Another enticing advantage was the fact that building on industrially zoned land was less restrictive in terms of building standards and planning requirements. Unlike other [City] neighborhoods, [Central] had little community scrutiny of individual projects. As a result, live/work projects were built in an ad-hoc manner throughout the area.

This city planning department documents the housing developers' decision to make money by executing development projects in Central geared to housing wealthy young professionals wanting to locate to the city. These developers chose Central to take advantage of the fact that the working-class community there had not heavily scrutinized or disputed development projects in the past, and because the neighborhood's industrial zoning meant lower building standards and fewer requirements for construction and urban planning in Central. Alejandra, a student researcher in the study, and a long-time resident of Central, describes the process of gentrification and displacement and how she witnessed the spate of new development in her neighborhood:

> A lot of corporate buildings are going up and not enough things for youth to rise up ... I just seen all these new buildings out of nowhere starting to pop up, like, everywhere I go. It's just new buildings starting to come up. There are places I used to go to—where I have memories in—just gone. It's like it was a piece of me that was destroyed ... And it's like you've destroyed something that was valuable to people that live here. You've made it something ugly. It's like killing a rose. It's like calling a dead rose pretty—trying to make it pretty. It's just destroying every little bit of memory. It's just not where I grew up. It's not where I have my memories. It's not where I started. It's not where I started to become someone who I am now. I mean, how is it gonna look if production keeps doing what it's doing?

In continuing to describe how she experienced and understood the gentrification process and the resulting displacement of people in Central, Alejandra reports:

> On Pine Street and Washington was a house we used to live in. And one of the buildings got burned down and they destroyed our house and put in restaurants and a hotel that's hecka expensive, housing that's hecka expensive. And, I mean, I used to *live* there. I have memories of me growing up. When I was practicing my basketball—dribbles down the hallway—playing with my little brother and my sisters and everything. Having my brother teach me new moves—how to shoot and all this. And then practicing my softball throws and all. I had memories just practicing and practicing in that house 'cause there was no park there and I was too young to go to the Rec [Center] by myself. And it was just like that. And they tore our house down. And every time I pass by there I see it and I think of when I was little running down the hallways just dribbling a basketball—dribbling any type of ball I had. And they tore it down and put something else up just to get more money out of it ... They just build stuff that they think will bring more money in. And, I mean, it has, but it's not what *we* want to see.

Alejandra observes that the desire to make money is the impetus behind the new development projects in her neighborhood, which have destroyed homes and displaced families without any regard for the residents who live there. As a result of the beginnings of neighborhood gentrification, anti-displacement organizing campaigns formed and developed in Central.

As a result of the community-building that occurred during these anti-displacement campaigns, several organizations affiliated with Central Youth United were founded. For example, the person leading the anti-displacement campaign became the director of the newly formed Central Community Organizing Alliance. The Central Community Development Center was also established during this time. Sister Space, a youth development organization that provided two young women to the CYU project, was also formed during this period. The Central Community Organizing Alliance, the Central Community Development Center, Sister Space and Representing Ourselves all serve on the Central Youth Task Force, which created and funded the Central Youth United youth participatory action research project that is the focus of this book.

Background of the Central Youth United Project

The Central Youth United project began with the legacy of the first PAR project with young people in Central, a youth-led community needs assessment carried out in 2001–2002, conducted by a different group of young people in Central. Youth Voices also provided training and technical assistance in participatory action research with young people to this first youth-led PAR project in 2001–2002. This project was organized by a community coalition and involved seven high school students, aged 14–17, who ignited a multi-year urban planning, design and development process that the community organized to meet their recommendations. In the first project, the action components of the PAR project were to create a final report, a video, and presentations of their research-based findings and recommendations. The action phase of the PAR project entailed that young people present their recommendations to adult organizers, community leaders, policymakers and elected officials in order for the adults to implement their recommendations.

The 2001–2002 PAR project found that over one-third of 12- to 18-year-olds had been kicked out of the recently built mall and public park, which were part of recent neighborhood redevelopment initiatives. The survey data indicated that these young people were being displaced from the neighborhood venues typically enjoyed by teenagers. This youth-led PAR project found that their neighborhood needed safe recreational spaces for youth. After conducting 194 surveys of young people aged 5–18 and analyzing their data, this first youth-led community needs assessment drew findings that culminated in four core recommendations to improve Central: (1) construct a new elementary school campus; (2) build a new public park; (3) create a new middle school in Central; and (4) create a youth center.

After the young people had presented their 2002 PAR recommendations to the community, a coalition of parents, teachers and other community members participated in a successful community organizing campaign to implement the first of the young people's PAR recommendations and build a new elementary school campus. In addition to its bilingual Spanish/English program, this elementary school boasts the only dual-immersion bilingual Tagalog/English program in the United States. This school was housed in a dilapidated building that had not been renovated since the 1950s. This organizing campaign win in 2003 resulted in the local Unified School District agreeing to build a new elementary school. Two years after the young people's PAR recommendation to build a new elementary school, this new elementary school building opened its doors in the fall of 2004.

This organizing campaign also took on the young people's second PAR recommendation. The mobilized parents and residents from the organizing campaign pressured the city's mayor, the Department of City Parks and Recreation and key policymakers to build a park as part of the new elementary school construction. The Central community successfully won its organizing campaign to build a new public park. The Central campaign organizers negotiated a shared-use agreement between the Unified School District and Parks and Recreation, and a four-acre park was built next to the new elementary school.

Mobilized parents, residents, teachers, youth workers and other adult allies fulfilled the youth-led PAR team's first two recommendations. Next, the Central community mobilized again to achieve the PAR project's third recommendation: create a new middle school. After a difficult and protracted battle with the city's Unified School District, the mobilized community finally won its organizing campaign to open a middle school serving grades 6–8 as an extension of the existing elementary school, which served grades K–5. Four years after the youth presented their PAR recommendation to create a new middle school in the Central neighborhood, the new middle school in Central opened its doors (in the fall of 2006).

The coalition of organized parents, activists and residents in Central succeeded in achieving three of the four PAR recommendations penned by high school students in their PAR report. This coalition successfully constructed a new elementary school building and campus, created a new public park for community use and created a new middle school, serving grades 6–8. The final, fourth recommendation—to build a youth center—had not yet been fulfilled. However, taking the young people's PAR recommendations seriously, the Central Youth Task Force secured money to conduct a feasibility study for a youth center. In 2006, the Task Force began planning to secure funding and identifying community partners to support a second youth-led PAR project, which would be framed as a youth-led needs assessment of Central. This is how the Central Youth United project examined here came into being.

Overview of the Central Youth United Project

The Central Youth United (CYU) project spanned seven months. The Central Youth Task Force hired Youth Voices to provide training and technical assistance to support the CYU project. The Task Force's purpose in securing funding and starting a needs assessment was to determine the current need for a youth center and to determine the scope and features of youth needs for youth center programming. Funded by a grant from the Department of Children, Youth and Their Families, this community needs assessment's findings and recommendations were based on a comprehensive participatory action research process led by young people. All CYU team members were from Central, with the exception of one student researcher from a similar neighborhood that borders Central.

Their research methodology timeline included eight steps:

1. understanding the project's context, setting goals and developing a research question;
2. developing a research design and selecting a research methodology;
3. developing focus-group research tools and developing research skills;
4. creating a data collection plan and collecting data;

5. organizing the collected data;
6. analyzing the data;
7. creating the final report, a PowerPoint presentation, poster-board visual aids and final presentation;
8. presenting the research findings and recommendations at a town hall meeting to an audience of over 60 community stakeholders.

The CYU team's research question was: What do youth really need in Central? Central Youth United's student researchers conducted focus groups with over 80 youth and adults who live, work and receive services in Central. Victor remarked that the reason why he came to the project every week was that he liked helping other young people, helping to improve his neighborhood and using data for community change:

DW: So, why do you keep coming back to the project every week?
V: Because I always like talking about kids and how to help them, giving them data about how the neighborhood is.
DW: What do you like most about the project so far?
V: That we're getting a lot of data.
DW: Why's it important to get data?
V: 'Cause data helps you change things. It can show you what you need to do and what you don't need to do.

The PAR team's presentation highlighted the team's finding that young people in Central consistently reported the lack of a safe recreational area in their neighborhood reserved for youth. The team reported that the recreation center is dominated by adults, who have brought violence into the space, and that most young people do not feel safe going there.

Further, the student researchers found that although there is a newly built park that is open during daylight hours, the high crime rate in assaults and drug trafficking there (which Central is notorious for), coupled with the extensive police harassment of teenagers in the park and streets, prevents young people from using this area. The team's data showed that over half of young people's housing complexes have no recreational area. Lastly, the team's focus groups revealed that they are routinely kicked out of the new neighborhood mall developments and that teenagers cannot afford movie theatre tickets, which only offer children rates and adult rates, the latter being $12 a ticket.

Through their data analysis process, the research team found a pattern of young people's displacement from recreational spaces in Central. Data from the PAR team's eight focus groups showed that many youth reported feeling unsafe in their streets and in their neighborhood. On the basis of their data, the action research team strongly recommended the creation of a youth center that could provide a safe space offering activities and programs for young people. Alejandra expresses her belief that when there are no positive opportunities or resources for teenagers, they can be tempted to engage in more harmful activities. She explains that the research team's community needs assessment report recommends building a neighborhood youth center, because doing so would address the systemic issue of structural and economic disinvestment in programming and resources for youth. Alejandra asserts that positive developmental outcomes for young people require an investment in youth programs that provide them with the tools to support positive outcomes:

> When you go to high school, there are no more [sports] teams. You only can play for your school, but when school's out, you wanna play for other teams. There's only AAU [Amateur Athletic Union] leagues, and AAU leagues cost too much. And for people who live down here in Central, it's too expensive for us. We barely can afford to have an apartment here and put food on the table and pay our bills and go to school and have stuff for school. We can barely afford to do that. And then to pay for an AAU team on top of that? That's not even for us. So kids that are entering high school (or are in high school), they start to do drugs or sell drugs and all this, following the wrong path. They might just end up not going to school at all. And for some of the kids who are staying in [school], they're trying to fight every step and step of the way, but they can't fight no more because they don't have enough tools that they need.

The PAR team recommended that a local youth center be constructed as the first priority in their set of research-based recommendations.

Among the research findings in Central Youth United's final report, the team found that: (1) Central is "a progressive neighborhood with a deep sense of community," although it is underserved and needs more resources; (2) Central is unsafe to walk through and needs a safe space for young people; (3) Central lacks affordable housing and its residents are being displaced; (4) community-based organizations need to work together to prevent gang violence; and (5) high school students are frustrated that they have to travel outside of Central to attend school, because the neighborhood lacks a high school. On the basis of these findings, the CYU team's core recommendations are as follows:

1. create a youth center;
2. provide affordable housing and home ownership programs;
3. create a neighborhood watch initiative;
4. create a high school.

Relating personally to the theme the team uncovered in their data that there should be a neighborhood high school, Alejandra remarks:

I have to always wake up early in the morning to get ready and leave the house by 6:30, so I can be to school on time. And that is not a good thing ... The schools are all in different neighborhoods where it takes me a long time to get there. Whereas there used to be better schools here ... Waking up early just gets tiring after a while because I don't have regular classes. I have a lot of honors classes and there's a lot of work. And at home, I have a lot of homework to do ... and I don't get to sleep until 10:30 and then I have to wake up at 5:00. It's really hard for me.

Alejandra's experience echoed the information that the CYU researchers collected from high school-aged young people in their focus groups about the difficulties of traveling outside of Central to attend school.

These findings and recommendations were presented during CYU's final presentation, which they organized as a community forum. CYU's culminating community presentation was attended by an audience of over 60 youth advocates, young people, policymakers, media representatives, service providers, elected representatives and funders. The CYU youth research team's presentation was filmed, and included refreshments and poster-board displays, a Power-Point display and a slide show with a hip-hop music soundtrack, a formal presentation of their findings and recommendations, and a question-and-answer session fielded by the student researchers. For example, a representative from the Department of Children, Youth and Their Families scheduled a meeting with Youth Voices to plan how her department could fund a second cycle of the CYU project. She was interested in funding an extended action phase to implement the team's recommendations.

Highly impressed with the CYU's team's research-based recommendations and their urgent desire to open a local youth center, the Central Youth Task Force convened an emergency ad hoc meeting on site immediately following the presentation. The Task Force called this impromptu meeting in order to allow one vocal CYU student researcher who expressed strong interest, Alejandra, to join their Task Force right away. Within moments after CYU's presentation, the Task Force invited Alejandra to join their group and sit at their meeting table to share her vision for the next steps the Task Force should take.

The Central Youth United's presentation sparked great enthusiasm among the adults in the neighborhood. The Central Youth Task Force asked the CYU research team to present their recommendations at an upcoming community forum. Central Community Organizing Alliance representatives, who sit on the Task Force, had begun planning a community forum and rally at City Hall to demand that elected representatives fund a youth center. The Central Community Organizing Alliance is the same grassroots community organizing non-profit that had followed up on the 2001–2002 youth-led needs assessment recommendations to build a new elementary school campus, construct a new public park and create a new middle school in Central. This same organizing nonprofit's interest in implementing CYU's recommendations was a good sign for the student researchers' community development goals.

Immediately after the team's presentation, this same group, the Central Community Organizing Alliance, demonstrated that it was taking this youth-led PAR team's needs assessment seriously. However, it took time to accomplish these past community development successes. It took two years to build the new elementary school, over two years to create the park and four years to construct a brand-new middle school. Yet, with the returning support of the Central Community Organizing Alliance and the Central Youth Task Force, the prospects that the community will mobilize to implement the student researchers' recommendations are promising.

Central Youth United Student Researcher Profiles

Table 3.1 lists the Central Youth United participants by demographic information and by their role in the PAR project. Student researchers identified their age, gender and race or ethnicity on a questionnaire at the start of the project. A brief profile of each student researcher follows.

Jocelyn

Jocelyn was the primary instructor for this project and identifies as Filipina. She met with the team twice weekly for a total of four hours. She was 32 years old at the time of the study. Jocelyn has worked with several youth development organizations over the past several years. Most recently, she worked with a youth development organization for girls and young women. While undertaking the position as primary instructor for Central Youth United, she also

TABLE 3.1 Central Youth United Students and Instructors by Role and Demographics

Name	Age	Gender	Race/Ethnicity	Role
Jocelyn	32	Female	Filipina	Primary instructor
Rashna	29	Female	Pakistani	Secondary instructor; Youth Voices trainer in PAR methods
Terrence	16	Male	African American	Student researcher
Jason	17	Male	Salvadoran and Mexican American	Student researcher
Miguel	14	Male	Filipino and Latino	Student researcher
Eric	14	Male	Latino and White	Student researcher
Victor	13	Male	Mexican American	Student researcher
Ameera	18	Female	Yemeni	Student researcher
Chenda	15	Female	Cambodian	Student researcher
Alejandra	16	Female	Mexican American	Student researcher

took on contract work with this youth development organization. In addition, Jocelyn had a part-time contract job as the teacher for an ethnic studies class focusing on Filipino Studies at a local urban high school, composed of one-third Black students, one-third Asian students and one-third Latino students. Jocelyn reported feeling stretched thin by her three part-time jobs while being the main project director and primary instructor. In addition to these work responsibilities, she was in the midst of applying to law school during the time the project was happening.

Rashna

Rashna was a trainer and consultant with Youth Voices, and she provided technical assistance, training and capacity-building to the Central Youth United project and to Jocelyn. She met with the team once weekly—half as often as Jocelyn met with them—to provide curriculum and training on the PAR process and to facilitate additional team-building activities using Youth Voice's curriculum. When Rashna provided these weekly trainings, Jocelyn's role shifted from being the primary instructor into a support capacity. In this role, she would interrupt to encourage student researchers to speak up, enforce team rules, or otherwise support Rashna's instruction. Only on a few occasions has Rashna taught the group alone. Her role in the project was to provide training on the PAR process and support to the primary instructor. Further, she was there to provide coaching to Jocelyn regarding planning, strategies and interventions, and to assess and support Jocelyn's role in creating a youth–adult partnership. Further, Rashna's role was to provide capacity-building support to Jocelyn on how to facilitate a youth-led process and how to institutionalize youth voice in the program planning cycle.

Rashna identified as a 29-year-old Pakistani woman and as a PAR trainer and instructor. She had worked at Youth Voices for over four years and directed its community health program, where she worked with marginalized young people in urban, public schools and in community-based nonprofits. She also provided organizational development, consulting on topics such as adultism, youth–adult partnerships, and nonprofit board development.

Terrence

Terrence joined the project right at the beginning and initially showed great promise as an actively engaged student researcher in the youth-led participatory PAR project. He is a member of Representing Ourselves. Terrence was the only African American student researcher in the project. He was 16 years old when he participated in the Central Youth United PAR project. He said that he loves his neighborhood and provided a thoughtful analysis of Central's strengths and the areas where Central needs to improve. He expressed pride in having an active role in improving Central throughout the project. Despite his sharp analysis, Terrence struggled academically in school, where he does not feel supported to succeed. A year younger than Jason, Terrence is one of Jason's closest friends. After Jason was suddenly hospitalized, Terrence's attendance dropped dramatically and he attended meetings only a few times afterwards.

Jason

With heritage from El Salvador and Mexico, Jason identifies as Latino—as Mexican American and Salvadoran—and also as a long-time member of Representing Ourselves. At 17 years old, he was older than most of the student researchers and proved to be a leader from the beginning of the project. All of the young men showed a high respect for him, and his social skills and popularity were evident from the start. Jason expressed a strong desire to help improve Central and articulated a pointed analysis of the forces and factors influencing his neighborhood. Jason had difficulties with school, which he did not find relevant to his goals. During the first phase of the project, his easy humor, mellow nature and charisma contributed a light-hearted, social tone to the project. Combined with his popularity, jokes and ready storytelling, his enthusiasm about the project's goals positively influenced the other young men on the team. Jason's early commitment to the project engendered in the other young men a sense that this project's aims were relevant and important. After a traumatic event led to Jason's hospitalization, which forced him to miss five weeks of the project, he returned to the project haunted by the need to recover, both emotionally and physically, and his relationship to the project changed and negatively impacted his own participation and group dynamics. Towards the end of the project, Jason was eventually fired from the CYU team because of his changed behavior and missed sessions.

Miguel

Miguel identified as Latino and Filipino and was 14 years old. He was one of the most engaged, enthusiastic and dynamic student researchers. Miguel's charisma and interpersonal skills made him well liked in the group, and although he was several years younger than Jason and Terrence, he often stood up for his own opinions to offer an alternative view. Miguel occasionally boasted about having been a member of Representing Ourselves since he was 8 years old. His participation in youth development programs became evident when he signaled that he was familiar with several of the team-building activities that Jocelyn and Rashna facilitated. Miguel was consistently enthusiastic and motivated to participate in project exercises. He even reprimanded Jason and Terrence on several occasions for their disengagement, and successfully refocused them. Miguel reported that he joined the project because he was passionate about helping to improve his neighborhood. Unfortunately, at the beginning of the project he had to leave Central Youth United because he had to move out of the neighborhood after his parents decided Central was unsafe for him.

Eric

Eric identified as Latino and White, and at 14 years old he was one of the younger members of the project. Eric reported having difficulties in school and said he often cut classes because he found school to be boring. At the beginning of the project, his earnest and sincere disposition was evident in his enthusiastic, positive comments and active participation in all project activities. As the project wore on, he developed an interpersonal conflict with Jason that went unresolved. This caused increased tensions in the project. Additionally, Eric was going through family problems at home as well as having problems in school. Towards the middle of the project, Eric stopped coming to the project and Jocelyn fired him because of his large number of unexcused absences.

Victor

Victor was a member of Representing Ourselves. Victor was the only one of the five young men from Representing Ourselves to stay on the project from its commencement until the end. Victor identifies as Mexican American and was the youngest member at 13 years old. While all of the other student researchers were in high school, he was still in middle school. He struggled in most of his classes in school and mostly received C and D grades except in math—one term he received an A in math. Victor is Alejandra's younger brother. Although Victor was quiet and seemed shy at the beginning and in the middle of the project, in the last phase of the project his participation in discussions was animated, confident and opinionated. He got along well with the other student researchers and reported in his interviews that he did not see any barriers to being the youngest member of Central Youth United. When he became the only boy remaining on the team, he said that he felt comfortable working with the three girls.

Ameera

Hailing from Yemen in the Middle East, Ameera identified as Yemeni and she also strongly identified with being Muslim. At 18 years old, she was the oldest member of the group. Ameera is an alumna of Sister Space, a youth development organization in Central located blocks away from the project, and she recently received the latter's annual college scholarship award, which afforded her the opportunity to attend college. After team members expressed interest in applying to college, Ameera gave a talk to the group about the college application process, in which she encouraged others to consider applying to college. She does well in school and plans to be a dentist. She lives in the same low-income housing complex as Victor and Alejandra, although she did not know them before joining this project. Ameera enjoyed working with Victor and did not hesitate to stand up for the team expectations and admonish either the young men or the young women when they were off-task. She seemed to get along well with everyone, and she and Victor were probably the only two group members who did not experience a major interpersonal conflict with one of their peers over the entire seven months of biweekly meetings. Ameera asserted that her participation in Central Youth United opened up her eyes to her responsibility to help her community.

Chenda

Chenda is a current member of Sister Space, and she holds this organization in very high regard. She does well in school. She identifies as Cambodian and although she participates in youth programming in Central, she is the only team member who does not live in Central. She lives in a low-income housing complex in a predominantly low-income, African American neighborhood that borders Central. Her neighborhood faces issues similar to those the Central Youth United team's community needs assessment describes. Chenda is 15 years old and very serious about her participation in the Central Youth United Participatory Action Research project. A dedicated and reliable student researcher, she was known by her fellow team members to be a hard worker. She revealed in her interviews that she has a low tolerance for unfocused behavior. Chenda is somewhat shy in groups, but voiced her critiques and recommendations for the project during our three interviews. She reported that she did not vocalize this feedback to either of the two project instructors. Chenda and Ameera were enthusiastic about working together in paired work.

Alejandra

Alejandra joined the project almost one-third of the way into its process. She is a member of Representing Ourselves (RO), a violence-prevention, youth development and civic engagement nonprofit organization located in Central. She was the only young woman from RO. Alejandra identifies as Mexican American and as an avid sports player. She is enrolled in mostly honors classes in school and does fairly well in school. She told me that she was invested in this project because she wants to help her neighborhood and stop the violence in Central; she personally knew five young people who had been shot. She is 16 years old and Victor's older sister. Alejandra never hesitated to issue instructions to her younger brother and all of the other boys in the project. When she came on board, all of the young men's teasing of her little brother, Victor, scaled down significantly. Alejandra also proved to be fearless in admonishing Jason and Eric, or anyone else, when they became unfocused, challenging them directly to pay attention and follow the group agreements. This approach worked well in focusing the young men. Alejandra's serious, tough demeanor caused the other two young women to be intimidated by her at first, but after they got to know her, they worked well together. Alejandra was the most vocal, confident and celebrated presenter during the question-and-answer session during the team's final presentation to community stakeholders.

Profiles of Organizations Affiliated With the CYU Project

The Central Community Development Center (CCDC)

Since 1997, the Central Community Development Center (CCDC) has worked to serve its mission to "strengthen the social, physical, and economic well being of the Filipino American community and the [Central] community with special attention to the underserved segments of the community." True to its mission to develop both the Filipino American community and the wider Central community, only one of the eight young people of color who were referred to join Central Youth United's PAR project by the CCDC's partnering organizations had a Filipino heritage. The CCDC's main purpose is to develop the Central community by increasing access to economic, health and social services by developing culturally relevant programs and by collaboration with existing programs.

By providing a community center, CCDC also aims to "strengthen community ties, facilitate the sharing of resources and expertise among service providers in SOMA, and to build leadership skills and the capacity of service providers to effectively provide relevant social services to the community." In addition to regular programming, the community center provides sliding-scale housing to low-income residents, a food bank, a senior citizens' center, a computer lab and a bookstore focused on Filipino culture. The Central Youth United PAR project examined in this book met at the CCDC community center. The CCDC also funds and convenes the Central Youth Task Force, composed of several youth-serving nonprofit organizations. I interviewed Janice, Executive Director of the CCDC, who reported on the history of Central and the background of the project.

The Central Community Organizing Alliance

The Central Community Organizing Alliance (CCOA; a pseudonym) was founded in 2001 by a group of grassroots organizations, following the anti-displacement community organizing campaigns to save residents' homes and small businesses. Its mission "is to build and support a strong, organized community that takes collective action to achieve equity for the low-income, people of color, immigrant and working class communities in [Central] through organizing, leadership development and community planning." The CCOA is a member of the Central Youth Task Force. After hearing the Central Youth United PAR project's presentation and recommendation for a youth center, the CCOA ultimately invited CYU youth representatives to join the Central Youth Task Force. The CCOA committed to organizing Central community members to fight for a youth center. I interviewed both Malaya, the CCOA's Director, and Michelle, Director of Community Planning, to explore the history of community action in Central and background of the CYU project.

Representing Ourselves

Representing Ourselves is a youth leadership development, violence-prevention and civic participation program that provides training and activities for young people in distressed communities who are either "at risk of engaging in criminal activities or have been involved in the juvenile justice system." Since its inception 13 years prior to the Central Youth United PAR project, Representing Ourselves' mission has been to involve marginalized young people in self-advocating for their own needs. Representing Ourselves' theory of change is that "by providing youth with valuable tools, leadership skills, and opportunities for safe interaction and community civic engagement, they will become leaders and advocates for change within themselves, their families, and their communities." Its training sessions and programs take place in schools, community centers, through street outreach and in a local juvenile detention facility. Representing Ourselves referred five young men and one young woman to the Central Youth United project, all of whom participated in CYU. I interviewed Emelda, a coordinator and senior staff member at Representing Ourselves, to get her perspective on the Central Youth United project, and the participation of the five CYU team members her organization referred to the project.

Sister Space

Sister Space (a pseudonym) is a youth development program for girls and young women in the Central neighborhood and other nearby neighborhoods. Its vision is to advance "generations of strong and creative women who realize their potential, live healthy lives and make a positive impact on their communities." It provides a safe space to cultivate the leadership of "Latina, African American, Asian, Arab, Pacific Islander, White and multiracial" girls and young women aged 11–24. Sister Space aims to "support the growth of low-income and immigrant girls and young women of color in urban communities" who speak languages other than English at home. Sister Space offers culturally relevant and gender-specific leadership development programs incorporating arts education, mentorship and life skills. Sister Space connects girls and young women with a community of supportive adults who help them use their skills to address issues they face in their lives and to create community change. Sister Space referred two young women to the Central Youth United project, both of whom participated in CYU. I interviewed Linh, a program coordinator at Sister Space, to gain her perspective on the CYU project and the growth of the two young women referred by her organization.

The Central Youth Task Force

The Central Youth Task Force is hosted by the Central Community Development Center (CCDC). The Central Youth Task Force is composed of the CCDC, the Central Community Organizing Alliance, Representing Ourselves, Sister Space and a local after-school program. In addition to its member organizations having referred all eight of the student researchers in Central Youth United's PAR project, the Task Force created and funded it. Realizing that there was no current community needs assessment and a lack of youth voice in community development and planning, the Task Force commissioned the PAR project with youth, which was also framed publicly as a youth-led community needs assessment. The Task Force contacted Youth Voices and contracted with it to provide training and technical assistance in participatory action research for the Central Youth United project. I interviewed a total of five adult members of the Task Force, who are all affiliated with the Central Youth United project.

Youth Voices

Youth Voices (a pseudonym) was a nonprofit intermediary organization that provided training, consulting and technical assistance in PAR with youth and youth-led evaluation. Youth Voices' purpose was to support PAR projects, particularly ones composed of marginalized young people—youth of color, low-income youth, immigrants, and lesbian, gay, bisexual, transgender and questioning (LGBTQ) youth—to create the conditions for social justice. Funded primarily by philanthropic foundation grants, Youth Voices envisions a world in which "young people and adults share knowledge and power to create a more just, sustainable and democratic society."

Youth Voices had three initiatives focusing on education, community health and youth organizing in California's Bay Area and Central Valley regions. Using its interactive, experiential-based popular education curriculum, Youth Voices built the capacity of PAR teams to take lead roles in identifying, planning and implementing action research projects for community change. Youth Voices also provided coaching to adult allies to help them learn how to support and guide young people and their youth-led projects. In addition, it provided consulting to school districts, alliances, coalitions and networks on ways to institutionalize youth voice, youth participation and youth-led PAR projects as part of the annual planning and assessment cycle of organizational systems.

Youth Voices assigned Rashna to provide training, consulting and technical assistance to the Central Youth United project to support its PAR process. Drawing on its history of providing training and technical assistance in the first PAR project with youth in Central, a youth-led community needs assessment in Central five years earlier, Youth Voices drew up a contract with the Central Community Development Center, which hosted, created and funded this second PAR project with youth in Central, the CYU project. The Central Youth United PAR project with young people was also conceived as a youth-led community needs assessment to understand the current needs of the Central neighborhood.

4

A PEDAGOGY OF PRAXIS

Connecting Reflection and Action

Introduction

This chapter describes what I term a *pedagogy of praxis*, a teaching approach that occurred within the participatory action research (PAR) project. This chapter foregrounds the PAR curriculum and instructional practices, and applies the framework of a pedagogy of praxis as a way to understand the PAR curriculum and pedagogy. The key themes in this chapter include the motivations for youth involvement, empowering marginalized young people and supporting youth voice, the synergy between action and learning, honoring the expertise of young people regarding their communities and experiences, building community across diverse groups of young people, and young people as critical agents of change. The points of tension for analysis and discussion include the ways in which the pedagogy of praxis framework was supported through the instructional approaches and curriculum in this collaborative inquiry project.

The PAR project offered effective opportunities and supports that allowed student researchers to take risks and be vulnerable in order to develop teamwork and their analysis skills. These structured curriculum activities that involve taking risks and being vulnerable also benefited the development of research skills as they conducted their research project that would culminate in a collective action plan for positive change in their local community. For example, the community mapping activity highlights how learning was situated in the student researchers' lived experiences. Rashna, the secondary adult instructor, remarked about this activity, "They did really good with the [community] mapping activity. Anytime they had to talk about the neighborhood or community, they're really into it and they're pretty successful at it." Students owned their expertise about their communities through these activities and showed that they were invested in their community and its fate when given the opportunity to share their knowledge and apply it towards developing an action plan to improve their neighborhood. For example, in the "Community Mapping" exercise, student researchers were excited to contribute landmarks and other assets in their neighborhood to their maps of their community.

In the Community Mapping exercise, the student researchers had to get into pairs to create a map of the Central neighborhood community on a big piece of butcher paper. Eric had just started with the program and he was paired with Ameera. As the pair began to select colored markers and draw symbols of their neighborhood on their maps, Eric and Ameera quickly realized that they held radically different perspectives about their neighborhood. Eric expressed his dismay that Ameera wanted to draw the local public library on their community map, exclaiming, "But no one goes in there! I don't want the library on our map." Ameera responded quickly to his assertion, proclaiming, "Yes, they do. I use the library all the time to study. And so do a lot of people." Eric looked away, shaking his head subtly and indicating embarrassment that his map would have the library on it. Then he sighed and consented, exhaling a soft "Fine."

A few moments later, Eric's concentration was broken as he was disrupted from carefully shading in another local building in yellow marker by Ameera's sudden protesting remark, "You're drawing the gold tooth shop on our map?!" Eric explained that this was an important landmark in Central and that everyone he knew either was a customer there or was saving money so that one day they could get gold fronts. Ameera began to chuckle, saying, "I don't know a single person who has even *once* thought about going in there." Eric's arms dramatically dropped to his sides and his head slumped in apparent exasperation and defeat. She responded with, "But okay, it's fine. We can keep it." He nodded his appreciation for this agreement and went back to quietly and intently coloring in his landmark. He was so focused that he didn't notice Ameera watching him color for a few seconds longer, then sighing, looking away and picking up her next marker.

This exercise, designed to tap into the funds of knowledge that each student researcher had about their neighborhood's assets, both drew out their expertise about what was important to Central residents and displayed their different experiences and perceptions of Central. Commenting on the community mapping activity, Rashna shares how she was stumped when Terrence and Miguel's map and Jason and Victor's map only showed one main street that ran through Central: Washington Street. Rashna recalls how she expected them to see the same boundaries of Central that she saw—the ones that were displayed on an official city map. She remembers the moment that she realized that she needed to listen to how they saw their neighborhood even when it didn't match her previous understanding:

> It was interesting because I would ask, "Tell me what the boundaries of Central are? Tell me street to street. Washington Street to what? This street

to what?" And they were like, "It's Washington Street." They were so adamant. And finally you have to just be like, "Right. This is Central to you: Washington Street." That's one of those places where I think you have to take this in, step back and be like, "Right. I'm asking you to map your community. This is what you see as your community." And if I mapped my community, I probably wouldn't want to map it based on someone telling me, "What are the gridlines?" But my community is my street. So I had to say, "You're right. I'm asking you to tell me. Let me *let you* tell me."

Rashna realized that in her attempt to situate learning in the residents' own knowledge and experience, she was bumping up against her own assumptions that her knowledge was correct and theirs was not—even though she didn't live in Central.

Rashna talks about the ways that the mapping exercise led to larger-group discussions about issues not directly represented on each pair of student researchers' maps. She says:

They don't bring up a lot of times the issues about the condos and the gentrification. But if you ask them little questions about it, they can talk about what happens, who those people are, the ways that they get looked at by them, the ways those people call the cops [on them] or the ways the cops take pictures [of them]. Stories come out. And that's always been interesting about them. It might not be in the most conscious place where they're gonna draw it out on the map, but if you ask them about it, they'll usually tell you, "Yeah, this is also a part of it."

After realizing that she needed to consistently step back to really hear the young people's perspectives about their own neighborhood, Rashna discovered that posing questions about Central led to additional stories and analysis about larger issues that directly impacted them, such as gentrification, police surveillance and the new condo dwellers' attitudes towards them as working-class teenagers. The Community Mapping activity was followed up with the CYU team's participation in a walking tour of Central. Jocelyn took advantage of an existing program that has college student volunteers serve as tour guides and relay the history of Central up to the present. As a result of discussions based on both the mapping activity that identified community assets in Central and the walking tour explaining Central's history, the research team was able to decide on a research question for their study: "What do youth *really* need in Central?"

The PAR curriculum and teaching approach included a participatory, active curriculum in which the two instructors provided opportunities and supports for student researchers to participate in decisions to design and plan their project. Ameera contends that she learns better when adults scaffold her participation in interactive activities where she can contribute her ideas. She asserts:

> I think doing it ourselves is better because first of all, we're coming up with the ideas. And also, you get to talk, move around. You just put yourself into the job, not just sitting and taking ideas from someone else that are theirs.

In the PAR process with young people, student participation and active learning are promoted through an interactive process in which young people's ideas are supported through structured, curriculum activities.

Participatory Action Research as a Structured Teaching Approach

The *pedagogy of praxis* framework describes the experiential, participatory teaching and learning approach, which connected an analysis of community issues with action to address these issues. In this pedagogy of praxis (Freire, 2001; Gadotti, 1996) approach, young people are engaged in praxis, connecting theory and action. A pedagogy of praxis connects critical reflection about student researchers' own social conditions with collective action to transform those conditions. Centering student researchers' prior knowledge through dialogue and a participatory process, a pedagogy of praxis gradually builds research and strategic thinking skills. A pedagogy of praxis scaffolds student voice, agency and participation to contribute to reflection on community needs to develop an action plan to address community needs. Through the PAR process, young people draw on their prior knowledge and experiences to identify salient issues their communities face and participate as decision-makers who direct the topic and trajectory of their curriculum by deciding what topic will be the focus of their research.

The youth-led PAR process includes cycles of reflection and action and further reflection (Atweh et al., 1998; Freire, 2001; Ginwright, 2008). The usage of reflection and action in a pedagogy of praxis usage aligns it with current PAR scholarship and research on young people's examination of the root causes that shape their communities' current conditions and application of their action research findings to embark on an action to improve those conditions (Cammarota & Fine, 2008; Cannella, 2008; Ginwright, 2008). Greene (2008) asserts that PAR projects with youth connect theory with action as opposed to theorizing in which students reflect on ideas, "abstractly beyond the world of human experience," without applicable consequence (p. 45). Thus, in linking theory with action, the PAR process seems especially important for educational research, given the current realities facing schools, in which educators often struggle to engage student interests in academics. As Ginwright (2008) contends, "research is most useful when young people develop skills both to explain systemic causes of issues that shape their lives and to act to transform those conditions" (p. 21).

The PAR process in the Central Youth United project involved participatory, structured activities that centered student researchers' input, experience and analysis to impact the design, planning and implementation of the PAR project. For example, before selecting their research topic, student researchers first engaged in a community mapping activity and then participated in a local walking tour of their neighborhood in which university students presented the neighborhood's history. These experiential learning exercises drew on student researchers' existing knowledge and presented new information and open-ended questions to allow the student researchers to consider their neighborhood's historical context and identify neighborhood assets and past and present issues facing their neighborhood. The Community Mapping activity included facilitated discussions by both instructors, in which the student researchers contributed their experiences with safety and violence in the streets, police harassment, gentrification, and a lack of access to resources and affordable social services such as health care, secure housing, opportunities to make a livable wage and job training.

Key decisions were made through student participation in hands-on exercises that hinged on active, collaborative learning. An example of participatory learning activities is the PAR team's process for selecting the research methods they would use to collect data. First, the team engaged in a collaborative learning activity in which they divided into pairs to work together to draw on their prior knowledge to create working definitions for each possible research method they might choose: surveys, interviews, observations, PhotoVoice, focus groups. Next, they participated in an experiential exercise in which they rotated through five learning stations to take a survey, use an existing interview protocol to interview each other, analyze fieldnotes from participant observations, evaluate images that visually document conditions created through PhotoVoice, and use a focus group guide to pose questions. Then, the student researchers identified pros and cons of each of the five possible research methods based on their experience in the previous exercise with surveys, interviews, observations, PhotoVoice and focus groups. Finally, the two instructors guided the student researchers through a discussion of the benefits and drawbacks of each research method, based on these experiential activities, to collectively decide which method would best answer their research question. Both instructors supported student participation through structured opportunities for student input on key decision points in project planning and design, such as identifying the topic of their research project and their selecting methods for collecting information.

CYU's Purpose and Goals, and Motivations for Joining the Project

Jocelyn is the primary project instructor who meets twice weekly with the group, totaling four hours per week. As an adult instructor and project curriculum developer, she discusses her vision for the project. Jocelyn's vision focuses on building skills and leadership development, and engendering a desire for young people to give back to their community. She asserts:

> My vision is that they learn all these different skills and I hope that whatever they learn that they take it on and remember and use it later on in their life. And I think that can help them grow up into a leader ... I think the first step is for them to get involved, and once they get involved, it's having a lot of mentors in terms of adult allies. But also to still be a mentor to other youth to help them grow. And then the youth being mentors, too, to the adults. So I can see this group of young folks becoming leaders and hopefully really remembering what they learned in this particular setting, but not just using it to give back in the community, but also using what they learned to give back in their school ... Victor was like, "Well, I wanna be someone that all the kids look up to." So I guess my vision is to see them become mentors to other youth in the community.

One of the project's goals is to promote an ambition in the student researchers to give back to both their community and their school, and to develop their mentorship and leadership skills. In alignment with Jocelyn's vision for learning outcomes for the student researchers, research shows that involvement in youth-led PAR projects can have multiple benefits for young people (Atweh et al., 1998; McIntyre, 2000). One thrust of the PAR project with young people is that it holds significance for young people, encouraging them to work towards improving their community (Morrell, 2006).

Rashna, the secondary adult instructor of the PAR curriculum, is from Youth Voices, an intermediary nonprofit that supports youth-led PAR projects through training and technical support. Every week, Rashna provided instruction in the PAR curriculum and technical assistance on the PAR process to CYU. A Pakistani woman in her late twenties with a bachelor's degree, she had been working at Youth Voices as a PAR curriculum instructor, trainer and consultant for over three years and also had experience as a curriculum developer and workshop facilitator. Rashna summarizes what she sees as the overall charge of the project. She reflects:

> I think Central Youth United's mission is to be able to both talk about what young people need in Central and then to address those needs. And whether that's through them doing that work or through giving their recommendations to other key stakeholders and saying, "You need to address this issue." I think that's what their work is about.

As part of the action component of their PAR project, Rashna envisions the Central Youth United team taking action to hold community stakeholders accountable for implementing their action research recommendations. As a secondary instructor of the PAR curriculum, Rashna sees her role as being to provide skill-building training for the PAR team and build Jocelyn's capacity to be an adult partner with student researchers. She discusses her role in providing a training curriculum that enables student researchers to define the solutions to the problems they face. She asserts:

> I think that we work from more of an assets-based approach and this idea that *all* young people have something really important to say. And that the folks that are the most impacted by a situation or oppression or whatever the issue is, need to be the ones defining that issue and coming up with the solutions ... Youth Voices runs from this really core belief that if you're impacted by something, you have the answer—more so than anybody else. So I think we run from this empowerment model and have young people work on something bigger than themselves, even. And actually create social justice or create conditions for social justice within their schools and communities ... And it is about people defining their own lives and coming up with the solutions and choices that *they* need versus us.

Rashna envisages her role as a PAR curriculum instructor as being to facilitate a process whereby the student researchers are valued as the most knowledgeable people to identify solutions that meet their own needs and their community's needs. Student researchers are empowered through the PAR curriculum process to see that they have agency to work collaboratively to create the conditions for social justice in their schools and communities. Whyte (1991) emphasizes that a fundamental principle of the PAR method deems that people who are closest to the issues they face have the greatest understanding of these issues and should take a lead role in developing effective solutions.

Emelda is project director at Representing Ourselves, one of the two organizations that referred youth members to CYU. Like Rashna's, Emelda's vision for the youth-led community needs assessment is to center student voice. A graduate from an Ivy League university, Emelda is a Latina in her early thirties who was raised in a working-class, predominantly Latino, neighborhood that borders Central. She has extensive experience over the years coordinating and directing youth development programs as a youth worker, workshop facilitator and dedicated program staff member. In these roles, she has worked with diverse young people with limited resources and successfully guided them to claim their visions to learn, grow and get their lives back on track. Emelda explains CYU's purpose:

> The thing that I really like about the [CYU] needs assessment is that it's young people talking to other young people about what they want and

what they need. And I feel like there are so many different things adults like to tell young people: what they need and what they want. And, yeah, we have the experience. And they say hindsight has 20/20 vision. So we have experience, and there are reasons why adults say things. But I think it's really good for young people to talk to other young people and find out what it is that they really want and what they really need to help them be happier and healthier.

Emelda envisions a youth-led needs assessment in which young people, those closest to the problems youth face, gather information from other young people on youth needs in Central.

The Central Youth United members were attracted to join this positive youth development program because it aligned with their values and visions to be agents of positive community change. The CYU project was designed as a PAR project that involved research to develop an action plan to address community issues and work towards positive community change. The PAR project's purpose was relevant to what young people value, such as their vision for community improvement. This connection between student researchers' values and visions and the project's purpose and goals led to enthusiasm about the project, motivation to join and commitment.

The process for joining the project entailed a referral from a community-based, nonprofit youth development organization and an application process. The student members of the PAR project were all referred to the project by one of two local youth development nonprofit organizations: Sister Space, which focuses on girls' development; and Representing Ourselves, a youth development organization focusing on young people who live in neighborhoods that are facing disinvestment in infrastructure and social services. The student candidates had to fill out a short, one-page application and answer a few brief questions. These questions included "Why did you want to join this project?" and "What is one goal you would like to reach through your participation in this project?" When I asked the student team members to describe the project and its purpose, many of them emphasized the project's goals and vision for community improvement.

All the student researchers reported in their interviews with me that they became involved in the project because the project's goals matched their values, and their vision to improve their community. Chenda, a student researcher who lives in the Spencerville neighborhood that borders Central, sees the project's purpose as creating a safer neighborhood for young people and their families. She explains:

> Central Youth United is a group of students who are reaching out to the community to help find the means to improve the community from what Central is right now. And [it's] trying to provide a safer area—more

[areas]—for the public and for students to use its resources ... I'm part of this project just for the youth.

This vision of improving their community by creating safer public spaces with resources for young people is a theme that resonated across interviews. Concurring with Chenda, Victor, another student researcher, underscores his vision to help engage young people with more opportunities for them to participate:

DW: Can you describe the purpose of Central Youth United?
V: [To] ask people questions, see what they would like to see in Central for the youth, to get them out of the streets, to see what we can do. Instead of going to jail, the youth can go somewhere else.
DW: Okay. What's your role in Central Youth United?
V: My role is to help the community. That's my role in this project.
DW: And what keeps you coming back to this project every week?
V: [I'm] trying to get more stuff for the youth to do in Central.

This project is relevant and legitimate for student researchers because it affords an opportunity for young people to effect meaningful change to both improve their community and acquire more resources to engage youth.

Ameera, the oldest member in the team of 13- to 18-year-old student researchers, clarifies the importance of the project in helping other youth in Central. She explains:

> It's a youth needs assessment. We're helping youth in Central to get what they want. For example, to help them to get more places to be involved ... And also to benefit my community. I live in Central and this program will do something to help it. So this program will help the youth in Central.

The Central Youth United project is relevant to student researchers because it will assess youth needs and help improve conditions for other young people. Alejandra, another of the student researchers, expresses what she sees as the aim of the project. She remarks, "We're trying to improve Central by having youth do it—putting all this information together about youth who live in Central. And we're youth who also live in Central. And we can relate to [the] people we're interviewing." Alejandra describes the purpose of this project as providing a process for youth who live in Central to gather information from their neighborhood peers and put the information together to help improve the community. Student researchers view this project as legitimate and meaningful because they seek an opportunity to improve their community. The PAR process offers an opportunity for student researchers to work collaboratively with other young people and adult instructors to conduct research and analyze community problems in order to design and implement an action plan that aims to address community issues and result in positive change in their community. This connection between analysis and action maps onto a pedagogy of praxis framework, which aims to connect reflection and action. The PAR curriculum and teaching approach sustains a pedagogy of praxis in which young people are supported in developing their analysis and strategic thinking skills, and designing and implementing a plan of action. Through the youth-led PAR process, student researchers contribute an analysis of their prior experiences to identify local issues and gradually develop their sense of agency to impact their environments and participate as decision-makers. Student researchers act as decision-makers both within the research project process and beyond it as they analyze their research findings to make recommendations for next steps to adult decision-makers. Importantly, through dialogue and an interactive process that supports student participation, the PAR process supports a pedagogy of praxis in which young people connect their analysis with action aimed towards positive community change.

A Community-Building Curriculum to Promote Collaborative Inquiry

The first stage of the PAR project curriculum required that the instructors spend time cultivating a sense of community among the student researchers. This community building process was important because it successfully created a safe, supportive learning environment to promote collaborative learning. Adults facilitated a team-building curriculum to build community across diverse backgrounds, especially across race and ethnicity, gender, sexuality, class, nationality and religion. The conditions of safety, respect and trust created through the team-building curriculum were essential in enabling student researchers to take risks and be vulnerable, and promoted participation. Creating a sense of trust and safety is among the key factors in creating effective programs that achieve positive youth development outcomes and create opportunities and support for youth development (Pittman & Wright, 1991). Overall, team-building was successful in allowing students to experience a different way of participating in a community than is typical in traditional classroom learning to collaborate in reaching their learning goals and overarching project goals.

Team-building activities were included in almost every workshop, twice weekly, as part of a process to build relationships and community across diverse experiences, sociopolitical locations and backgrounds. For example, team-builders began on the first day with an exercise called "Four Corners." To begin this activity, Rashna, the adult facilitator, announces to everyone, "I will read a statement. Then you have to move to one of the four corners of the room depending on whether you agree or disagree with the statement." As she explains the rules, she is pointing to the four flip-chart papers she has posted in each of the four corners of the room, labeled "strongly agree," "agree," "disagree" and "strongly disagree." She instructs that she will call on people from each corner to share their opinions. She emphasizes that everyone must remember the ground rules the team created for this project, especially "no put-downs" and "agree to disagree." Rashna reminds them that she will read one statement at a time and then they will move about the room to indicate their perspective, followed by a discussion. Throughout the activity, Rashna read each of the following statements:

> I believe that all youth are lazy.
> I believe that youth have good ideas.
> I believe that youth in Central care about their neighborhood.
> I believe that most adults know what's best for youth.
> I believe that people listen to what youth in Central have to say.
> I believe that young people have the power to create positive change in Central.

The loudest, most enthusiastic eruption of opinions occurs in the discussion that follows after Rashna reads the fourth statement, "I believe that most adults know what's best for youth." After this statement is read, everyone silently moves to the sign that represents their opinion about this statement. It is almost equally divided between "strongly agree," "agree," "disagree," and "strongly disagree." Rashna first calls on Terrence, standing under the "strongly agree" sign. He shares, "Well, I think that kids these days get into trouble a lot and sometimes we need adults to steer us on the right path." Next, Rashna calls on Jason, who is standing in the "disagree" area, and remarks:

> Yeah, it's true that some kids are on the wrong path, but not everyone. But even when we're doing things we know we shouldn't be doing, we still know the path we want to be on. Maybe if my social worker didn't talk down to me or flash on me, I could hear what she was saying better.

Chenda, standing under "strongly disagree," is called on next and she offers:

> Well, I don't think that *all* adults are right *all* the time. My history teacher is real disrespectful to me even though I give her respect and I do all my work and I try to participate in discussions. She disrespects the whole class, but our principal doesn't even believe us or do anything about it.

Chenda's comments ignite a flurry of hand-waving from Miguel, who is standing next to Chenda in "strongly disagree." After being called on, Miguel offers:

> Okay, what about if your teacher just assumes that they know what's best for you but it's actually not best for you? Oh, and what if an adult at a

youth organization just assumes that you don't know anything when actually you could be helping them with their vision, but they don't really
listen? That's why I'm in "strongly disagree" right here!

After a lively discussion in which people strongly disagree but no one is dismissive of anyone else's ideas, Rashna gathers the group to talk about the purpose of
this youth-led project. The team-building curriculum promoted a sense of
respect and trust among student researchers that allowed PAR members to
participate in group discussions and even be vulnerable at times by sharing their
emerging beliefs and perspectives without fear of humiliation from peers. The
ability to participate in group discussions and curriculum activities in a learning
environment characterized by trust built confidence in themselves and each
other as they began to move through the PAR process of engaging in collaborative research. The pedagogy of praxis approach demands that student researchers link theory and action, so developing a sense of trust and community in
sharing their perspectives, respectfully disagreeing with others, and theorizing
together are essential to both the PAR process and participating in a pedagogy
of praxis. Therefore, the team-building curriculum was essential in building a
sense of trust for the student researchers in sharing their views and experiences
with a diverse group who came from a range of backgrounds and were likely
not hold to the same viewpoints.

As referenced in Youth Voice's memorandum of understanding with the
organization that hosts the project, the Central Youth United curriculum
process is designed to team-build. Three key components of pedagogical
approaches successfully created an engaging learning environment characterized
by trust and safety: (1) Teaching and learning is highly structured. (2) Pedagogical approaches are interactive. (3) Teaching and learning is experiential. In
the CYU project, young people are highly engaged in pedagogical approaches
that provide experiential, interactive, structured activities that center dialogue and access their prior knowledge. This participatory, interactive learning
served to scaffold youth leadership skills in project design, planning and
implementation. From her perspective as the primary project facilitator,
Jocelyn believes that team-building is a key goal of Central Youth United. She
declares:

> I think it's more than just a [community] needs assessment. I feel like the
> needs assessment is the result of this process that got youth together from
> two different organizations that don't really work with each other ... I
> think also it's about building a team.

Jocelyn sees the needs assessment as the final product of the process, but values
the importance of building a team between two organizations that are isolated
from each other. One of the student researchers, Ameera, clarifies why it is

important for her group to build a team. She explains, "We started together not knowing each other at first, so at every group meeting there was team-building, where we got to know each other, work with each other." According to Youth Voices' project proposal, these team-building activities are an intentional component of Youth Voice's training curriculum to build a cohesive group that is capable of sustaining momentum over the span of the project, approximately equivalent to the length of an academic year. The main strategy the two adult instructors employed in team-building was the use of structured, interactive activities.

The "Medicine Wheel" activity was designed to build teamwork across diverse work styles. The medicine wheel symbol derives from indigenous epistemological systems. At the start of the activity, Jocelyn explained that the medicine wheel is an important symbol and set of concepts established by Native American knowledge systems, primarily from the Plains First Nations peoples, and that it still plays an important role for them. Jocelyn then passed out a handout to everyone that had a large circle with four colorful quadrants. In one quadrant was a buffalo, in another was an eagle, in the third was a deer and in the last one was a bear. She explained to the group that each animal has different characteristics, remarking:

> The buffalo is one of the leaders and wants to get things done, like a taskmaster, but they need to learn how to work with other people. The eagle is a visionary: They have big visions, but they don't really use their own hands to put it in place. The deer is more the compassionate and understanding animal—a team player. The deer is often attuned to other people, but this sometimes means the deer may be sensitive to other people's judgments. And then the bear is one that's really traditional and just does it by the book. The bear is a rule-follower who may sometimes judge themselves and others to determine if everyone is following the traditional rules.

After the group had listened to the descriptions of the different characteristics and work styles—a taskmaster, a visionary, a team player and a traditional rule-follower—they had to figure out which animal represented their own working style. Ameera began laughing, remarking, "I'm a buffalo! I love to do things and get them done!" A few people smiled around the table, nodding their heads in agreement with her remark. Chenda muttered, with a tone that hinted at some admiration, "You do get your work done—even by yourself." Ameera responded with "Yeah, but I need to learn how to work better with other people." Then Victor declared, "Hey, I'm a deer, no doubt!" Jason responded, teasing him, "You're a team player? Are you sure about that?" Jocelyn addressed this comment, saying, "Maybe when he's goofing around with you, he doesn't seem focused on the team, but let's hear an explanation from Victor. What makes you a deer, Victor?" Victor affirmed that he was a deer, arguing, "Listen, I have understanding towards other people. That's how I am." Miguel offered that he was an eagle, rationalizing, "Well, people say that I have good ideas, like leadership, even though I may not always follow through with my vision on my own." Jocelyn smiled and asked, "What are you, Chenda?" Chenda responded with "I'm a deer, so I'm emotional and I don't like to be put down. So if you don't put me down, then you can work with me." This early activity allowed the PAR team members a chance to self-identify their personality characteristics and work styles, and realize the strengths and possible blind spots in the diversity of work styles on the team.

In reflecting on the "Medicine Wheel" activity, Chenda clarifies the importance of team-building activities. She declares:

> It is important to know your environment, between the adults and the youth, together. We work together, we get to know each other, and for that it's good that we're communicating. And we're not quiet or anything and not knowing each other. It's best to know what's around you and how their personality works ... It gets us engaged. We talk more. We giggle. We laugh. We talk to each other.

Team-building and relationship-building activities allow the building of relationships between peers, and between youth and adults, through laughing and communicating.

Jocelyn reflects on the significance of the Medicine Wheel activity to help both the instructors and the student researchers to accept and acknowledge team members' different participation styles. She observes:

> Medicine Wheel was way in the beginning when they're just getting to know each other. Victor was a deer. Ameera was a buffalo. She loved to do things and get things done: "Just give me the instructions and I'll do it." And buffalos tend to just do by themselves. And so I could see her changing into the different animals during the project.

Jocelyn's strategic use of this exercise allows the peer group, as well as both instructors, to recognize that everyone brings their own work style to the group, which are packages with both strengths and potential pitfalls. In the Medicine Wheel activity, diverse work styles and traits the group members bring to the table are recognized and valued as assets. When team members have the opportunity to be self-reflective about their work styles and the strengths and potential blind spots that may come with each package, their work styles were able to change throughout the duration of the project. Chenda affirms the importance of team-building activities in which they had to get to know one another. She remarks, "I like the team-building, where you get to know each other and then you have to work together to get to something. And you have to direct something. Or solve something … It gets your attention." Through the process of working together to achieve a goal, the student researchers get to know each other more deeply by participating in team-building activities.

A Gradual Process to Bolster Marginalized Students' Voice

One of the key components of the PAR process with young people as a teaching strategy is to bolster student voice, which aligns with the pedagogy of praxis framework. Elaborating on her use of experiential, interactive exercises, Rashna, an adult PAR instructor, discusses her strategies to bolster student voice:

> What I've seen is that young people are used to their voices being really silenced, and their opinions not mattering too much. And so you can't just bring a group of young people together and necessarily expect that it's gonna be okay, like, "It's your floor. Go ahead." It's a slow process and it's really one of building skills and leadership capacity and empowering people to feel like they have something important and meaningful to say and that they will be listened to—even if they're not agreed with—that they will be listened to.

Reflecting on the process of promoting youth voice as a PAR instructor, Rashna considers:

> I think sometimes we get into a setup if we want to integrate youth voice, and then we'll just grab any youth we can and put them at the table and then say, "Go!" And it's a big setup for everybody. It's [actually] a really slow process.

The adult facilitator's role is to facilitate this gradual process to support youth voice, agency and participation at the decision-making table. In describing the adult's role in supporting youth voice, Alejandra, a student researcher, confirms that a key factor is the adult facilitator's ability to guide the student researchers through the steps in the process. She explains:

> The facilitators really just listen and they really try to progress us [to] each step—every time we're here—to try to get us to the final point. And they're not just leaving us on the first level. They're just taking their time, slowly, level by level.

The gradual progression through the steps of the participatory action research process is a key factor in successful strategies to support student voice.

Participatory action research has emphasized that politically and socioeco-nomically marginalized people possess expertise about the root causes of the conditions their communities face (Morrell, 2008). The educational philosophy of Paulo Freire is well cited by current scholars and researchers of PAR with young people as contributing to PAR's theoretical legacy (Cammarota & Fine, 2008; Torre et al., 2008). In his work on alternative research methodologies, Freire (1982) observes:

> The silenced are not just incidental to the curiosity of the researcher but are the masters of inquiry into the underlying causes of the events in their world. In this context research becomes a means of moving them beyond silence into a quest to proclaim the world.
>
> (pp. 30–31)

Freire asserts that marginalized research participants possess expertise that can both benefit the direction of research projects and build agency within these research participants. In practice, both of the terms "participatory action research" and "popular education" are often used to describe an interactive, empowering pedagogy that facilitates a participatory process in which learners interrogate their own prior knowledge and experiences in order to contribute their ideas, perspectives and experiences, and deepen their analysis. Scholarship in the field of education often refers to this pedagogical approach as critical pedagogy.

A Pedagogy That Supports Youth Participation and Active Learning

The pedagogy and curriculum in the Central Youth United project provided support and opportunities for student researchers to give input, take risks and be vulnerable, which developed teamwork, strategic thinking skills and research skills. This learning environment was characterized by structured, interactive pedagogical approaches in which learning was situated in young people's prior knowledge. Another example of research skill development is exemplified in the "Focus Group Facilitation" activity. In this activity, some student research-ers role-played their upcoming focus group facilitation roles by asking questions from the student researchers' focus group guide. Other student researchers role-played the focus group participants.

In this Focus Group Facilitation exercise, Rashna points to the agenda she has hung up in two-toned lines alternating between red and orange marker, and instructs some people to role-play being focus group facilitators and others to be participants. Eric begins to role-play the student researchers' upcoming facilita-tion roles by asking questions from the youth-created focus group guide. All other research team members actively role-play community members in Central and provide answers about what young people in Central need.

To debrief the activity, Rashna directs the group to elicit answers about "dos" and "don'ts" for facilitating focus groups. Rashna asks, "What did Eric do as a facilitator?" A few hands spring up and Rashna calls on one: "Okay, Chenda." Chenda vocalizes matter-of-factly, "Well, he paid attention to us." Rashna records this on flip-chart paper in baby blue marker, while asking, "Anything else?" Ameera proposes, "Yeah, his body language showed he wanted to hear answers from us." Rashna responds, "Uh-huh," while writing down this contribution and then calls out, "Alejandra?" Alejandra suggests, "You were conversing with us." She writes down her exact words in baby blue marker. "Good. Jason, did you notice anything that we did as facilitators that worked well?" Jason responds, "Hold on; I'm thinking." Then he offers, "You were feeling us; you paid attention." "Feeling us" is recorded on the over-sized paper. Rashna asks, "What else?" Alejandra shouts out, "Good eye contact." She writes this down, asking, "All right, anything else we did?" It is quiet for a few moments as everyone seems out of answers. "Victor?" He puts forth, "You were serious about your questions." "Yep. Great. Other things?" "Well," Ameera begins, "You asked good follow-up questions." "That's right. Like what?" She hesitates and Chenda jumps in, "You asked 'who, what, when, where and why.'"

After this debrief and cataloging of focus group skills that Rashna elicited from the team, she unveils another flip-chart paper with the title "Focus Group Questions." She relays, "One question Eric asked from our practice focus group that you all had trouble answering was 'How would you change Central?' So how else can we ask that question differently for the real focus groups?" Rashna then writes down all their responses to revise their focus group questions on the flip-chart visual (see Table 4.1).

The final part of this exercise is to fill in a flip-chart table with the "don'ts" of focus group facilitation. Rashna used an experiential activity first, in which

TABLE 4.1 CYU Focus Group Facilitation Lesson Visual Aid

"Dos" of Focus Group Facilitation	*Focus Group Questions*
Paid attention to us; conversating [sic] with us	How do you see Central in the future?
Feeling us; good eye contact; serious about questions	Will the new buildings going up affect youth in Central? Why or why not?
Good follow-up questions	Do you trust people in Central? Why or why not?
Asked "who, what, when, where and why"	What's the perfect neighborhood that you can imagine look like?

they see what it feels like to be participants in a focus group. She then followed this up by asking them to revise their focus group guide.

The pedagogy of praxis and PAR curriculum was designed to support student researchers in contributing their input to participate in decisions about the research project through structured, interactive activities that situated learning in young people's prior knowledge. Student researchers developed research skills through participatory activities grounded in their own experiences. In this example, student researchers learned how to conduct a focus group to collect data through role-playing this new role and then analyzing their own experiences. Through learning through their own mock experiences as focus group facilitators and participants, student researchers saw that they were capable of analyzing "dos" and "don'ts" of facilitation participating in a learning process in which they offered their own insights based on their experiences and analysis. In this way, student researchers were facilitated through a process in which they taught each other tips about how to perform successfully in a new role, while building their confidence that they would succeed in this new role that was expected of them. Showing the marginalized student researchers that they do have a valuable analysis and can apply their knowledge to evaluate unfamiliar situations enables students to see for themselves that they are competent, and capable of taking on new roles and responsibilities. This process is crucial to empowering marginalized students in order for them to build their academic skills.

Structured Activities to Elicit Youth Voice, Experiences and Perspectives

Increased youth participation means that an interactive curriculum needs to slow down the process to take the time needed for young people to have a role in meaningful involvement in project planning, leadership and decisions. Victor commented that his voice was heard when he took the lead in preparing a budget and presenting his budget during a meeting with potential funders. Victor sees taking a leadership role that has a meaningful impact on the project as an indicator that his voice is heard:

DW: Can you think of a time where your voice was heard?
v: I liked talking about the budget [at a meeting with potential funders].
DW: The budget? Okay. What was your role with the budget?
v: 'Cause I was the person that added all the stuff together. So, I liked the part where we did the budget.

Student researchers view their voices as being heard when they take an active lead in roles that carry meaningful responsibility. Such meaningful responsibility impacts the project's success, failure or direction.

Jason cites a time that his voice is heard as occurring in another focus group role-play activity. In this exercise, Jason played the role of being a focus group participant. Jason described a real event he witnessed, and recalled that team members listened attentively to his story.

DW: Does anyone know of a time when you were speaking and you were heard?

J: Yeah, all year. When we were practicing the focus groups ... I talked about things that I've seen. People were listening.

In this activity, Jason played the role of being a Central resident participating in CYU's focus group. Rashna agrees that this time was one of the few moments in the project where Jason contributed his perspective and his voice was really heard. She recalls:

> I think some of the deepest moments in the project were when I would—and the site facilitator [Jocelyn] would—run their focus group with them. So we would take their focus group guide that they had created and we would run it for them. To model facilitation, but then also, because it was like, "Well, you're Central youth, what do you say to these answers?" ... I feel like those focus groups were some of the moments where Jason, in particular, would focus for almost the entire thing. And he gave a lot. He spoke a lot and I think that was really powerful. I think you finally saw and heard his voice.

Rashna observes that Jason was highly focused and engaged when team members listened to his stories.

In this focus group facilitation role-playing activity, Rashna points to the agenda she has hung up, with the list of activities alternating between red and orange felt marker. She instructs that everyone will role-play being participants in the focus groups and that Jocelyn will role-play the student researchers' upcoming facilitation role. Jocelyn asks questions from the focus group protocol, or guide, that the student researchers have compiled. There are some lukewarm answers as the group warms up. Then Jocelyn asks, "What have you seen that you would change about the Central environment?" No one has a ready answer. Then, Jason calls out, "Ooo. Hold up, I got one for that one." He begins saying that one time he was just walking down the street and he "saw this lady walking along the edge of the roof of the SROs." SROs are single-room-occupancy hotel rooms rented by the week or month at a low rate. They have the reputation as serving as a type of privatized, makeshift housing development for people who have few or no other housing options. Another Central resident, Emelda, on staff at Representing Ourselves, reported in her interview that Central residents sometimes witness people jumping from the SRO rooms to commit suicide. Jason continues:

> And I was with my friend, and for some reason I was noticing her walking along the edge of the roof, because she was really close to the edge. And then, she just jumped, man. And I shouted out, "Oh, my God!" to my friend, and I pointed, and he looked up.

Jason is partially covering his mouth with his hand as he reveals what he witnessed next. He discloses:

> We just stood there: watching her falling through the air. It seemed like a long time, too. And then she just landed on the sidewalk. Right in front of us—like ten feet [three meters] away. Oh, man. We couldn't believe it. It was horrible. For real. Her blood was everywhere on the sidewalk, spilling from her head. I mean, it was bad. Really bad.

Jason shakes his head slowly, solemnly. It is quiet for a few seconds while everyone digests this tragic information. Then Eric asks what the lady looked like and how nearby she was to him. No one asks whether the woman lived, because it is clear that she did not. Rashna discusses this activity as one of the memorable moments in the project where the researchers' stories were heard, and as a result, everyone was engaged, present and focused. She recalls:

> We did this practice group with them where Jocelyn facilitated their focus group guide and they were the participants, and that was kind of a cool moment of them just talking about their neighborhood, and they brought up a lot of information and really talked about what was going on. And everybody was really grounded and present and listening to each other and really sincere in how they talked about what was going on.

The interactive nature of the structured activity supports team members' active participation and provides a venue for Jason to share his knowledge of what happens in his neighborhood and what it all means for young people. When student researchers experience subjectivity in these activities, they are highly engaged and "grounded and present and listening to each other" in a sincere way.

Further, when the student researchers are in the "expert" role, even in a role play, they confidently voice their experiences and knowledge about circumstances in their neighborhood that need to be addressed in a neighborhood that has been economically and structurally abandoned by the city's services. If the student researchers had merely read about the possible impacts of poverty, abuse, addiction and structural violence in low-income neighborhoods, it is unlikely that they would be as interested in connecting their micro-level experiences to macro-level forces in the larger society. Also, if student researchers had received handouts or viewed flip-chart papers listing the "dos" and "don'ts" of focus group facilitation, they might not have been as engaged, or have developed their skills to the extent that they did. These structured, participatory activities were effective because the students learned about focus group facilitation by experiencing it and then generated their own list of "dos" and "don'ts" based on reflecting on their experiences.

Teaching Strategies to Guide and Build Knowledge Producers

The teaching strategies and curriculum included a participatory curriculum in which student researchers design and plan their project in order to learn new research skills. One example of learning new research skills was evidenced by the "Food Matrix" data analysis activity. This activity took place after student researchers had already conducted focus groups with youth and adults to collect data pertaining to their research question. At this point in the PAR process, student researchers were positioned to learn how to analyze their collected data. Rashna trained the student researchers in data analysis, including how to understand the data as evidence in order to draw findings. She explains the pedagogical strategies behind the Food Matrix data analysis activity. In the PAR curriculum, an instructor acts as a guide who draws on their own set of knowledge, experience and curriculum tools to help facilitate learning. She reflects:

> I sort of see myself as like: I'm bringing tools and I hold a certain knowledge set. I've learned a curriculum and I've learned things based on the experiences I've had in [PAR] projects. And so I bring that into the room with me. And I try to use that as a guide or a tool and offer that up in really concrete ways.

Expounding on her pedagogical approach, Rashna gives a specific example of the Food Matrix data analysis activity:

> For example, today we're learning data analysis. So, I'm not gonna do a PowerPoint on data analysis, but we're gonna talk about foods and *you're* gonna rate them and you're gonna talk about what you see up here in terms of these ratings and what's the meaning behind it. And as I'm facilitating this, I'm gonna barely think about what *I think* the meaning behind it is. I'm gonna concentrate on what *you're saying* and come up with the follow-up questions based on *that* versus what I'm thinking about it.

Rashna discusses her role as that of a guide who instructs through drawing out student researchers' experiences. While lectures can certainly be an important part of teaching, she emphasizes that she does not solely rely on lectures to convey information to the student researchers. Instead, to prepare them to analyze data, she facilitates a process in which she has students draw on their own prior knowledge of foods and rate them in order to see that they are already familiar with rating and evaluating information. This interactive teaching process is designed to draw out student researchers' prior experiences in order to analyze them. Importantly, in this instructional approach Rashna does not consider her own thoughts and analysis of the foods discussed, but, rather, concentrates on the student researchers' input and then poses follow-up questions to further draw out their thoughts and analysis. In this teaching and learning process, she is not concerned with transferring the content from her head into the students' heads, but rather facilitating a process in which students' lives are the context for learning and analysis.

This teaching approach demands that the curriculum taps these young people's funds of knowledge (Moll, Armanti, Neff & González, 1992), their prior knowledge and competence based on their life experience. A funds of knowledge approach to teaching views working-class and poor communities in terms of their strengths and assets (González, Moll & Amanti, 2013; Moll & Greenberg, 1990). Drawing on student researchers' prior knowledge, the teaching approach in the PAR project is empowering because it allows student researchers to draw out their own ideas and analysis based on their prior knowledge and experiences. Rather than a top-down model of teaching new research skills, this pedagogy and curriculum shows student researchers that they already have the building blocks for research skills. They then understand that they can apply their existing skill sets to develop expertise in data analysis—a new skill set. Rashna explains further her pedagogical rationale for her PAR curriculum trainings:

> I try to keep [PAR] trainings open and with room for a lot of discussion from them ... I think that Youth Voices tries to have this popular education approach where the knowledge should come from the group of people. And I think a lot of our curriculum facilitates that.

In this PAR curriculum and pedagogy, the instructor relies on discussion to build upon student researchers' prior knowledge to learn a new academic skill set. This pedagogical approach and curriculum is grounded by a popular education approach. In a popular education approach, the principle is that the student researchers hold expertise and knowledge about the causes of and solutions to the problems they face. Similarly, scholarship on participatory action research finds that an underlying assumption of the participatory action research model is that those closest to the issues studied are the most helpful sources to devise research-based solutions (Fals-Borda & Rahman, 1991; Whyte, 1991). Relying on a participatory action research model, a pedagogy of praxis contained two overlapping asset-based teaching approaches to build academic skills: drawing on student researchers' funds of knowledge, and a popular education approach that tapped this knowledge and expertise for reflection and analysis through a participatory, facilitated process in which the text is student researchers' lives. The PAR process connected this reflection to their action project on the basis of their data analysis and research findings.

In the Food Matrix data analysis lesson, student researchers learned experientially by first analyzing "mock data" to draw findings by using supporting evidence. To guide them through this process, Rashna begins the lesson by telling them that today they are going to learn about how to analyze data by first creating "mock data." They will then develop research indicators to code this data. She explains that the mock data will come from them, prompting: "What foods do youth choose to purchase in Central?" She first points to a blank chart drawn on big flip-chart paper and asked them to name three foods they usually buy in Central. They agree on three foods: burritos, pizza and fried rice. Rashna writes these into the blank chart. She says, "Think of three categories that you could use in order to rate which of these foods is your favorite." After much prompting from Rashna about adequate categories, or indicators, that could evaluate all three of their identified foods, they finally select taste, smell, and price. She explains that "taste," "smell" and "price" are their indicators that they have developed to assess their chosen foods: burritos, pizza and fried rice. Finally, they are tasked to verbally fill out the remaining nine boxes in the matrix: the taste, smell and price for each of their three foods. Rashna uncaps a green marker, ready to write down their answers in the matrix. She then prompts, "Okay what is the taste indicator of burritos?" Alejandra calls out, "Spicy" and Victor volunteers, "Juicy." While it began as a blank chart without foods or indicators to measure them, the final chart, recording their "data," turned out as shown in Table 4.2.

After they have filled out the three food categories and three indicators to measure these foods, Rashna says, "Now you will draw findings using evidence from the 'data' in your chart." She asks them, "What's one piece of data that supports, "People buy foods that they believe smell good and are inexpensive?" She reminds them to answer this question using evidence from the "mock data" that they just created in their chart. Alejandra offers, "Well, the data says that

TABLE 4.2 Food Matrix Activity Listing "Data" and "Indicators"

Food	Taste (indicator)	Smell (indicator)	Price (indicator)
Burrito	Spicy; juicy	Smell of flavors gets you hungry	Can be expensive; cheap at taco trucks
Pizza	Too greasy but hot; tastes hella good; can burn your mouth	Smells like fresh bread; makes mouth water	Very cheap; cheapest of all three foods
Fried rice	Dry; smokey	The smell is okay; doesn't draw you in	Can be cheap; some places charge

people buy pizza because one, it 'makes the mouth watery' and two, it 'is very cheap.'" "That's right!" Rashna exclaims, writing this sentence on the flip-chart paper underneath the chart. In this way, the research team was introduced to the concept of creating indicators to code data and the idea of using evidence from these data categories to analyze the data and draw findings.

After their data analysis training, the research team began data analysis by deciding that the indicators they would use to code their focus group data were "safety," "environment," "community," "resources for youth," and "schools." Discussing her pedagogical approach to supporting youth voice, Rashna reflects:

> I believe that decision-making is one of the biggest parts of youth-led work and youth having a voice. That's the power of the things that we do. And the decisions that get made in a lot of ways mean that young people are really giving their input, giving their information, and then, actually, also making the call about how something should go. To me this is really integral to the process of developing youth voice in a really meaningful way—not tokenizing it.

In order to avoid tokenizing youth voice, but rather to develop authentic youth voice, it is important that student researchers provide input on project decisions that have a meaningful impact on the direction of the project. When reflection and analysis were tied to action to improve their community through a pedagogy of praxis, student researchers were invested in participating in the curriculum activities. Student researchers exhibited high levels of participation and agency through a curriculum and pedagogy that required their meaningful input in their PAR project's design and implementation. These empowering pedagogical approaches highly engaged student researchers as decision-makers and knowledge producers.

Conclusion: A Pedagogy of Praxis Approach

Young people are highly interested in contributing to investments in their communities. When there is a connection between the project's vision and their values and vision for community transformation, this leads to motivation and high participation. Highly structured, experiential, interactive pedagogical approaches build trust and safety. Such interactive teaching strategies enable risk-taking and lead to youth engagement. This chapter described what I term a *pedagogy of praxis*, which occurred in this student-driven participatory action research project. A pedagogy of praxis connects critical reflection about one's social conditions with action to transform those conditions.

Young people were highly engaged in pedagogical approaches that provided interactive, structured activities that centered their voices, experiences, analysis and vision to take action to improve their communities. This experiential teaching and learning approach, a pedagogy of praxis, involves student research-ers in creating their own theories about the nature of the problems they aim to fix and then engages them in directing a research-based action plan to address them. For example, student researchers directed each step of the PAR process to create the research question and the research design, such as sample size and data collection methods. Eventually, they conducted data analysis to draw find-ings and present their recommendations. These key decisions were made through interactive, hands-on workshops in which student researchers engaged in group exercises and dialogue about solutions that built upon their prior knowledge. This learning process was situated in their lived experiences about their neighborhood's needs.

A pedagogy of praxis linked reflection and analysis to action to improve their community, resulting in student researchers' having high levels of investment and participation in the curriculum activities. Adult support of student voice and participation entailed structured opportunities for student input on key decision points in project planning and design. In order to develop authentic youth voice, the curriculum and pedagogy challenged student researchers to contribute to project decisions that significantly impacted the project's direc-tion, design and scope.

When the project's purpose and goals match young people's values and visions for community change, motivation to join is high. A pedagogy of praxis was an effective teaching and learning approach that further generated motiva-tion and active participation from the student research team. The pedagogy of praxis process consisted of asset-based teaching approaches to build academic skills: drawing on student researchers' funds of knowledge and a popular educa-tion approach that tapped this expertise for reflection and analysis through a participatory, facilitated process in which the text is student researchers' lives. The PAR process connects reflection about the conditions in their community and their causes to an action project that they develop and implement on the basis of their data analysis and research findings. Student researchers' levels of participation were highest when they had meaningful input in designing, plan-ning and implementing a participatory action research project in alignment with their own goals for community change. As an approach to teaching and learn-ing, a pedagogy of praxis generated a high level of student engagement and commitment to participate.

5

SITUATED LEARNING

Change Agents in a Meaningful Purpose

Introduction

This chapter analyzes the components of curriculum design and pedagogy that built student researchers' academic skills through their participation in roles that entailed collective decision-making, relational leadership, peer mentorship, group accountability, ownership and agency. It explores a form of learning, *situated learning*, that emerged and operated in the participatory action research project with youth. The chapter provides an analysis and discussion of *relational leadership*, a complementary instructional process to situated learning in which student researchers shared ideas and power with peers and instructors through a collaborative, participatory decision-making process. The Central Youth United (CYU) participatory action research (PAR) project built upon student researchers' sense of accountability to their community and promoted student researchers' sense of themselves as agents of community change by providing opportunities and supports to use their action research findings in the service of community improvement.

Youth Input and Decision-Making: Contributing Ideas and Experiences

In the Central Youth United case, both decision-making and leadership involved a collective dimension. In the facilitated team discussions, the youth research team contributed ideas, debated alternative project designs and directions, and negotiated to reach consensus on each key decision points throughout the group project. Key decisions entailed selecting the research topic; deciding whether their research method should be interviews, surveys, focus groups or observations; analyzing their data to draw research findings; and presenting their recommendations for action. Adults then facilitated a consensus-building process to allow team members to negotiate and debate so as to arrive at a decision that everyone could support. Student researchers began to understand their leadership as enacted by sharing ideas with other group members to participate in a relational process of collaborative decision-making.

There was a meaningful shift in the way leadership was both embodied and conceptualized by the young people. At an early stage in the program, most student researchers did not yet describe themselves in their interviews as leaders or key players in project decisions or planning. However, midway through the program and towards the close of it, young people described their leadership in the group as evident through the sharing of ideas, decision-making power, and leadership with their peers to shape the design and direction of the project. Reflecting back on the skill set she developed over the entire course of the program, Alejandra comments that she learned to share her ideas with the larger group. In a focus group with her fellow student researchers, she summarizes the leadership skills she deemed the young people learned:

> The leadership skills we learned: Speaking out, working together as a team, to not be scared, to not be shy, to show your ideas, and to just speak out. And then, if you have an idea, just say it out. Just don't keep it inside 'cause it probably could be a good one.

Alejandra views her increased ability to speak her mind and share her ideas with the group and work together as a team as an acquired leadership skill. She also learned through the PAR project that young people should not be shy or afraid to share their ideas because they might actually be valuable and beneficial to a group inquiry project.

Similarly, Victor describes his role in decision-making as sharing his answers and opinions in the group process by responding to the instructors' problem-posing method: "Sometimes I help make decisions. I show my opinion. You feel me? I have an opinion on the questions they ask. They ask questions—I'm gonna have an opinion." Young people participated in decision-making when they shared their opinions to help decide how the project should move forward. Ameera summarizes her view of her fellow student researchers' role in partici-pating and sharing their ideas and experiences. She reflects:

> Through this project I found out that the youth that I'm working with, they're really participating: They have experiences; they're sharing. They have these great ideas. But we need some people to come and gather all the youth, let them share their experiences—teach them. [The youth will] have great ideas and others can benefit from them.

Leadership functioned through a distributed process in which each team member shared ideas and perspectives through group dialogue designed to gather input to make collective decisions about tangible next steps. The student researchers saw that their ideas and decisions directly impacted the PAR project's scope and trajectory. While the young people participated in discussions to bring their ideas to bear on the project decisions, the adult role was that of a guide to facilitate the process of sharing ideas, experiences and opinions to benefit the PAR team and ultimately the wider community the PAR team aimed to improve.

In this project, the sharing of opinions appeared to enable the group to realize its process and propel forward decision-making and peer learning. Jocelyn, one of the two CYU instructors, also expressed this idea that young people displayed their leadership when they contributed to group discussions:

> I think when we would have discussions on different topics—either with me or Rashna—was when they were being a leader. And sometimes it was like pulling teeth, but once they got into it and once we got their experiences out of it, then it was like one of those sessions where they're like, "Oh, wow! Why does it gotta end right now?"

The student researchers were enthusiastic about wielding their leadership and their responsibility to further the project's goals through participating in project discussions and contributing their ideas and experiences. Chenda also viewed her active participation as sharing her viewpoints and experiences in discussions. She described her active leadership role when she was "speaking in front of them, standing up and speaking what I think or explaining something ... giving my ideas, my opinion, my experiences." In the Central Youth United project, being a leader entailed that young people shared ideas, experiences and opinions in relationship to others to propel forward the collaborative project. This demonstrates a conceptualization of relational leadership that rests on sharing ideas, opinions and viewpoints to collaborate on decision-making during project planning discussions.

Relational Leadership: A Dialogical Process in Communities of Practice

The student researchers articulated and enacted an alternative conception of leadership in which leadership is shared among members of the group. Rather than leadership developing individually in each student researcher, their leadership developed in relationship to the other team members through sharing ideas in a collaborative decision-making process. This investigation terms this concept *relational leadership*. A central element of relational leadership is that it entails sharing ideas through group dialogue, which aims to build consensus to reach a collective decision.

Student researchers disagreed with the notion that one individual holds leadership. They did not conceive of a bureaucratic model of leadership in which a wise, benevolent, solitary hero figure wields power over the group to "assess problems, propose alternatives, and make rational choices" (Baldridge, Curtis, Ecker & Riley, 1977, p. 21). For example, Alejandra maintained that leadership is distributed among group members. She insisted:

> Everybody should try and take a part in leading the group. And put their own little personality ... into their leadership ... It isn't like going to school, where all you do is listen, listen, listen. You have to actually be ... saying stuff.

Leadership was seen as being equally distributed among individuals in the group, who each contributed their own unique styles and abilities to the group process. The student researchers shouldered responsibility for their own participation, exhibited an awareness of monitoring their own participation patterns, and felt accountable to the team to participate in decisions.

Group Accountability Within Relational Leadership

Part of this collaborative nature of leadership included being accountable for another team member's active participation in project decisions and discussions. This sometimes entailed rallying other young people's motivation and enthusiasm in contributing to the group. As Alejandra explained:

> I'll be like, "Oh, come on, let's get to it, let's do this." And I'll be like, "Oh, yeah, we could do this." And when I come up with a lot of ideas and it just flows from my head, that's how I think I'm a good leader.

Again, sharing ideas in the group planning process was seen as a mark of good leadership in this project. In discussing her leadership role, Alejandra expanded on her role in inspiring others to become motivated:

> I get everybody around me pumped up. And then if I say something, another person thinks another thing, and then it just comes into a big idea, and a big discussion about it. And just pointing little things out and making new questions and doing new things that we haven't done. And then people be like, "Oh, that's a good idea." And then they think about it and then they get another idea. It just progresses.

This notion of leadership as contributing to sparking new ideas in others and moving the group process forward came up frequently in interviews with the student researchers. This feature of leadership—inspiring leadership and contributions from others—exemplified the team's conceptions of relational leadership. They defined a salient component of leadership: promoting leadership in others and contributing to distributed leadership. Jocelyn believed that after some young men left the team, the increased support from the young women enabled Victor to develop his skills and become an actively participating member of the team. She mused on Victor's transition from novice to expert and the impact that this heightened support had on Victor's development:

> I've seen him grow ... to really becoming this young researcher and understanding what we're looking for. It took a while, but I feel like, you just tell him, "Okay, what does this mean?" And he knows it. You just gotta get it out of him. And I see the young women stepping up to it, too. Before, they would just answer for themselves. But now when they see Victor and they don't want to answer *for* him and they kind of help each other in that process now. They're like, "What do you think?" And so I feel like they've grown as a team rather than just as individuals.

In shifting from a group to a team, young people became aware of other people's participation and then adjusted their own participation to be sure not to either dominate the conversation or refrain from contributing their ideas. This allowed room for democratic participation. Chenda recounted her efforts to step up when she found a lull in the conversation and to step back to enable other member's voices to be heard:

> Today, mostly I was talking ... when it went dead silent or something, I just started popping up with stuff ... When Jocelyn asks us a question, I wanted to see if [the other youth] would answer it first because most of the time I was answering it. And then, since they didn't answer, I just stepped it up and started answering so Jocelyn wouldn't keep on asking the same questions. And then, sooner or later, they'd come up with answers as we'd go on.

She allowed others to contribute their ideas by altering her own participation to fit group needs.

Inspiring Teamwork and Engagement in Others Through Relational Leadership

In this project, collaborative decision-making was most apparent within structured, interactive group activities that fostered active participation in team decisions. One example of sharing input in a structured exercise occurred during a team-building activity called "Hot Lava." In this activity, the two teams lined up facing each other and were told that the 25 feet (8 meters) between them was hot lava. Rashna gave each team two pieces of typing paper and told them that these pieces of paper were stones that they could step on to make it across the hot lava to the other side. Each team had to work together to figure out how to work together to use their stones to get their whole group safely across the hot lava. Explaining the rules, Rashna warned that if one person's foot slipped off the stone, their entire group had to start over. As both teams began to brainstorm possible strategies to get across the lava, an excited buzz escalated to a loud humming sound bouncing off the walls of the room.

The first team attempted to slide across the hardwood floors, using their imaginary stones—the two pieces of typing paper—as if they were a set of skis, but these competitors kept losing one paper ski and falling into the imaginary hot lava. The second team spread out their two stones like lily pads in a toxic stream, leaping into the air to land on the stones and make it safely across. This team's second-to-last person across took up the paper stones, crumbled up these into two balls of paper, and threw them across the hot lava to their last remaining teammate for them to use to cross safely. Scoring a win, this winning team's reaction resembled the dramatics of winning a national sports championship. They jumped about, shouting, "We won! We won!" A smile and nod from one of the adult instructors, Rashna, acting as judge, validated their victory.

Discussing her decision-making role and agency in directing her winning team, Chenda took credit for persuading them to apply her strategy, which was to use their stones as if they were lily pads to leap across to safety. She told me about her decision-making role, leadership and agency in this game:

> I just spoke my mind. And I had my turn and then I directed them. There was some leadership there. I stopped everyone and I sort of told them what to do in the game. I gave them my opinion of what they should do ... Then I stopped them for a couple seconds because they were talking and I said, "Hey, you guys, we should do it this way." And then someone else, they did a leadership move, too, and they were like, "No. We should do it this way." Each one of us was trying to find a way to win—actually bring the whole team to the other side.

Her leadership and decision-making role here are signaled by the fact that she spoke her mind to share her ideas and influence the group by advocating for her strategy through negotiating with other members. She did not emphasize the outcome of her negotiations; instead, her decision-making centered on her process of relating to others. Further, while she displayed leadership and agency to impact others and manipulate her surrounding environment, her leadership was not diminished by that of her fellow team members, and she shared her leadership role with others. This form of shared leadership demanded that the team function collaboratively to reflect, strategize and negotiate to agree on an approach in order to experience success and ultimately to agree on a community action plan.

Positive youth development (PYD) research has identified key youth development needs that PYD programs should aim to scaffold with programmatic opportunities and supports. Specifically, programs should provide opportunities to form friendly, durable relationships with peers and adults, and to develop a sense of mattering, opportunities for skill-building and mastery to develop confidence, structured opportunities for decision-making, and opportunities to connect to community resources, contribute to one's community and develop a sense of efficacy (Eccles & Gootman, 2002).

Peer Mentorship as a Component of Relational Leadership Development

In addition to the age range in the group, which was from 13 years old to 18 years old, there was also a range of literacy levels and work habits. At age 13 and still in middle school, Victor was the youngest. Ameera, an 18-year-old freshman at a nearby state university, intentionally mentored Victor during the project. While it appeared to take the efforts of several people to help maintain Victor's engagement, it may be understandable, as he was significantly younger than the rest of the group members and he engaged in regular fits of unprovoked giggles. While Victor may have struggled to concentrate on the tasks at hand and pull his weight in the group, his co-workers took the charge from their two instructors to make an effort to support him.

According to some team members' accounts, keeping Victor on task was an effort that involved fellow student researchers. Chenda offered her opinion: "I think Victor's got some good answers. He participates well. He may goof off at times, but then it's just to make fun of the subject that we're doing." Another team member pointed out that although he may be a bit unfocused at times, others intervened to instruct him to be more productive. Victor's older sister Alejandra, a 16-year-old high school sophomore, also had a role in attempting to keep her younger brother focused. Ameera observed, "His sister always encouraged him to do, telling him, 'Victor, do this. Do that.' Sometimes he did it, sometimes not. It depended on his mood." Ameera was not the only one who noticed other people's efforts to encourage Victor to be productive. Jocelyn, one of the adult instructors, also noticed that team members supported Victor. She believed that the team imitated the two adult co-facilitators, who shared their workload. Jocelyn observed:

> Ameera and Chenda would give [Victor] a task—they knew how to give him a task—like "Glue the pictures" or "Write this down" or "Type this up" or "Do this and that." And I felt like it was evenly distributed. By

that time they all learned how to distribute the work—with Rashna and I showing by example.

Jocelyn shared that she and the other adult facilitator were intentionally modeling how to distribute their workload. As Jocelyn mentioned previously, she asked the older girls to support Victor by distributing tasks to him. Ameera recounted one example in which she gave Victor a task when Jocelyn was not present. They had to conduct outreach to community-based organizations by distributing stacks of flyers, announcing the team's final presentation of their community needs assessment findings and recommendations. She recalled:

> When we went to distribute flyers, I told Victor, "Take this stack of flyers. Give it to people." He didn't do it. He just kept them in his hand ... He said, "I don't know nobody here." I told him, "It's okay. Just give the flyers to them and leave." He's only 13, so that's okay.

With the support of his outreach partner, Ameera, Victor was eventually able to overcome his hesitation to interact with strangers and distribute stacks of flyers to local community-based organizations. This outreach activity, structured by Jocelyn, also entailed that Chenda and Alejandra partner together. Even though they sometimes had conflicts, Jocelyn thought that pairing them together might ease the tensions that sometimes flared up between them.

Jocelyn often partnered Victor with either Ameera or Chenda in paired work exercises in an effort to keep him focused and productive. Victor, Chenda and Ameera all commented on their positive experiences in these mentoring relationships. While Ameera and Chenda took up an active role in mentoring, Jocelyn mentioned that, as the instructor, she activated this process through intervening by pulling each girl aside and telling them that as team members they were partially responsible for maintaining a group dynamic that was conducive to learning. Jocelyn shared that this was an intentional approach to peer mentorship. She reflected:

> The whole seven months after we said, "Ameera, you need to teach someone to help you do that. Don't do it all by yourself," she got it. But I always have to remind them. Even Chenda would just take the pictures herself and I would say, "*You* supervise Victor. You help *him* help *you.*"

Jocelyn believed that it was a group responsibility to keep everyone learning and on track, and ensure that they mentored each other to ensure the project's success despite the diversity in ages from 13 to 18. She instructed the highly motivated researchers to take up this responsibility and support their fellow team members who were struggling to stay afloat.

From her perspective as an adult instructor, Rashna believed that it was hard for Victor not to follow the lead of the older boys when they were being unfocused, but that when the older boys were not present, Victor was able to actively contribute answers. Rashna noted:

> When it was just [Victor] and the young women, he would be on it—answers, answers, answers—lots of information to contribute. But when the boys came around, he was a fool. He would just follow along. I mean, he's in the seventh grade and here are these older boys and he would follow along and be dumb and goofy.

Jocelyn also noticed that Victor had trouble keeping focused when he was paired with the older boys when they were distracted, and that Victor sometimes felt lost working alone. She often arranged for Victor and Ameera to partner together. Jocelyn recalled:

> Especially when I put him together with Ameera, you know, I can see Ameera become his mentor in terms of like, "Okay, Victor, come on, let's do this together." And I purposely do that so they can mentor each other ... 'Cause she was the oldest and he was the youngest.

Ameera recalled using positive reinforcement with Victor to encourage him to write follow-up questions for the focus group protocols. She discussed her approach to propel Victor's motivation to contribute to the group process:

> I just kept patient. I just held myself. I can get un-patient really quickly ... I was always encouraging him, so if he did anything, I would say, "Oh, good job, Victor. See, that was a great idea." He liked to be encouraged, so I kept doing that to him. And so I made him think about an idea because if I took all the jobs over from him then he wouldn't do anything. Maybe if we divided [the jobs] then he felt more responsible. And I was just encouraging, "You're doing good, just continue."

Ameera described how she supported Victor's skill development as a team contributor. She continued to note that in addition to her supporting of his participation, his contributions were eventually incorporated into their focus group protocol. She remembered:

> One time ... we had to create [focus group] follow-up questions, so he was my partner. So he came up with all these questions, and then I was saying, "Good job! That was a great question." ... Some of his questions were really applied and we used it with the focus groups later on.

Aware of her leadership role in motivating her peer to contribute, Ameera helped encourage Victor's input into this final product. She was also aware that "if I took all the jobs over from then he wouldn't do anything." Members of this team were more actively engaged and accountable when they were charged with being responsible for a part of the work. Pairing up the student researchers to create dyads that had to hold each other accountable worked well to maintain their attention. Ameera conveyed in the following example that holding one's peers accountable to staying on task was directed not only towards Victor, but also towards others. She remarked:

> It was kind of cool because you tell them what to do, like, "Hey, you stop doing this and do this. Start doing that." Even though they didn't always listen to me but then I just felt more responsible to get them back focused ... I wasn't even thinking to do that until one of the facilitators told me to. Jocelyn said, "Hey, you work with them, so if you tell them to get back to work they might listen to you more than they do to me." So I was like, "Okay." So then I tried it. One time, Jason just wouldn't focus. I told him, "Hey, you'd better get back to work because we have only one more hour left." And he said, "All right."

Jocelyn explained to me that she purposefully sets out to create a space that feels fair and equal in terms of the distribution of the workload. She commented:

> I have to create a space where people could feel like they're not the *only* ones doing the work. And so, I think now that we have a smaller group it is easier to distribute the work and if one was slacking, then they've all kind of been like, "Yo, come on, get on it."

Creating a democratic space for taking risks was an intentional strategy. This democratic learning environment proved to be conducive to learning.

Emergent Leadership Roles: Situated Learning

A central tenet of situated learning is that an effective way to learn is through collaborations that involve active participation and applying knowledge to actual situations (Lave & Wenger, 2003). The Central Youth United project employed situated learning approaches through interactive group activities in which emerging student researchers applied their research skills to their local neighborhood context. Situated learning involves participation in communities of practice, in which members learn essential skills, standards and behaviors as participants in these communities (Lave & Wenger, 2003; Wenger, 1998; 2000). In this PAR project, the participatory action research team functioned as a community of practice in which student researchers learned research skills and standards, and learned to behave as emerging researchers. Through a process identified as "legitimate peripheral participation" in situated learning approaches, novice learners shift from the periphery of activity in communities of practice towards taking up central roles as experts who inhabit the culture of communities of practice (Lave & Wenger, 2003). The student researchers moved from being novice researchers to becoming expert researchers capable of designing and executing a research project using situated learning approaches that were collaborative and interactive, and applied knowledge in authentic situations.

Overwhelmingly, student researchers reported that their leadership skills developed throughout the project as a result of taking on new leadership roles. In particular, having to facilitate the focus groups with another team member seemed to have quite an impact on the young researchers. Towards the end of the project, Chenda reflected on how her leadership developed over time throughout the entire needs assessment process. She remarked, "My leadership grew with public speaking, having to do your own focus group that you could do yourself and not have to have someone else talk for you." In a similar vein, midway through the project Victor recalled the aspect of the project (up to that point) that had had the greatest personal impact on him. Citing his role leading the focus groups, Victor names this experience as allowing him to grow into this leadership role:

> What affected me the most was we ran our first focus group. I was nervous that day. I was *really* nervous that day. I don't know—I never did one in my *life*. And then after, I felt better. I was like, "Oh, I'm gonna get used to this." Before you judge, like, "Oh, I don't like doing this stuff," you gotta do it yourself ... I started getting used to it and then I did better and better and better ... 'Cause if you get used to something, then you can improve in it.

Although it may have seemed daunting before he actually tried it, Victor reflected that it was through trying something out for the first time, followed by repeated practice at being in this new role, that he became "better and better and better." He explained that for his learning, he has first to be presented with an opportunity to take on a new role (in this case, facilitating a focus group). The experience of adjusting to this new role first allowed him to build his confidence and then improve his performance.

Of course, Victor also went through weeks of training and practice, including participating in role-playing activities, before actually being thrown into this new role. If the instructors had just given him the opportunity to be in a new leadership role without first giving him adequate preparation, then he might have been set up for failure. Indeed, in addition to holding high expectations for student abilities, instructors provided structured supports to enable student researchers to be prepared to take on new roles.

All of the student researchers noted that adjusting to perform in their new leadership roles resulted in improvements in their ability to run focus groups. Jocelyn noticed another factor that contributed towards their improved focus group facilitation skills. While observing them facilitate, she recognized aspects of their facilitation techniques that she was familiar with. She concluded that the young researchers applied what they learned about facilitation through observing the adults. She recalled:

> It's like they're trying to imitate me and Rashna. It was crazy. Like when we would ask them questions and we would probe them for answers ... and just different ways that we would facilitate, I could see them doing it. It's weird. I felt like I was looking in a mirror.

Jocelyn's observations imply that, without realizing it, the adults were providing a model of facilitation styles, which became apparent when they noticed the student researchers incorporating their own techniques while leading the focus groups.

For example, Chenda and Ameera co-facilitated a focus group of nine elementary students at the neighborhood school, and applied their new facilitation skills to collect data. Chenda and Ameera strolled into the elementary auditorium, where they met with three teachers who had arranged to allow several students from their fourth-grade classrooms to be excused to participate in the focus group. As co-facilitators, Chenda and Ameera had the nine girls sit in a circle of chairs and asked them questions from the team-designed focus group protocol, prodding the shy students to contribute their views on topics such as how safe they felt in the neighborhood and what resources they might need.

They applied the follow-up question probes they had practiced in the group sessions to elicit information from their focus group participants: "Can you give an example of that to help me understand what you mean?" "From your experience, can you think of a time when that happened?" The co-facilitators' probing questions sounded strikingly similar to Rashna's and Jocelyn's probes when the adults role-played the focus group facilitators. Ameera and Chenda even executed the non-verbal cues they had practiced in their earlier training sessions. The non-verbal cues the girls implemented included nodding their heads encouragingly when focus group participants struggled to articulate their answers, maintaining a neutral facial expression when something controversial was said, and maintaining eye contact to indicate that they were paying close attention.

One 11-year-old girl discussed the significant number of homeless people on the streets in Central and how she felt unsafe when drunken homeless people yelled at her as she walked alone down Washington Street on her way home from school. Chenda applied her facilitation training to press further to elicit more information, and probed, "Can you say more about that?" The elementary student responded that she believed that the solution to resolving this safety issue was not limited to building more homeless shelters with extended city services. Rather, the solution ultimately was for elected officials to strive to "give the homeless people homes." This led other focus group participants to discuss the need for city officials to commit to building affordable housing for all people in their neighborhood, including people without homes. Throughout the focus group, both Chenda and Ameera applied their new knowledge from their focus group trainings through acting in new facilitation and leadership roles.

The research project involved several central principles of the situated learning framework (Lave & Wenger, 2003). For example, learning new knowledge and research skills entailed learning in authentic contexts, through participatory activities and in collaboration with peers and adults. Further, student researchers moved from newcomer roles in which they were unfamiliar with the nuances of research design and methods to gradually shouldering increasing responsibilities to shift towards embodying expert roles as members of a community of practice. At each step in the research project, adults facilitated interactive activities to train the youth team in research skills, and the team had to decide on crucial aspects of the research design such as their research question, research sample, methods (interviews, surveys, focus groups or observations), analytic themes during data coding and analysis, and the drawing out of research findings and recommendations for action. The youth project's process entailed that young people actively participated in decisions, reflected on the ways in which they participated, and took accountability for their role in participating in group decisions. Relational leadership entailed contributions to the group process, responsibility for one's participation, accountability to the group, and responsibility for others' contributions.

A Sense of Ownership

Recognizing their ownership over the project seemed to indicate a feeling of pride in the student researchers that this project was theirs and that it was youth-led. Feeling a sense of ownership indicated that student researchers were proud of their work because they felt that they owned the group's work. Chenda articulated her definition of ownership: "To me, ownership is being part of the group, being proud of being in this project, being proud of the name, stuff like that." Ameera explained that she felt complete ownership over the project because the student researchers were responsible for each step of the project's process.

DW: How much do you think that the Central Youth United project is your project?

A: 100 percent.

DW: Yeah?

A: It's mine. It's mine. And it's the others' also.

DW: Okay. Why do you say that it's yours 100 percent?

A: Because we are the ones who worked on it. We did this. We presented. Even though [the project] wasn't our idea, it's like we were the hands that did all the things ... We put all this together. We did the research. We went out there. We asked the questions. We collected all the data. We collected all the information and that's how we came to our presentation.

Developing a sense of ownership occurred through the gradual recognition that not only did the student researchers collect the data and present it to community stakeholders, but they were leading the direction, scope, planning and design of the PAR project. Rashna discussed occasions when the youth research team displayed project ownership in the public sphere. She observes:

> In the focus groups that I've seen them facilitate, they're not only stepping up and talking about their project, but doing it in these ways that were really skilled around how they talked about it. Like, "I have ownership of this project. I'm not gonna divulge everything that's going on to you." And when someone asks, "So, how's it been going?" to say, "It's been really great—we're doing our focus groups now." They are able to skillfully bring out the positive and I think they have a sense of "This is my project; I'm protecting it. I'm gonna make it sound good." So that kind of seemed like a way that they held ownership.

Ownership is evidenced by the ways in which student researchers protected the reputation of their project by representing it in a positive light in public situations.

Adult Role in Increasing Project Ownership

Alejandra commented that the student researchers had ownership over this project because they made project decisions at key decision points in the research process. She explained:

> We're not expecting for adults to do it *for* us. Adults are teaching us, yes, but at the same time, we're putting in all the work: *We* came up with the questions, *we* came up with [the decision] that we're gonna do the focus groups. We came up with everything: how we're gonna do it and how we're gonna put our information together. Adults are just guiding us through the way.

Student researchers understood that they were the ones making key decisions at key decision points in the project and that the adult role functioned to teach skills and guide the process. Indeed, student researchers were involved in selecting a research question and topic, research methods, analysis of the information, and creation of the final report and presentation. They were aware of their leadership and agency in making decisions about the project design. PAR team members brought their ideas to bear on the project's planning. This expanded their self-concept about their own capacities and capabilities. Victor discussed how the adults' role helped him acquire new skill sets through modeling new leadership roles, teaching skills, and fielding questions.

DW: What have the two adults, Jocelyn and Rashna, done that's been helpful for you in this project so far?

V: Showing us, "This is what you have to do," and then showing us, teaching us stuff. By showing us an example of how you set up a focus group. So, next time we know how to set up one.

DW: Okay. Can you tell me how that looked? What were the adults doing?

V: Helping me answer some questions instead of just telling me what I have to do.

This approach stands in stark contrast to a more conventional approach in which adults issue instructions—for later assessment—with minimum scaffolding support. In this PAR project, instructors provided tangible guidance and structure to scaffold youth learning.

Ameera described this collegial model of youth and adults working in partnership towards common goals with adult guidance. She remarked:

> The adults, they're great. They're the one hand of the project and the youth are the other hand. So one hand can't come up by itself. We need two hands. So, they have the questions, they guide us and we go through the points that we want to succeed on. They guide the activities. They give us their help.

Adult guidance was an important part of youth-led work and helped support strong, viable and collegial youth–adult partnerships.

Ultimately, Rashna was convinced by the student researchers' reasoning to include focus group data from adults who work with young people in Central. She explained how she stepped back to allow the team to decide on their research sample even when their decisions went against the outcome she recommended. She articulated that, ideally, not only should adults' roles be to provide guidance and support, but they should also step back to allow young people room to step up. Rashna asserted:

> I've had experience doing these projects so I wanna guide you to make sure you don't trip up where another group has tripped up. And so

sometimes around that process I might have to step back, like, "You might do it in an entirely different way than this [other] group did and you might have challenges, but it might prove really successful ... I can give you my suggestions around my experience with it, but ultimately, you have to decide." At first I was like, "Why would you ask adults what youth really need in Central? You need to talk to young people." So I think that was a moment where it was like, "Right. You can make that decision. You *should* make that decision."

In this PAR project, adults acted as supports to young people's decision-making and leadership by stepping back at times—specifically, in circumstances where youth judgments were reasonable and feasible, but might not reflect the adult facilitator's preferred choice. Allowing room for student researchers to make meaningful decisions to direct the project may entail taking risks. The students may either make mistakes or prove that their decisions worked better than expected.

The data analysis phase is a point during the action research process where the young people noticeably begin to take more ownership over the direction of their project. There were six pieces of flip-chart papers hung about with the written categories "school," "environment," "resources for youth," "community," "safety," and one marked "?" for uncategorized data. The activity asked that the researchers read the quotations, handwritten on Post-it notes, from this set of focus group data in order to code them into six themes. They categorized all of this data by placing the Post-its into one of these six categories, each represented by its own flip-chart paper. All of the young people involved in the project reported that engagement levels were significantly higher when they reached a meaningful goal with adult support as part of a larger project that had real consequences in their environment. Ameera contended, "It's not that interesting when you just see everything done for you. The good thing is, you work hard on it to get it, then you can see it and understand it." In reaching a consequential goal through structured, interactive activities with adult support, this increased level of engagement enhanced understanding.

Rashna explained that she noticed the team, particularly Alejandra, feeling an increased sense of ownership and engagement during the data analysis phase:

> During data analysis, Alejandra said to me, "Oh, I'm really smart, aren't I? I *get* it!" And it was just really awesome. You know, this is a young person who you really had to work to engage her, but in this moment, she was just so happy. I had not seen her feel that happy. And she was really owning the project as her own. They all were like, "Oh, this is *our* analysis, this is what we have to say about Central."

A high peak in the action researchers' ownership occurred during the data analysis phase when they remarked, "This is our analysis." Rashna saw data analysis as a moment in the project at which the researchers felt ownership over the research findings, and therefore the direction of the project. Alejandra described the role of Rashna, as one of the instructors, in helping her understand how to analyze the data to create data analysis themes. She implied a sense of empowerment that she is competent, and capable of coding and analyzing the results of their research. Alejandra explained:

> If we don't understand something, all of us as a group—as youth, adults—will be like, "Oh, it's like this and da-da da-da." They just help us with little things that we don't understand. Things we haven't learned. They're just there 'cause they've already been through it. They're adults; they've experienced it. For example, when we came up with the themes. After we did the focus groups, they told us to look at our notes, and then look at major things that people kept saying over and over and then we put them into themes. We wrote [the quotes] on Post-its and we put them into categories. Then we could see what they said and see what we need in Central.

Alejandra described the importance of having adult support and guidance scaffold her understanding of analyzing data to come up with themes or patterns in the data. Ownership over the work seemed to increase when the group reached the data analysis phase. The experience of contributing to the collective data analysis process showed the team that their analysis directly shaped the research findings and recommendations that will appear in their final report. Data analysis was a point in the project when it began to dawn on the research team that the PAR project assessing community needs was their own work and that their fellow community members would hold them responsible for their findings and recommendations.

Developing Agency, Commitment and Accountability

The student researchers in this project developed a sense of accountability for their project's outcomes. They also felt a sense of responsibility to the neighborhood community that they were studying. The team felt accountable to use the information they collected to best represent their neighborhood's needs in their final presentation. Thus, team members became committed to realizing the project's goals. Reflecting on how team members increased their accountability to each other in order to complete their community needs assessment, Jocelyn observed:

> The past few months that they've been doing their research, they've been really accountable to each other to finish it. Because as they started interviewing the youth in Central, well, I can remember at their first focus

group I could see light bulbs just flashing in their heads. And they realized then, "That's why we're asking these questions: to address some of these issues they're talking about in the focus groups."

The research team developed a sense of ownership to the project and its goals, especially because the project's purpose is to make a difference in their community. The Central Youth United researchers described the ways in which the research project and their collected data provided evidence that validated their own thoughts about community problems that needed to be addressed. In light of the team's collected information, some research team members became clear that there were issues in dire need of attention in Central.

Student researchers also developed a sense of accountability to their community to be a part of the solution and take action to improve their neighborhood. As Ameera explained:

> I never thought about my community. I thought that someday we'll just move ... so I didn't really feel responsible about Central ... I didn't even think about changing Central. So coming here just opened my eyes to see that I could make a difference.

Ameera then recalled that it was the focus groups that developed her sense of accountability to the Central community. These experiences motivated her to follow-through with the project's final presentation of its recommendations. This project engendered in Ameera a sense of agency and accountability to help improve her community. She noted:

> After doing all the focus groups where everybody says that Central is unsafe, a lot of homeless people, it's underserved—those were basically all my ideas ... So from that point on, I'm like we all agree—we all notice— that Central is not really good, so I felt responsible. I was doing this project, so I felt even more responsible because I was trying to help come up with something at the end that would help Central ... so it was my responsibility to take advantage of this work I'm doing.

Hearing her ideas about neighborhood needs reiterated by focus group participants stimulated Ameera's sense of responsibility to improve Central. Student researchers developed their sense of accountability to community members through interacting with them in their focus groups.

Jocelyn affirmed that after the team members interacted with youth and adult community members during the focus groups, their sense of urgency and accountability significantly increased. She observed that team members felt accountable to their focus group participants, who charged the researchers with a responsibility to use their collected data with integrity. She recollected:

As soon as the focus groups were done, I felt like they started to feel like, "We need to finish this because people are waiting on this stuff. There's a reason why we're here." 'Cause people would challenge them at those focus groups, like, "So you come in our community and ask all these questions, so what are you gonna do then?" You know, and they come and look at me and I'm like, "Well, it's up to you. We're just trying to gather this information to find out: This is what we need." And so then they started to feel more like, "Oh, this is a big thing." And when we started planning this presentation they're like, "We actually have people coming?" You know, and then they're like, "For real? I'm scared." ... So that's where I felt like they had a lot of pride, in terms of what they're doing.

Conducting research in their own neighborhood, this team of student researchers were challenged to make good on their promise that they would attempt to use this research to develop a final report that wove together an accurate picture representing their neighborhood's challenges, resources and needs. The PAR process, in which the expectations of their neighbors were communicated to the student researchers, helped hold this group accountable both to each other and to others in their neighborhood.

Stakes were higher for the research team when other people expressed anticipation that the researchers would use their data responsibly to gather information to help improve their neighborhood. This process of a PAR project with youth underscored the importance of creating a relevant, collective final product that aimed to improve their community. This community needs assessment and the PAR project will help advocate for increased resources for young people in their own neighborhood. In contrast to a classroom project done merely for a grade, which will not improve the classroom or school environment, their final product identifies and addresses their own community's needs. This PAR project demanded that other people—outside of the research team—might be impacted by the team's work. Therefore, the process of taking collective action towards improving their own neighborhood raised the stakes for collective accountability because the research team was also accountable to real people in their wider environment.

Features of Youth-Led Work and Challenges

Youth Voices is an intermediary nonprofit organization with expertise in training and capacity-building to support youth-led PAR projects. Some Central Youth United project members reported that they felt that it was a youth-led process. In our interview, I noted that Chenda uses the term "youth-led" to describe their process, so I asked her to give her definition of the concept of youth-led work.

DW: And when you say "youth-led," what do mean?

C: Youth-led: When mostly the youth would lead the group. They would plan, direct, and work together—teamwork—so that's what youth-led is for us.

Youth-led work occurs when young people direct, plan and collectively lead the group process. Ameera described the Central Youth United project, clarifying as follows:

> It is led by youth because everything we do is our opinion. We came up with the name of the group. We came up with the research question. We came up with the research tool. It's all decisions that we're coming up with.

Supporting a youth-led process engenders a sense of pride and confidence in the student researchers that they have mastered useful academic and leadership skills valued by schools and society. After the close of the project and their successful presentation to over 60 members of their community, student researchers understood that they were capable, competent and worthy of respect. A youth-led process requires an adult presence, adult guidance and adult support. Explaining the adult's guiding role in this process, Chenda explained:

> It's all our opinions, but Jocelyn's there just to guide us through the process ... It's youth-led, but it's just the adults are there to supervise. We need their supervision of the youth and our decision-making. The [adult] leaders get the information.

In this youth–adult partnership within this youth-led project, adults supported youth leadership by guiding and supporting youth decision-making throughout the process.

Challenges in Supporting a Youth-Led Process

One challenge the Central Youth United project faced is that its design did not support a youth-led approach to the highest degree possible. In pre-planning or ongoing planning, the adults did not report considering how to support or train student researchers to facilitate part of the meeting agenda or even a whole meeting agenda. These Central Youth United trainings happened twice weekly over a period of seven months. Twice weekly, the adults prepared every agenda for the trainings and never significantly shared facilitation roles with youth team members. As Ameera noted, "There are some parts that aren't led by youth. So every time we come, we have an agenda that's ready for us and we do it. So that's the part." Chenda agreed that the student researchers could rotate facilitation of the day's agenda. She remarked:

> If each person could do the Monday or Wednesday agenda, let's say Victor does that. Let's see. Rashna gives him the agenda and he could try to follow the agenda and put his shoes in Rashna's shoes, or someone puts their shoes in Jocelyn's shoes and see how it works.

As Chenda pointed out in a later interview, this type of experiential learning may have boosted team members' acquired leadership skills:

> We haven't had a chance to really be in the facilitator's shoes. Even though we're facilitating different focus groups, it would be interesting if we facilitated *our* group to see what we could work on as a facilitator during focus groups and in public speaking … [This might look like] giving us a role ahead of time to know what we're supposed to be facilitating, so we could be prepared and keep [our facilitation] on topic, and so we would know how it feels to keep on topic like how Jocelyn does it, and Rashna. Just to feel a little [of] what they might feel and improve it.

One challenge in the project was that young people did not have the opportunity or support to lead a project activity or meeting session—especially in light of the fact that Youth Voices, the consulting and training organization that employs Rashna, has a training curriculum that could easily be taught to young people, as it is taught to adult trainers new to the organization. It seems ironic that a project aiming to be youth-led did not include time and support for any youth-led activities during the twice-weekly meetings.

Conclusion: Situated Learning and Building Agency

Young people are usually not asked to contribute their ideas in order to develop, direct and plan their classroom lessons, curricula or learning units in school. Instead, only a handful of young people, usually student government leaders, are typically asked to contribute their input to school-wide decisions, planning or policies (Hart, 1997). As advocates of youth development, educators and educational researchers, we want young people to learn and grow. Young people learn and grow through their participation in leadership development opportunities, supported by caring adults and structured, supportive contexts (Pittman, 2000). Usually, we think of leadership development as an individual trajectory. Indeed, youth development literature, including positive youth development (PYD) literature, has historically discussed leadership development as occurring along individual developmental pathways in order to reach a set of desired leadership competencies (Scales & Leffert, 1999).

Yet, conceptualizations of youth development strategies in the literature have changed over time as the youth development field has shifted its focus from individual developmental trajectories towards the contexts of youth development programs. Current PYD research has extended its focus to include the program features that provide opportunities and supports for young people to gradually engage in increasing leadership responsibilities and roles (Damon, 2004; Huber, Frommeyer, Weisenbach & Sazama, 2003; Larson, 2000; Pittman, 2000; Scales & Leffert, 1999). Thus, the PYD field and its frameworks are moving away from individual developmental pathways to focus on leadership competencies young people reach, not in isolation, but within supportive programmatic settings. However, PYD research has scarcely described the process of leadership development in these supportive program contexts: components of this process, how these strategies look, or their limitations or benefits.

In the Central Youth United case, an adult-supported youth leadership development process was central to the successful youth leadership skills and outcomes of this project. In this leadership development process, young people benefited from structured opportunities to practice leadership roles and responsibilities. The CYU project promoted leadership development. Second, there is a collective nature to the leadership development process. Third, collective decision-making processes and the sharing of ideas in discussions were central to leadership development. Fourth, both instructors in this project supported youth leadership development by providing structured, interactive and experiential learning exercises that required decision-making and meaningful participation. Fifth, the young people developed a sense of accountability, ownership and agency because these interactive activities supported their voice and empowerment. Sixth, when young people experienced high degrees of accountability, ownership and agency, their levels of participation, motivation and commitment greatly increased.

This chapter reveals that young people's leadership skills were successfully developed through adult support, curriculum and structures to scaffold a participatory group decision-making process. These research findings align with prior research that identified the core features of youth development programs as: (1) development of youth voice, skill-building and mastery; (2) adult support for efficacy and responsibility in positions of leadership; (3) a structure that supports youth input and participation in decision-making; and (4) youth leadership in decisions that impact project design, development and execution (Connell, Gambone & Smith, 2001; McLaughlin, Irby & Langman, 1994; Perkins & Borden, 2003; Pittman, 1996; Zeldin, 2004). Perkins and Borden's (2003) study suggests that young people's active engagement as decision-makers is one of the most significant indicators of effective positive youth development programs.

Furthermore, student researchers increased their confidence and expanded their self-conceptions of their leadership, academic abilities and agency to impact their settings. This participatory, experiential, project-based learning process created a space for students to take risks and make mistakes. This learning process successfully supported young people in inhabiting new leadership roles. Student researchers developed their leadership skills through building relationships with others and developing leadership skills such as peer mentoring. When young people were trusted with responsibilities, they took accountability for group learning. They were open to learning from peers and reflecting on the ways in which their participation encouraged others to contribute to the group process. These findings align with prior work that delineated core sets of youth development competencies—such as safety, trusting relationships, a sense of belonging, group membership, mastery and social contribution—that PYD programs should scaffold with programmatic opportunities and supports (McLaughlin et al., 1994).

Developing relational leadership involved youth input in project planning and design. Further, relational leadership required taking responsibility for one's own participation, monitoring one's own participation patterns, being accountable to the group and encouraging others' contributions. Further, student researchers felt a sense of ownership over their work and the overall project, and that the ability to participate in the public sphere led to accountability to others. These youth-led PAR project members even experienced a sense of accountability to people beyond the youth and adults in the project. Guishard and colleagues (2005) find that in PAR projects, student researchers' interactions with their own study participants often engender a commitment to ensure that the action phase of their research project meets identified needs.

The Central Youth United case involved a training curriculum designed to support young researchers in designing the research plan, creating focus group protocols, conducting focus groups, analyzing data and drawing conclusions to present to community decision-makers. In this project, the establishing of successful youth–adult partnerships demanded that adults play active roles in supporting and guiding youth-led decision-making processes and leadership development. Adults took on roles as youth allies to support young people's development and to empower them as leaders through a relational process. Similarly, critical youth studies frameworks find that young people, characterized as a politically, economically and socially marginalized group that holds an asymmetrical relationship with adults, benefit from adult support and advocacy (Griffin, 1993; Lesko, 2012; Wyn, 2000; Wyn & Whyte, 1997).

Adults in the Central Youth United project saw their work as serving as youth advocates and allies, and thus being supportive of young people's growth and development, by identifying power differentials and taking action with other adults and young people to work towards equity in youth–adult partnerships in both thinking and practice. One of the limitations in developing young people's shared leadership in this youth-led project seemed to be that the two project instructors did not consider sharing decisions with student researchers when the instructors were designing and leading project activities. Even with this limitation, which might have inhibited the best possible outcomes for leadership development, young people in this project successfully developed their leadership skills.

One factor that shaped positive developmental outcomes was the role of adults in supporting and guiding student researchers' input and leadership in project decisions. In this case, the adults' role in facilitating the leadership development process enabled young people and adults to work in partnership towards their project's goals of becoming civically engaged and improving their neighborhood community. This finding aligns with key principles in youth development practice: that youth–adult partnerships serve to contribute vision, insight and direction in community problem-solving for thriving institutions and communities.

Situated Learning

In situated learning approaches, the learning of new knowledge and skills occurs most effectively through participatory, collaborative interactions that involve applying knowledge within authentic contexts (Lave & Wenger, 2003). In the Central Youth United project, learning occurred through participatory, collaborative activities that demanded that the student researchers use their new research skills to conduct research in authentic contexts to be found in their local neighborhood community. A key component of situated learning entails participating in communities of practice, in which participants learn a set of core skills, behaviors and standards (Lave & Wenger, 2003; Wenger, 1998; 2000). In the CYU case, student researchers learned the standards, behaviors and skills of research and learned how to conduct a credible research study with human participants. The situated learning framework entails that novice learners move from the periphery of activity towards the center to become more active in the culture and roles of communities of practice, and begin to act to inhabit the role of an expert, which is a process known as "legitimate peripheral participation" (Lave & Wenger, 2003). In the CYU project, the team of student researchers participating in the PAR project served as a community of practice and they moved from being novice researchers to becoming expert researchers capable of designing a research project, collecting data, analyzing data to draw findings, and presenting their findings and recommendations to community stakeholders. Situated learning occurred in the CYU case through a teaching and learning approach that was participatory, collaborative and action oriented.

Connecting Ownership, Agency and Motivation Through Communities of Practice

Young people became highly engaged, motivated and committed to the process when they experienced a sense of ownership and agency over their work. This finding aligns with frameworks for conducting PAR with young people, which find that young people gain a sense of ownership, accountability and agency through participation in group decision-making processes in which they realize the limitations and possibilities of their leadership and participation (Atweh et al., 1998; Cahill et al., 2008; Cammarota & Fine, 2008; McIntyre, 2000; Morrell, 2008). Further, when young people had the opportunity to take collaborative action in the public sphere, there was a significant increase in their sense of accountability in terms of helping others and improving their environments.

Positive Youth Development and Participation

Research suggests that in order to enable young people to participate as active, contributing members of a democracy, previous, gradual participation in adult-supported decision-making responsibilities is necessary (Gibson, 2001; Hart, 1997). Recent research on positive youth development (PYD) programs recommends that they provide skill-building practices and opportunities for youth participation in increasing decision-making responsibilities and leadership roles (Camino & Zeldin, 2002; Eccles & Gootman, 2002; Perkins & Borden, 2003). High-quality organized activities and programs have been identified as an ecological asset that can potentially enhance young people's development (Eccles & Gootman, 2002; Kirshner, 2007; Strobel, Kirshner, O'Donoghue & Wallin McLaughlin, 2008). One study found that students reported low levels of attention, concentration and investment during traditional schoolwork and homework, yet the same students reported high engagement while participating in quality youth programs (Larson, 2000). Other studies on the impact of organized activities in terms of increased youth voice, youth participation and agency in school and non-school settings show that these organized activities are contexts in which young people build their competencies and apply these developed skills in authentic settings (Kirshner, 2007; Mitra, 2004; 2009; Strobel et al., 2008). A substantial body of research has investigated the features of organized activities—such as participatory, collaborative, action-oriented approaches—as potentially supportive contexts for youth development when there are structured opportunities for youth input, adult support for decision-making and leadership roles, and collaborations with adults and peers (Connell et al., 2001; Kirshner, 2007; Larson & Angus, 2011; Larson, Walker & Pearce, 2005; Mahoney, Eccles, & Larson, 2004; McLaughlin, 2000; Mitra, 2004; Perkins et al., 2003; Zeldin, Christens & Powers, 2013). However, more research is needed that builds upon and extends this important research on PYD program organized activities, settings and their outcomes to provide a close investigation of the curriculum and instructional practices that can help to engage young people and develop their academic skills and sense of agency.

Participatory action research (PAR) with youth shows itself to be another viable method that uses organized activities to develop young people's decision-making and program-planning skills as change agents (Atweh et al., 1998; Cammarota & Fine, 2008; McIntyre, 2000). Studies within the emergent field of

PAR with youth have begun to delineate some of the processes and practices of PAR projects with young people (Cahill et al., 2008; Cammarota & Fine, 2008; Morrell, 2008). To build upon this vital research, more research is needed that examines instructional strategies, curriculum design and structured programmatic supports to increase young people's participation as decision-makers and leaders. Additional research is needed that investigates how young people understand their participation as decision-makers, leaders and agents of change, and which strategies youth perceive as supportive of their emergent capacities. Such research may help us better understand what practices are most effective in engaging student researchers in decision-making roles and responsibilities as leaders and change agents. Therefore, to build capacities for decision-making and agency, towards the goal of preparing young people to develop the skills needed for them to participate as active members in a democracy, it is important for research to expand its focus to study relationships between youth involvement strategies, instructional practices and curriculum, and student researchers' perceptions of their participation as decision-makers, leaders and agents of community change.

In a similar manner, youth development research has found that people are motivated to tackle challenges when they perceive themselves as having ownership and agency over their actions (Deci & Ryan, 2000; Eccles & Wigfield, 2002; Ryan & Deci, 2000). Other research in developmental psychology that employs the applied developmental systems theory (ADST) framework finds that healthy, adaptive functioning occurs when individuals not only adjust to institutions and social systems as they currently exist, but also learn to transform institutions and their social contexts to support the self (Lerner, Brentano, Dowling & Anderson, 2002). In other words, for healthy developmental outcomes young people need opportunities to contribute both to their own development and to the development of their social contexts. Other research has found that including a civic activism or social justice component to youth leadership development strategies is a viable and successful approach to supporting young people's healthy development (Ginwright & Cammarota, 2002). In the CYU case, the project's curriculum and teaching process involved *relational leadership*, a collective, relational model of sharing power and decision-making that entails sharing ideas through dialogue and structured activities, and was central to successful situated learning. This case also involved situated learning to build the capacity for decision-making and leadership and to build a sense of agency.

6

PROMOTING SOCIOPOLITICAL ANALYSIS SKILLS

Introduction

"We had to answer questions—and they were really hard—around when we discriminated against people's race or sexuality and gender and all this stuff. And you just had to answer them honestly. And I think it went well," observed Rashna, the secondary instructor in the Central Youth United (CYU) project. In a similar vein, Ameera, a student researcher, remarked, "I liked about it that we are actually mentioning it. Some people never mention this stuff ... And we always hear it and we listen, so now we get to talk about it, and hopefully we can change it." Ameera explained that she appreciated the brave conversations about difference as part of the curriculum activities because they were breaking the silence about the discrimination they faced and identifying solutions to address it.

This chapter discusses the development of a specific form of critical thinking skill, *sociopolitical analysis skills*, which occurred through the teaching approach and curriculum that the two instructors implemented. In this participatory action research (PAR) project with young people, sociopolitical analysis development occurred as an intentional pedagogical strategy in which student researchers connected their personal, micro-level experiences of sociopolitical inequities to larger, macro-level sociopolitical forces. Promoting sociopolitical analysis skills is an element of a *pedagogy of praxis*, described in the previous chapter, in which student researchers analyze community issues and connect them with an action plan to address these issues. Student researchers in Central Youth United were highly engaged in this component of a pedagogy of praxis in which they developed their sociopolitical analysis skills. The PAR curriculum enabled student researchers to engage deeply in conversations about social and political issues they experienced, and to think critically about the sociopolitical context of their research study.

The PAR process includes cycles of reflection and action and further reflection (Atweh et al., 1998; Freire, 2001; Ginwright, 2008). For example, the Freirean pedagogical framework holds three critical elements to participatory learning: (1) an active, dialogical approach stimulating critical awareness of sociopolitical factors; (2) program content relevant to the learner's interests and sociopolitical context; and (3) the use of teaching techniques such as deconstructing complex themes into smaller elements and codifying them with visual representations (Freire, 2001, p. 83). In the CYU case, group dialogue addressed solutions that built upon their prior knowledge about the young people's neighborhood's needs, solutions that were situated in their lived experiences. It was an important learning experience for the student researchers to have discussions about power with supportive instructors and other young people.

For example, the student researchers identified their social locations: where they fitted into society's hierarchy along the lines of race and ethnicity, gender, class, citizenship status, sexual orientation and other markers of identity. The student researchers then discussed the ways in which their various social locations can both privilege and marginalize them. As PAR researcher Ginwright (2008) notes, "research is most useful when young people develop skills both to explain systemic causes of issues that shape their lives and to act to transform those conditions" (p. 21). This particular concept of developing a critical awareness of the root causes of issues that directly impact them can also be described as developing a critical consciousness (Freire, 2001; Patel, 2012).

This group had student researchers who identified with a diverse range of ethnicities: African American, Mexican, Cambodian, Yemeni and Salvadorian. In their pre-surveys, CYU members identified with the racial categories of Black, Latino, Asian and Middle Eastern. The two adult PAR instructors, Jocelyn and Rashna, identify as Filipino and Pakistani respectively. These two instructors intentionally incorporated activities in which student researchers were challenged to question their own stereotypes and share their experiences about race and racism with this team. Engaging across difference on an equal basis was a first step in building trust. The instructors also expressed their intent to provide activities that allowed the student researchers to determine where stereotypes come from. They also intended student researchers to employ sociological thinking to examine institutions in society such as the mass media, family, school and youth groups, legal systems and government, the economy, religious institutions, police forces and the military. For some student researchers, the most valued skill they developed in this project was learning to connect with people of different backgrounds. At the close of the program, Ameera discussed what she had gained from her experience in the CYU project. She observed, "I think the most skills that I got were how to do focus groups and research projects, the presentation skills, communication skills ... How to communicate with people from different places, different ethnicities." As the student researchers built upon these initial connections, they were able to participate in learning activities to share their lived experiences of discrimination, as well as their own prejudices. This enabled student researchers to engage with each other across their differing backgrounds to draw deeper connections between their experiences and lives. They were also able to better understand sociopolitical concepts by grounding their analysis in their previous encounters with discrimination.

For example, in one activity that Jocelyn designed, there were flip-chart papers placed around the room labeled with five racial categories of Black, Latino, Asian, Middle Eastern and White. On large flip-chart papers, everyone had to write down stereotypes they had heard about each racial group, including their own. Ameera remembers the saliency of this activity for her:

> [In the activity] you have to go around and write, "What do you hear about this group? What's your first expression or feeling about this group?" We had to put [down] all the hate slurs, the bad stuff, about that community or group. It was kind of sad to hear and see all this bad stuff said about that group. But I liked about it that we are actually mentioning it. Some people never mention this stuff. It's a shame, but it's what's happening these days. And we always hear it and we listen, so now we get to talk about it, and hopefully we can change it—at least in Central Youth United ... The goal was to see how the media influences us. For instance, the news—how they treat these racial groups—or you see that the media is wrong.

Ameera emphasizes that although this exercise facilitates a difficult conversation, she appreciates that instructors are creating a space where they can discuss hate slurs and distortions about racial groups presented in the nightly news and the mainstream media. She points out that hateful words and actions unfortunately happen and that students hear such things on a regular basis, and so benefit from talking about it directly. She also expresses that her experience discussing difficult topics such as stereotypes and oppression builds her sense of possibility, hope and agency such that she can act to transform these stereotypes and change them, at least in her team of student researchers. Ameera mentions her hope that in Central Youth United the student researchers can change the discriminatory patterns of behavior towards each other. Understanding the ability to either reproduce macro-level power inequities or interrupt them within their micro-level learning environments enables young people to develop their own "political clarity" and analysis (Bartolomé, 1994). Following the activity, Jocelyn read these identified stereotypes aloud so that these stereotypical assumptions could be examined through a facilitated discussion.

It was particularly significant for the student research team to analyze the ways in which everyone is affected by power and wields power over others.

For these student researchers, developing their capacities for sociopolitical analysis entailed talking to other team members and to the two instructors in order to validate and understand their experiences of discrimination. They also learned about the ways in which their actions based on stereotypes might unwittingly discriminate against others and reproduce structural inequities. This realization motivated the team to work together to take actions towards creating the conditions for social justice within their team and in their neighborhood.

Student researchers experienced discussions of power as important strategies for building their participation, leadership and agency. Many student researchers expressed an appreciation for a supportive space in which to discuss with other teenagers and their instructors injustices that functioned in their lives. They also expressed disappointment that teachers had not previously supported them in analyzing their stories of discrimination in classrooms or in non-school learning settings that aimed to support their learning. The student researchers were developing an important critical thinking skill by being able to name their experiences, understand that their experiences are not representative of everyone else's experience and realize that their perspective is an asset in the group dialogue.

A Dialogic Approach That Taps Funds of Knowledge to Actively Construct Ideas

Scholarship on pedagogical approaches aiming to develop learners' agency emphasizes that tapping into their existing funds of knowledge (González et al., 2013; Moll, 1992)—the resources of prior knowledge, perspectives and values that are situated in their lived experiences—helps increase their sense of control over their learning by viewing their perspectives as assets (Chow, 1999; Heath, 1983; Kenway & Modra, 1992). Similarly, Bartolomé (1994) suggests teachers employ a "humanizing pedagogy" that includes students' experiences, history and perspectives in their approaches to teaching. A central tenet of scholarship on critical pedagogy suggests that learners critically interrogate their own experiences and identities to understand how their views and needs are systemically reinforced, contradicted and sustained by larger sociopolitical forces (Giroux, 1983). Scholarship and research on pedagogy finds that a "dialogic approach," or group dialogue, which situates learning (Kenway & Modra, 1992; Lave & Wenger, 2003) within students' lived experiences, identities and perspectives is a sound pedagogical approach to develop their self-conceptions as change agents (De los Reyes, 2002; Ellsworth, 1989; Freire, 1998; Gore, 2003; Ladson-Billings & Tate, 2006; Morrell, 2004; Shor, 1992). For example, Freire (2001) describes his "culture circle" approach to literacy development as requiring learners to critically "read the word" to increase their literacy while simultaneously taking an active, creative role in constructing their own ideas through dialogue to enable them to critically "read the world," through analysis of the world they inhabit.

Student researchers in the Central Youth United project built their sociopolitical analysis skills and developed a sense of agency through pedagogical approaches that connected reflection about their community's needs with the implementing of action projects to meet these needs. This connection between micro and macro levels helped the student researchers develop their sociopolitical analysis skill sets.

One interactive activity, "Five Communities," was intentionally designed to build trust and teamwork to scaffold collective decision-making and collective, distributed leadership. In this activity, the primary instructor, Jocelyn, has everyone select some markers and a piece of colored construction paper. She then points to a pile of small scissors and an array of colored construction paper. She instructs that everyone has 20 minutes to draw (or cut out of colored paper) five symbols that represent five communities to which they belong. In the Five Communities activity, the action researchers decided to draw symbols representing their family communities, racial and ethnic communities, country they were from, mosque or church or school communities, sports teams, social cliques and affiliations, and other youth programs. Jocelyn mentions that the Five Communities activity is an example that explains her rationale behind providing team-building activities. Her goal is for student researchers to connect across diverse backgrounds and social locations. She comments that this activity "shows your personality through each community and how you're different in each community. Yet, you belong to not just one, but more than one community." Jocelyn mentions that a learning goal for this activity is to acknowledge that each person belongs to multiple communities and to show "how you're different in each community." Observing this activity compelled student researchers to consider the qualitatively different roles they may hold depending on different contexts: at home, at school, at Sister Space, at Representing Ourselves or at Central Youth United.

In another activity that centered discussions of race and ethnicity, the research team and both instructors had to answer questions on slips of paper they drew from a hat. These questions asked them to divulge a time that they discriminated against another group on the basis of multiple identities. Rashna, the secondary instructor, was present for Jocelyn's activity as a participant herself and recalls her observations:

> We had to answer questions—and they were really hard—around when we discriminated against people's race or sexuality and gender and all this stuff. And you just had to answer them honestly. And I think it went well … I remember there were a lot of questions about race—you know, "Have you discriminated?" And then it would be with certain people, like against Asian Americans. I remember a discussion around Arab/Muslim discrimination and I was really happy because I feel like we don't talk about that hardly ever after post-9/11, and it's so real. And I felt

happy that it was part of the discussion with these young people because assumptions came up and we have somebody who is Muslim in the group. So that felt really powerful.

Rashna describes her experience of participating in an exercise that tackled difficult topics of discrimination. She also explains that it was difficult to be vulnerable and take accountability—in public—for the ways in which she discriminated against other groups. Being accountable to students and being vulnerable with them is not something that teachers are often encouraged to do in schools. However, in this case the benefits included a noticeable change in the sense of safety to take risks to learn and the level of trust that developed between instructors and student researchers and then between student researchers. These activities centered individual identities and discrimination due to race, class, gender, sexuality, citizenship status and religion. These learning exercises were designed to build relationships and connections across diversity and across team members' varied perspectives and social locations.

Both student researchers and instructors had to push themselves outside of their comfort zones to be vulnerable and share about their participation in recreating social injustice. Rashna shares her experience of mutual risk-taking and vulnerability as creating "trust in the room" during that activity. For both instructors and student researchers, one important part of the program was building these connections across diverse identities and backgrounds. Creating connections with people from different places, different ethnicities and different backgrounds helped build a sense of community and team in the group. Further, understanding the ways in which social injustices affect everyone served to expand both instructors' and student researchers' analysis of their own relationship to issues of race, discrimination and social justice. Eventually, the Central Youth United inquiry project led to a community action plan to create a youth center in the neighborhood.

Developing Sociopolitical Analysis Skills

This concept of developing sociopolitical analysis skills aligns with and extends the work of psychologists Watts and Guessous (2006), which emphasizes the importance of youth developing a critical awareness of their relationship to their sociopolitical context, which they term *sociopolitical development* (SPD). Their study defines SPD as "the evolving, critical understanding of the political, economic, cultural and other systemic forces that shape society and one's status within it, and the associated process of growth in relevant knowledge, analytical skills, and emotional faculties" (p. 60). Research finds that successful sociopolitical development involves four elements: (1) a critical analysis of authority and power; (2) a sense of agency to take action that makes an impact; (3) structured opportunities for action; and (4) developmental outcomes of commitment and action (Watts & Guessous, 2006; Watts, Williams & Jagers, 2003).

Similarly, studies on PAR with youth find that student researchers develop a more nuanced understanding of the social problem their project investigates when they are able to connect an identified micro-level issue to larger, macro-level sociopolitical contexts (Cahill et al., 2008; Cammarota & Fine, 2008; Cannella, 2008; Fine et al., 2003; Morrell, 2008; Torre et al., 2008). For example, one study finds that PAR projects with young people are most successful in developing a sociopolitical analysis of the social problem under study when the student researchers participate in training designed as "a democratic environment to empower youth, by expanding and building on their emerging commitments to social change through inquiry" (Guishard et al., 2005, p. 45).

Ladson-Billings (2014) observes that those historically disadvantaged by educational inequities should benefit from a quality education and develop the tools to critique the status quo, and those who are advantaged by educational inequities should develop skills and analysis that will enable them to critique the origins and foundation of their own privileges. In the same vein, A. Howard (2008) found that deconstructing privilege and interrogating its unfairness is a crucial component in learning, and developing a critical analysis. Other researchers have found that interrogating privilege and its interpersonal and societal impacts is an important part of the PAR approach for student researchers representing diverse backgrounds (Torre et al., 2008). Further, Torre et al. (2008) concludes that if privilege goes unchallenged in learning settings that bring together people from diverse identities, who each experience both privilege and oppression, such learning environments are in danger of reproducing social hierarchies and inequities. The sociopolitical activities in Central Youth United aim to address social hierarchies in order to create a more equitable learning environment. Ginwright (2008) finds that PAR as an art and method can create a space for a collective reimagining of our world that stresses "democratizing knowledge," "critical inquiry of everyday life," and practices that engage young people in "democratic problem solving" (p. 14). Aligning with scholarship both on critical pedagogy and on PAR with young people, in the CYU case student researchers developed their sociopolitical analysis skills when they explicitly connected their micro-level experiences to larger, macro-level sociopolitical factors and forces as problem-solvers and decision-makers.

The CYU project intentionally incorporated curriculum and strategies that promoted sociopolitical thinking that connected their personal experiences with wider social, economic and political inequities. These teaching techniques that aimed to cultivate sociopolitical analysis skills provided several benefits to the student researchers: (1) a forum for student researchers to share and validate their personal experiences of prejudice and discrimination; (2) opportunities to think critically outside of their own individual experiences to connect with others' experiences and perspectives; and (3) structured support to channel their feelings of alienation and frustration with these experiences into a constructive commitment to collective action aiming to create a more just society.

One example of sociopolitical analysis development strategies in action in the CYU project was the "Three 'I's of Oppression" activity. This activity entailed several phases drawn out over multiple team meetings. Jocelyn singled out the Three "I"s of Oppression activity as a good example of an activity she uses to foster strategic thinking about the sociopolitical context of the student research- ers' community needs assessment. Following the PAR curriculum, Jocelyn's teaching approach incorporated a discussion of the root causes and solutions to problems the student researchers faced in order to help them think strategically about the action component of their participatory action research project. That is, student researchers needed to think strategically about ways to find research- based solutions to the team's research question, "What do youth really need in Central?" Jocelyn refers to these types of PAR curriculum activities as "political education activities," distinguishing them from traditional research skill devel- opment activities and team-building activities. Jocelyn discusses why she facilit- ates activities designed to help the student researchers relate their lives to their research context, explaining that is important to

> have them understand their living environment or their conditions or even their community. So we taught about oppression. We learned about the different "-isms" from bad [derogatory] words that they used to dif- ferent things that are institutional. So them understanding that part and then seeing, "So how does that relate to Central? How does that relate to you as a person that lives in Central? How does it relate to you as a Mexican American? Or "How does it relate to you period?" And so *having them bring out their personal stories* was really good and then being like, "Well, why are we doing this research?" Because it's about you and it's about where you live. So I think at the end, they kinda went, "Oh, okay, I get it." And so it's learning about themselves first and then learn- ing, "Okay, now that you know that there's all these things that are messed up personally, locally, globally, then what do you do about it?" And so that's when they chose, "Well, this is what we want to do to address: The youth's needs in Central. [Jocelyn's emphasis]

In a focus group, almost all student researchers named this Three "I"s of Oppression activity as among those that had the most impact, and one that was among the most interesting, relevant and engaging. This may be because stu- dents do not often have an opportunity to discuss their experiences of discrimi- nation in the classroom as a part of the school curriculum in a safe learning environment. Perhaps more importantly, traditional curricula may not offer opportunities in which these experiences of discrimination are the subject of examination and analysis through structured activities designed to acknowledge the realities of discrimination while also pointing to the abilities of students to act with others to work towards creating more equitable social spaces and institutions. As we saw at the outset of this chapter, Ameera indicated that this was why she found the activity to be important to her when she described an activity designed to foster her sociopolitical analysis skills. She recalled:

> We had to put [down] all the hate slurs, the bad stuff, about that community or group. It was kind of sad to hear and see all this bad stuff said about that group. But I liked about it that we are actually mentioning it. Some people never mention this stuff … And we always hear it and we listen, so now we get to talk about it, and hopefully we can change it.

Chenda also shares that the Three "I"s of Oppression activity is one of her most memorable activities in the project. She recalls the activity:

> There was an activity that for sure I remember with oppression. And we were discussing how we have interpersonal, internalized and institutional oppression. It's just describing oppression and how many things could influence you and what people influence you and how you change yourself. And if your environment is one way, it might impact you in the same way.

What is most striking about this activity for Chenda is the relationship between the macro-level oppressions, such as institutional oppressions in the wider environment, and their impact on an individual's micro-level experiences. These micro-level experiences include the ways in which individuals impact others or how individuals who have been impacted negatively by environmental factors might lead them to change themselves. Chenda articulates the connection between the macro level and the micro level in her remark that "[i]f your environment is one way, it might impact you in the same way." For example, an environment that is hostile to one's general presence and personal attempts to make contributions might make someone feel hostile as a result. Similarly, Cammarota and Fine (2008) find that student researchers are better able to analyze the social issue that is the topic of inquiry in their PAR project through understanding the larger, macro-level political and societal forces that shape their micro-level issue. Through these activities that facilitate difficult discussions about the political context of their community needs assessment, the student researchers draw connections between interpersonal stereotypes and institutional discrimination. Student researchers also participate in curriculum activities to analyze the ways in which people might internalize these messages and change themselves to conform to these stereotypes, or the ways they might change themselves to resist them.

In the first segment of the Three "I"s of Oppression activity, Jocelyn begins the activity by passing out a handout with examples and stick-figure drawings illustrating three forms of oppression: institutional, interpersonal and internal. Rashna later commented that perhaps there should be a fourth "I" of oppression, "ideological" oppression, to highlight the ideologies operating underneath the other three forms of oppression. Jocelyn then defines each of these three forms of oppression and gives examples. She defines institutional oppression as systems or institutions that perpetuate the stereotypes that some groups are better than others. She lists examples of societal institutions: the media, family, church, schools or prisons. Jocelyn then defines internal oppression as what happens when one begins to believe the stereotypes perpetuated by these institutions. She gives the example of a girl believing that girls are not smart. She defines interpersonal oppression as discrimination that occurs between two or more people, which stems from these stereotypes. She gives the example of a Black male not being hired, owing to an employers' discriminatory biases and beliefs. Everyone then participates in the discussion that follows, in which each student researcher shares their personal experiences of different forms of oppression they have encountered.

For example, Chenda discusses how she has experienced interpersonal oppression from a social clique of other girls at school who gossiped about her in middle school because she did not wear the latest fashionable, brand-name clothes. This leads to a discussion of how young women often internalize messages from the media about acceptable appearances for girls and women. The group begins to list what messages the media conveys about how girls and young women should look. The list they catalogue includes having manicured nails; accessorizing their outfits with a brand-name purse; being thin; having light skin, light hair and light eyes; and following the latest designer fashion trends for their slim-fitting outfits.

The three young men eagerly recall times when someone first introduced to them the idea that to be "real" and "hard" and "cool" they had to "sag their pants, wear hoodies, and be fitted" in casual wear accessorized with matching baseball caps and designer sneakers. This led Jason, Terrence and Miguel to discuss how they began to internalize the idea that "real" men had to dress a certain way. Victor gives an example of being in his kitchen the day before he entered middle school when his older brother walked into the kitchen and told him, "You can't tuck your shirt in or wear your pants like that anymore, man. It ain't cool and you ain't a little boy anymore. To get respect out here, you gotta sag."

The young men on the research team discuss how this situation and decide that this was an example of a form of interpersonal oppression—young men policing each other when one person steps out the box of what is deemed acceptable for a young man's appearance and behavior. Both the young men and the young women share the ways in which they learned what it meant to be masculine or feminine in Central, recalling aloud who told them these unspoken rules and when and where they learned them. They then list all of the institutions that helped produce and perpetuate interpersonal and internalized oppressions. Their list of institutions that convey these stereotypical messages includes television and the media, school and textbooks, the family system and the church or mosque. The student researchers then discuss ways that people within these institutions either reproduce oppressions by discriminating against other people or internalize or resist these messages for themselves. Next, Jocelyn elicits responses from the young men to share their experiences of one of the three forms of oppression. Jason, Terrence, Miguel and Victor all share their experiences with the police, who harass them regularly. They disclose that on an almost daily basis the police confront them to demand why they are walking down the street in their own neighborhood, the area where they live. They reveal that they are often stopped and frisked by the police in the daytime when they are minding their own business and on the way to visit a family member or run an errand for a family member. They share that whenever they attempt to go to the nearby mall, a new development patronized by the new, wealthy condo dwellers who have moved into their neighborhood, the police ask them why they are there and whether they are actually shopping, demanding that they leave and threatening otherwise to arrest them for loitering. They then name the ways in which the police stereotype them for their outward appearance: sagging pants, big hooded sweatshirts, matching baseball caps. They recount the ways that these experiences made them feel unsafe in their own neighborhoods—made to feel unsafe by the very police force that is supposed to protect and serve them as law-abiding civilians. Through discussing the patterns of their experiences with each other, these four young men determine that police brutality and harassment can represent institutional oppression.

These four Black and Latino young men demonstrated a sudden, palpable excitement to share a plethora of stories about their experiences regarding the hyper-policing of Black and Latino young men in their neighborhood and their feelings of betrayal and injustice due to these indignities. Their enthusiasm to share these stories indicated that they had not had an opportunity to be listened to in describing these painful, degrading and sometimes humiliating experiences with figures who wielded authority and power over them in situations in which they had little or no control. This organized activity provided a space for them to be listened to without being automatically dismissed as exaggerating their experiences or being blamed for them. Although all of the young women know many stories about the police arriving hours late when residents call for their protection in an emergency, many of them admit that they are unfamiliar with the extent and degree to which young men experience police harassment on a weekly basis. In contrast to the dominant narrative on police harassment and brutality, this activity allowed those who had not directly experienced being profiled by the police to learn directly from their peers, who had regularly experienced this in their neighborhood. In addition, some of their understandable anger and rage at these indignities was dissipated by having a space to talk through their humiliating experiences in a space where they were not brushed off as being mere troublemakers or wrongdoers. These exercises enabled the young people to strengthen their existing analysis of the sociopolitical forces impacting their experiences of police harassment in Central. It is important for the student researchers to be able to discuss this analysis together, because they can thereby acknowledge the realities they face, be validated in their experiences, develop empathy and responsiveness to others in connecting across difference, and build a shared sense of common challenges and possibilities to collectively address these challenges. These experiences were both engaging and challenging for the student researchers.

Schools that typically serve students marginalized by race, ethnicity and socioeconomic status often struggle to provide positive, engaging climates and opportunities for student engagement (Noguera, 2003). Research has found that to improve students' resiliency and academic achievement, schools should provide students with more opportunities for participation in activities that develop social competencies such as responsiveness to others and relationship skills (Wasonga, Christman & Kilmer, 2003). Schools may need to take a more active role in promoting skills such as responsiveness to others and building relationships across difference to promote safe environments for difficult conversations and learning, and might benefit from undertaking instructional practices, learned from organized youth programs, to build relationships across difference. The PAR curriculum entailed facilitated discussions about social processes in context and the systemic causes of injustice. Research shows that, particularly for marginalized young people, healthy development includes understanding social processes and the root causes of injustice (Ginwright & James, 2002; Watts et al., 2003). In addition, these structured, facilitated discussions are important ways to channel student researchers' frustrations about these experiences into ideas and plans for collective action that work towards increasing equity and justice in their local environments. Watkins, Larson and Sullivan (2007) found that organized youth programs can benefit youth development through activities in which young people interact across groups, develop sensitivity to difference, learn about other groups and injustices they have experienced, find commonalities in experiences, build relationships across groups, understand the systemic processes that create injustice, and develop a commitment to advocating for equal treatment and social action to fight injustice.

Both the young women and the two instructors validate the young men's feelings by acknowledging popular and academic investigations of police harassment that also view this phenomenon as a social justice issue. Rashna explains the teaching and learning principle behind these activities in which young people speak their truth about power abuses in a structured, validating exercise:

> I think when anybody is oppressed in some way, it's a really long process to come back and feel powerful around whatever that is, you know.

And I think that takes a lot of skill-building and support and trust in young people to speak what their truth is and let them speak it without correcting it, or rephrasing it, or reframing it, but what they say is valid and true to what their experience is (or what their peers' experiences are) or how their perspective on the world is.

Rashna's purpose in facilitating curriculum activities such as the Three "I"s of Oppression activity is to develop sociopolitical thinking, with the goal of empowering students from marginalized groups to use their voice and vocalize what is true for them about their experiences with oppression. As a PAR instructor of a student-driven process, her intention is to act in the role of an adult ally to build trust and support for youth voice. Through creating a space for student researchers to apply sociopolitical concepts to their own experience, this teaching strategy encourages them to speak their truths about forms of discrimination that they face, validates their experiences and perspectives, and provides skill-building activities to develop their analysis of sociopolitical forces that relate to these experiences.

This curriculum intended to provide trainings that engage both student researchers' experiences and their sociopolitical analysis of oppression in order to empower the student researchers. The two instructors in the Central Youth United project believed that empowerment is a component of youth development and is a youth leadership skill. The CYU project's curriculum and teaching strategies sought to empower student researchers through interactive activities and group dialogue that centered discussions of power as related to their own lived experiences. The CYU's curriculum and teaching strategies align with Kreisberg's (1992) theoretical framework, in which he posits that when educational scholars discuss theory and practices aiming to empower young learners, it can be limiting for such discussions not to address issues of power in their scholarship and practice recommendations. The CYU curriculum sought to empower student researchers by supporting them in discussing how issues of power impact their lives and to analyze their experiences as they relate to macro-level sociopolitical systems.

In the closing component of the exercise, PAR team members divided themselves into two groups to write and perform a short skit in the format of a television commercial, illustrating one of the forms of oppression the group had discussed. Jason, Terrence, Miguel and Victor were in one group and performed a skit about the police harassing them for doing nothing but standing on a Central street corner. Relaying their experiences with policing and being under surveillance by the police, the young men were tense and defensive at first, but the group discussion acknowledged their realities and placed them within the context of wider sociopolitical systems. The student researchers saw policing as related to wider sociopolitical systems because they pointed to the reality of systematic institutional discrimination against young men of color in U.S. society.

They further considered that institutions such as the police force would scrutinize the behavior of young men of color, owing to unquestioned stereotypes of men of color as threatening and dangerous. The young men of color on the PAR team understood that they experienced hostile surveillance and policing in the neighborhood where they lived because of social misconceptions that all men of color were dangerous, and potential criminals. While the realities of policing and biases in social systems may have been somewhat daunting at times during the discussion, through their own analysis the group arrived at a new conclusion: Sociopolitical systems are composed of humans and have changed over time; therefore, inequities in sociopolitical systems are capable of improvement through collective civic activism. The discussion then turned to ways in which they could stand with others to work to decrease bias in policing and to improve relationships between communities of color and the police.

After this group discussion, the young men noted that they were less traumatized because of their understanding that solutions were possible and because they were hopeful about being able to take action with others in order to make a difference and improve institutions within Central's sociopolitical system. They were especially interested in creating a neighborhood teen center where teenagers could safely congregate and socialize without fear of police harassment. For example, after being assigned to create a mock television commercial skit, Jason, Miguel, Victor and Terrence's group recounts and analyzes their almost daily experiences of police harassment in their small group. In creating and performing their skit, their demeanor becomes relaxed, as evidenced by their skit's humorous dramatization of the "real" situation of police harassment and its second scene enacting the "ideal" way that police officers should serve and protect them. Jason played the part of a friendly, helpful, supportive officer who serves as a keeper of the peace. The audience is asked to imagine that the scene is one where the police officer greets a group of Black and Brown boys dressed in matching, sagging casualwear on the street with:

> Good morning, fellas, you're probably on your way to school, now, huh? I know you might be running late to class, so I won't hold you up by asking for your ID like you didn't live here or belong here. If you need any directions or have a question, please ask me because I'm just here to protect and serve.

Jason, Terrence, Victor and Miguel giggle at their own creativity and humor embedded in the skit imagining ideal interactions with law enforcement.

Building on this team meeting, at which Jocelyn had facilitated the Three "I"s of Oppression, she followed up in the next meeting with a second part of this activity. For the second part of this activity, Jocelyn unfurled a flip-chart paper taped to the wall with the question "When have you felt mistreated by your race, ethnicity, class, gender, sexuality, disability, religion, country you're from or citizenship status?" She explained that the purpose of this exercise is to share personal stories that serve as an example of one type of discrimination, such as racism, classism, sexism, heterosexism, ableism (discrimination based on physical or cognitive disabilities) or religious oppression, or discrimination based on nationality or immigrant status. Jocelyn then instructed everyone to open their three-ring project binders to a loose-leaf sheet of paper and told them that they had seven minutes to jot down their story of discrimination, which they would all go around and share afterwards. She reminded them that their story could be any example of discrimination or oppression that they felt comfortable sharing with the group.

Jocelyn begins by sharing her example of discrimination. She relays her story:

> I was on the bus when I moved from my mostly Filipino elementary school in L.A. to a predominately White elementary school in the fourth grade. Just after coming to my new school, I entered the school bus one morning, which was full of only White kids. I saw an empty seat and started to sit down. "Someone is sitting here," one of the kids said, although it was obvious that no one was. I went to the next open seat a few rows back and the same thing happened. I kept at it for the last two remaining seats, asking the girls and boys on the bus to let me sit down, but each of the kids refused to let me sit, covering the empty seat with a jacket or sweater and saying, "Someone is sitting here already." The kids then started to make fun of me by saying in a mocking voice, "Ching chow ching. Ching chow ching," over and over. I wanted to cry, but I didn't want to give them the satisfaction. I was so embarrassed and hurt and angry inside, though. So I had to just stand there on the bus trying to block out their taunts of "Ching chow ching."
>
> After a while, the bus driver said that he couldn't start driving the bus until everyone was seated. I told the bus driver that no one was letting me sit down next to them but he said, "It's not my business. My job is just to drive the bus." The kids seemed like they could just taunt me all day without the bus moving anywhere. Finally, I saw an empty seat in the back without a jacket blocking it and I sat down. After that, no one talked to me or even looked at me for the whole ride to school that day and every day afterwards during my bus rides to and from school. It was like that until I found my two new friends, other Filipinos who later trans-ferred to my school.

At the close of her story, the student researchers ask all kinds of questions. They want to know about Jocelyn's friends, her time in high school afterwards, and whether other Filipinos transferred to her school later. There is an understood boundary within their questioning that doesn't get too personal or ask about related topics that might upset her. Jocelyn shares that one of the Filipino students who transferred to her school and was in her group of friends is now her husband. The student researchers are very interested in this since they talk to her husband when he comes to pick her up after the team meetings. She adds, "You would never guess now, but he was a big ole nerd in high school." She says she only thought of him as a friend back then, because "he had no game and he was super short." She confides that years later, after he had grown out of his nerdy phase, she realized that it didn't matter that he was short because "he was cute and wonderful and I wanted to start dating him." The group members are very responsive to her sharing, as evidenced by the flurry of questions. Jocelyn not only models sharing a painful experience, but even admits to her husband's former nerdy days (in a group where being a "nerd" is definitely not cool). However, she finally cuts off their questions, telling them, "We can talk more about this later," and then asks who would like to share next.

Jocelyn first set the tone by modeling what was appropriate to share, pointing out that it was okay to be vulnerable and to trust that the group would respect appropriate boundaries, and showing that they did not have to share everything if they wanted to keep more painful reflections to themselves. Further, Jocelyn modeled sharing a story that was not too raw, unhealed or traumatic—a story that she was still grappling with but one that, though still painful, she had a handle on. This showed that she was not expecting the student researchers to take care of her feelings, support her in making sense of her experience, or being in the inappropriate role of her therapist or care-taker. Rather, sharing a story that was once painful but had already healed indicated to the group that almost everyone has experienced some form of discrimination and that it is courageous to be able to share those experiences and discuss the conditions that created them with others through a structured process.

In this atmosphere that Jocelyn created by modeling risk-taking and vulnerability, it seemed unlikely that anyone would purposely say anything that might break the trust that was expected of them. Jocelyn's willingness to be vulnerable in front of the group of student researchers by sharing her personal stories through structured curriculum activities challenged traditional power dynamics between teachers and students. It allowed for the adult in the instructor role to show that she was not expecting vulnerability from the group of student researchers without herself being vulnerable, and it also showed her trust in the group and her expectation that they would be understanding and respectful when she was vulnerable. The student researchers responded to her trust in their capacity to be compassionate and understanding by showing their concern, empathy, validation and respect for her personal experience.

Later, Jocelyn reflects on how she experienced the exercise and how she began to learn more about their experiences. Recalling the Three "I"s of Oppression activity, Jocelyn shares that this "discussion was when they start to learn more about their own conditions, where they live." Jocelyn reflects that in this activity, the group "learned more about Ameera and where she came from, and Chenda and where she came from, and so it was interesting" to the students. She continues, "I think those kinds of conversations, when you bring out their experiences and then you share yours, get us to understand each other." This exercise helps build trust, understanding and collegiality between the student researchers and also between the student researchers and the instructors. This type of curriculum activity helps foster collegiality and turn the group into a team.

Jocelyn asks, "Who would like to share next?" A few folks raise their hands, eager to share their stories. Amani raises her hand first and begins:

> Well, you see I cover my head every day and it's because I am Muslim. My family came here from Yemen, where most people are Muslim and it is accepted there, without discrimination, just like Christianity is the major religion here and being a Christian is accepted here. Anyway, I always cover my head because that's my religion, and I never had problems with people about it. But after the 9/11 bombing and after all of the news stories reporting on terrorists, without also showing Muslim families who are against terrorists, things really changed at school. When I would walk down the hall to go to class, kids stared at me all the way down the hall, every period of each day. They would point and whisper, "There goes a terrorist." When I told my teachers that it is very hard for me to feel comfortable walking down the hall with everyone stopping their conversations to just stare and point and say things, they said there is nothing they can do. Not only at school, but walking to school and back, people on the street, even the homeless people on Washington Street, shout at me, "Terrorist!" or they yell at me, "Why don't you go back to your country?! We don't need terrorists here." One time, a man who was drunk in the street called out to me, "We'll bomb your country back to the Stone Age!" It's easier for my brothers walking to school and in the hallways at school because no one can tell that they are Muslim because they don't have to cover their hair.

After her story, Ameera fields a few questions. Acknowledging that it is "messed up," Victor admits, "To be honest, from watching the nightly news, they made it seem like all Muslims were terrorists, man, for real." This prompts Ameera to patiently explain to Victor that there are many different types of Muslims, just as there are many different types of people who are Christian or Jewish or Hindu or Buddhist or any other religion. Victor agrees, responding, "Well, I agree because I know there are some people in my mother's church who are just no good!" Victor and Ameera are laughing now as Victor concludes, "Okay, I guess I shouldn't believe everything I see on TV!"

Later on, Ameera reflects on how the learning environment felt to her and assessed that it was a space that allowed her to share her ideas. She explains:

> Every time I think an idea, I say it. It's taken into consideration. It might be wrong, but it was taken into consideration ... It was a free environment that you could just say whatever you want. Anything I wanted to say, I would just say it. You know, share the experience with other group members.

This open and safe learning environment was a space that allowed team members to take risks, be vulnerable, and share their ideas.

Chenda wants to go next. She tells her story about being discriminated against because she is a girl. She relates:

> I was at my friend's house and he lives in my same apartment complex, and my friend, he just got the new Xbox for Christmas. So he said we could play it, but he never really let me have a turn! He was so good that he could just keep playing and playing. Finally, when it was my turn, it would be over so fast because I didn't have any practice, so I wasn't that good. Even though he let my brothers learn how to play on his Xbox, he said since I was a girl, I shouldn't be playing it anyway. I was so mad because I really wanted to play.

After finishing her story, Chenda fields questions from her peers about her experience, mostly about how she felt at the time and inquiring about her current Xbox skills.

After everyone had told their stories about experiences that were once painful, no one was disrespectful, knowing that everyone would be in a vulnerable position when it was their turn to share their personal encounter with discrimination. It would be easy for someone to be judgmental, claiming that the discrimination was not significant or that the storyteller should have reacted differently in the situation—that they should have spoken up or remained quiet and walked away. However, the earlier curriculum that entailed team-building activities had helped develop a sense of trust, reliance on each other, and teamwork to accomplish a group task. Creating this group dynamic first before engaging in curriculum activities that would make them vulnerable allowed the young people not to be dismissive or skeptical or inattentive to each other's stories. This attentive, caring, compassionate group dynamic was built over time. This exercise allowed team members to consider and analyze the sociopolitical environment in which their experiences are nested.

The Three "I"s of Oppression activity is a type of interactive learning exercise that aligns with Freire's (2001) framework for participatory learning in which group dialogue centered on learners' interests encourages awareness of the sociopolitical context relevant to these interests and helps to sort and organize these experiences through visual representations. This learning exercise facilitated strategic thinking about the sociopolitical landscape that their project must take into account in order to identify Central's needs. The student researchers were encouraged to develop relevant, successful research-based recommendations for action by developing an inquiry project to determine young people's needs in their neighborhood, which culminated in a community action project to improve their neighborhood by creating a youth center. According to Youth Voice's mission statement, the thrust of its student-driven participatory action research project is to create a research-based community intervention to work towards "creating the conditions for social justice." As a result, the instructors included this activity to help student researchers think critically about the ways in which they might repeat or disrupt inequities as individuals or as a collective PAR project. The Three "I"s of Oppression activity contained several phases that extended over several meeting sessions and built upon earlier exercises. First they learned the terms and concepts and then they applied them to their own experiences through both large-group and small-group discussions. Next, in small groups they created skits about this discrimination in the format of a television commercial for further analysis and discussion. Finally, they told stories about discrimination and discussed them in order for individuals to generate a deeper analysis of their experiences and relate their experiences to others. Throughout the project, the group would refer to the skits or to other examples of discrimination from the storytelling activity when discussing issues such as police harassment of young men of color in their neighborhood, or other harassment that young women experienced in the street and the need for a safe place for young people to go with structured youth development programming. The discussions reflected a growing awareness that their PAR project should aim to address larger sociopolitical inequities and safety for young people in their neighborhood, particularly for young men of color, young women and other vulnerable groups of youth who felt unsafe because of the police, men on the street or others who negatively responded to their social location. Jocelyn explains the teaching goals of the Three "I"s of Oppression activity:

> The Three "I"s of Oppression activity is about understanding the different kinds of institutions in this society that get out messages. Things that we believe in and that kinda dictate our cultural values. There's the interpersonal oppression where you take all those different messages from media, TV, from church, from school, from books and then you're teaching your friends that or teaching your family members that and then you're kind of repeating the oppression. And then the internalized oppression is more like you trying to change yourself and conform to what you think is the standard of beauty or what a boy should be like or a girl should be like.

This activity enabled student researchers to consider where they and their project fitted within the wider sociopolitical ecology in which their community needs assessment is nested. Rashna shares her perspective on their pedagogical approach: using storytelling as an engaging learning tool. She says, "One thing Jocelyn and I tried to do was come up with more activities where stories could be told. Because they respond really well to each other's stories."

The Role of Vulnerability in Understanding Shared Challenges

Rashna summarizes the need for PAR instructors to exhibit vulnerability and transparency in order to participate effectively in a process to build youth–adult partnerships. She concludes:

> I believe that in organizing and in youth-led work there's got to be more transparency. And sure, you have boundaries and appropriate boundaries, but to expect one hundred percent vulnerability from a young person and give zero in return is just foolish to me. It's totally asinine and it's really unfair and it's not about creating equal power. And so I think there was just something really remarkable about that activity. Everybody has to get down to their bare bones and talked about when they've been racist, when they've had racism perpetrated against them. But really, really do it. And sometimes we all say some hurtful thing. I mean, I feel there was stuff called out about "terrorists" in that room, and I was just like, "Oh, my God!" But then you could address it.

These activities were designed to develop a connection between macro-level inequities and micro-level experiences. They demand that both student researchers and their instructors be vulnerable and take risks in order to be adult allies for their students and equalize power in youth–adult partnerships.

Jocelyn, the primary instructor, as well as each of the student researchers, reveal sensitive and vulnerable topics in sharing their stories. In order for the storyteller to be vulnerable, the teller has to take a risk and trust that no one will respond by being judgmental or dismissive. Referring to the Three "I"s activity, Rashna observes, "I think there was more respect in the room during that activity." After each person opens up by sharing a part of their story, a palpable sense of trust is evident in the room because it is clear that no one will intentionally disrespect another's vulnerable story in this space.

Despite the PAR team members' differences—in terms of gender, their relationship to the police and policing, whether or not they struggle with their home life, how they relate to school or other social institutions, and visions for their future paths—the team are left with a sense of cooperation and shared challenges. Ameera captures this feeling of trust built in this learning environment through the PAR curriculum in which student researchers felt comfortable to share their problems—experienced both in school and beyond school. She remarks:

I like how we all have the same problems. And now it's time for us to share everything together. You know, every problem we have in school and outside school, we come in here and discuss it and try to improve it.

The student researchers were aware that one goal of sharing their problems was to engage in collective work that aimed to address these issues and improve young people's situations in their neighborhood. The Three "I"s of Oppression activity not only helped student researchers to relate to each other's stories of discrimination, but also helped them connect the different oppressive social conditions that have shaped the experiences they have had, even though they come from different social locations. Jocelyn shared her trust-building pedagogical strategy, noting, "I think that building trust with them was really key. So then they trust you that you're not just telling them what to do. You're there, too, to help them." Both instructors are intentional about building trust between youth and adults in order to support student researchers' authentic and enthusiastic participation and understanding of shared challenges.

The critical, sociopolitical activities that developed an analysis of the community dimension of their neighborhood needs assessment required high degrees of risk-taking and vulnerability, and conditions of trust and safety. These activities aim to promote critical thinking about the sociopolitical ecology in which the Central Youth United project is nested and bolster the project's successful action planning in this environment. These sociopolitical activities served several pedagogical functions in the context of this PAR project. These exercises allow the student researchers to think strategically to consider: (1) an analysis and assessment of their project's community context; (2) the root causes of community problems and solutions to meet community needs; (3) how policies are formed and how to engage policymakers in their final presentation of research-based recommendations; and (d) how their PAR project might achieve its action goals in the wider community setting.

Conclusion: The Development of Sociopolitical Analysis

The participatory action research (PAR) process with young people as a pedagogical approach enabled student researchers to talk deeply about issues they faced. As part of a pedagogy of praxis, this PAR curriculum built on prior knowledge to promote critical thinking in the form of sociopolitical analysis. This sociopolitical analysis development process provided several benefits to the student researchers. First, the workshops provided a needed forum for student researchers to share and validate their responses to personal experiences of prejudice and discrimination, which included frustration, alienation and anger. Second, the student researchers were challenged to think critically outside of their own individual experiences of discrimination to draw connections with other team members' experiences and alternative points of view. Third, they were able to channel their feelings of alienation and frustration—resulting from their experiences of injustices—towards a more positive enthusiasm for working together collectively with the guidance of their instructors through activism aiming towards creating more socially just communities. In the Central Youth United case, the student researchers on the PAR team identified their activist project as working with adult decision-makers to create a youth center.

These student researchers were also able to achieve mastery over sociopolitical concepts and analysis that they had already encountered through experiencing discrimination and from their initial analysis of these experiences. This teaching approach enabled student researchers to connect their personal experiences of sociopolitical inequities with an analysis of wider sociopolitical inequities that exist in society and its institutions. In the CYU case, the young researchers benefited from participating in a structured, supportive, safe learning environment where they could acknowledge and accept the reality of social and political inequities. Importantly, this forum for learning and analysis enabled them to channel their frustration about inequity into collective action to transform these sociopolitical inequities. Cammarota and Fine (2008) emphasize that as a pedagogical approach, PAR provides young people with the tools to develop critical epistemologies, to build agency to transform their environments and to act to address social injustices.

The curriculum activities and teaching approach used to develop sociopolitical analysis skills demanded a learning environment characterized by safety and trust, owing to the nature of the activities, which entailed significant levels of vulnerability and risk. Research has found that creating a dynamic of safe, trusting relationships between peers not often experienced in classrooms is instrumental in promoting young people's successful growth and development for students (McLaughlin, 2000). In the CYU project, student researchers reported that they felt safe and respected enough to share their stories in the program. Ameera appreciated a forum to discuss difficult issues instead of avoiding tough topics. As we noted earlier in this chapter, she gained a lot from the activities that focused on racism, xenophobia and other forms of injustice. She recalled, "I liked about it that we are actually mentioning it. Some people never mention this stuff ... And we always hear it and we listen, so now we get to talk about it, and hopefully we can change it."

The team-building activities build relationships and a sense of belonging and group membership. It is important that these student researchers are able to participate in structured conversations in spaces characterized by safety, trust and respect with supportive adults. It is especially important to feel safe and respected when discussing sensitive issues that matter deeply to them and affect how they relate to others. The team-building components of the curriculum help develop relationships with peers and adult instructors and foster a sense of being a valued member of the team. Additionally, the student researchers in

Central Youth United were supported in improving their community by making a social contribution, a core youth development competency.

Creating a safe space helps student researchers to take a risk to promote learning. Additionally, supporting youth voice and participation entails youth input in project planning and on important key decision points in the project's process. The facilitator's role in supporting youth voice is to encourage, guide and draw out student researchers' input by building on what they already realize that they know. For example, Jocelyn explains that she employs an intentional trust-building pedagogical approach. As she acknowledged in an interview discussed earlier in this chapter, "I think that building trust with them was really key. So then they trust you that you're not just telling them what to do. You're there, too, to help them." As already discussed in this chapter, Rashna also acknowledged that she intentionally seeks to build trust and support with the student researchers. She says she builds trust in order to support student researchers in being empowered and in speaking their truth about power. She draws the connection between her trust-building pedagogical approach and supporting youth empowerment. Rashna explains:

> When anybody is oppressed in some way, it's a really long process to come back and feel powerful … that takes a lot of skill-building and support and trust in young people to speak what their truth is and let them speak it without correcting it, or rephrasing it, or reframing it, but what they say is valid and true to what their experience is … or how their perspective on the world is.

Both instructors articulate their intentional strategy to support young people's voice and empowerment by guiding them in exercises designed to draw out their voice. Both instructors and student researchers felt it safe to be vulnerable and speak their mind, and develop their analysis about difficult social and political issues in activities in which they are encouraged to use their voice. Finally, increasing student researchers' voice and empowerment are key factors in expanding their self-conceptions as agents of community change.

7

EMPOWERING YOUTH AS EXPERTS AND KNOWLEDGE PRODUCERS

Introduction

Throughout the United States, there is a current trend for youth development, civic engagement and youth-organizing nonprofit organizations to identify their organizations and programs as either "youth-driven" or "youth-led." In addition, within the field of participatory action research (PAR) with young people, research and scholarship discusses complications for adults in supporting youth-led PAR projects (Cammarota & Fine, 2008; McIntyre, 2000). Scholars have called for youth-serving organizations to redesign their organizational structures to provide organizational scaffolding to support young people in sharing in organizational decision-making power with adults (Zeldin, 2004; Zeldin et al., 2013). There is a growing trend for nonprofit youth organizations to raise awareness about adultism and its impacts on adults, youth, organizations and policies by creating interactive curriculum and organizational practices to allow young people to drive policy, school reform and community development efforts (GLSEN, 2004; Sazama & Young, 2001). However, despite the focus of practitioners in the nonprofit sector on adultism, and the work of adult allies to support of youth-led work, academic research and scholarship that examines adultism and the dilemmas and successes of youth–adult partnerships is scarce. Following this introduction, this chapter discusses two examples of successful instructor interventions to resolve interpersonal conflicts.

Successful Interventions by Instructors to Resolve Interpersonal Conflicts

In this case, there were some tensions in creating a youth–adult partnership, largely stemming from challenging group dynamics. It is certainly not surprising that group dynamics were at play in a group that met twice weekly, totaling four hours a week, for over seven months. The ways in which the two instructors responded to these group dynamics point to some of the tensions embedded in the tricky balancing act of attempting to create youth–adult partnerships. As the trainer from the intermediary organization Youth Voices, Rashna had the role of providing research training, technical assistance and capacity-building support to the Central Youth United PAR project. As an independent contractor who works in the youth development field, Jocelyn was the project site facilitator and met with them twice weekly.

Jocelyn was highly successful in intervening in group dynamics to resolve interpersonal conflicts between several team members. For example, when Alejandra first joined the project, she had trouble making friends with the other two young women, Ameera and Chenda, who worked well together. Jocelyn describes the growing conflict between Alejandra and Chenda:

> There was one [conflict] between Alejandra and Chenda because Alejandra was new and so she didn't really know the two girls ... So Alejandra was trying to get to know folks, but then she would kinda corner herself with just her brother [Victor] 'cause she only knew him. But then Chenda even told me, "I don't think Alejandra likes me." You know, they all talk to me individually, and so I was like, "Okay, I'll talk to her." So I talked to Alejandra individually, and I was like, "Do you not like her? What's your problem?" And she said, "No, I just come off like that, with no smile, looking serious." I'm like, "Okay, but sometimes people take it a different way, you know." So I try to help them see a different perspective. And ever since that talk, they sit next to each other and they clown around with each other.

Jocelyn views her role as an instructor to intervene in peer conflicts between team members to try to "help them see a different perspective." When this tension is brought to Jocelyn's attention, she takes up the task of resolving this interpersonal conflict. Jocelyn describes her strategy as one that emphasizes the importance of teamwork:

> I was like, "You guys are a team, and in order for you guys to finish this whole project, you need to learn how to work with each other. I'm not asking you to be her best friend. But you need to have a comfortable working environment so everything can get done." And Alejandra was

like, "No, I understand that." 'Cause, you know, Alejandra's a team player—plays all sorts of sports. But you just kinda have to put it in perspective: This is like a sport. You gotta have that team mentality you got out on the field—it comes in here, too. But it's just another kind of work. And Alejandra's like, "Well, it's true." ... I'll say, "Well, you need to work on you being nicer or you not making that person feel bad," and so then after that talk they would work it out. And sometimes you just have to remind them.

In her role as an instructor, Jocelyn sees intervening in conflicts between student researchers as part of her role. In this intervention to resolve conflict, Jocelyn's approach is to remind student researchers of what they already know inside but tend to forget to implement all of the time: Be considerate of your impact of other people in order to successfully work as a team. In this situation, Jocelyn applied a positive youth development principle, viewing young people as assets because she assumed that these two girls already knew how to act with teamwork (although they were not showing this knowledge at that moment), and she assumed that these young women had successfully resolved conflicts with other people in other settings for the sake of working together towards a common goal. If Jocelyn spent her energy on lecturing the two young women on ethics, or implied that these two young people failed to meet team expectations because they were inherently disagreeable people (or came from disagreeable families or neighborhoods), it would have been much more difficult for the two girls to hear and follow her feedback. As a result of Jocelyn's successful intervention, both girls realized that the tension was a result of their false assumptions, and this interpersonal conflict was resolved.

Another successful intervention Jocelyn mediated involved an interpersonal conflict between Eric and Jason and Chenda at an in-person interview to discuss their grant proposal. The youth research team drafted a grant proposal and budget for a youth-led grant-making program, Youth Funding Youth Ideas (YFYI), to extend their team's timeline and fund the action phase of their action research project. According to its website, the YFYI program's grant-making group is composed entirely of youth funders, aged 14–17, who evaluate proposals to grant funding to youth-led projects in high-risk environments that center "transformative leadership development." The youth-led grant-making group provides support, tools and assistance to the youth-produced proposals, and evaluates the progress and youth leadership development of their grantees. This decision-making group of youth funders invited the CYU team to an interview as part of the grant-seeking process. Since only young people aged 13–17 and under can apply for funding, Ameera, who is 18, and Jocelyn, the adult instructor, could not help the team write the grant proposal or appear for the scheduled in-person team interview. This meant that Chenda, Victor, Jason and Eric went alone to the grant interview with Youth Funding Youth Ideas.

During the interview, the three young men froze up and did not describe their project, neither using the talking-points they had drafted for this purpose nor answering any questions in the question-and-answer session at the interview's end. This meant that Chenda had to field all questions and take over the task of describing their team's proposal and goals. Afterwards, instead of thanking Chenda for covering them and representing CYU, Jason and Eric made fun of Chenda, calling her an "SVD girl," meaning a girl from the Spencerville District (SVD) neighborhood that borders Central. Chenda explains the nuances of racialized meaning behind their name-calling:

> They just disrespected me. When we were leaving the YFYI interview, Jason and them, they were teasing me and I was just mad afterwards ... Since Cambodians are populated in the Spencerville District neighborhood, they would always call me "SVD girl," and since I don't like that neighborhood, and there's a lot of people in that neighborhood that are not representing my culture, I sorta dislike that neighborhood. And I don't wanna be connected to that neighborhood 'cause it's a bad neighborhood, and I don't even live in there. And then, they called me "SVD girl," which I don't like because I'm not them, and they're calling me that because most Cambodians are there, so this is a racial thing.

Chenda explains that calling her an SVD girl constitutes a racial slur because she is Cambodian and the SVD neighborhood symbolizes a local neighborhood that is predominately Cambodian with a reputation as a "bad" neighborhood. Further, Jocelyn confirms that Central, which is predominately Filipino, Latino and African American, has a racialized neighborhood rivalry with the Cambodians who live in Central. Chenda remarks that their disrespectful slur is even more upsetting because she lives in a different neighborhood bordering both the SVD neighborhood and Central, which is populated mostly by working-class African American families.

After Chenda had approached Jocelyn to voice her feelings about this conflict, Jocelyn acted swiftly by talking with Chenda one on one and meeting separately with Jason, Eric and even Victor, who was a bystander to this incident. Jocelyn discussed with the boys the ways in which their comments were inappropriate, hurtful and disrespectful, and the boys realized the full implications of their words in negatively impacting their team member. Jocelyn further showed that she took these derogatory remarks seriously by making room in her tight agenda the following meeting to implement new curriculum that she had developed for this purpose. This included a whole-group refection activity to debrief those present at the grant interview. Rashna offers her perspective on the conflict, identifying the support that the young men may have needed in the grant interview to be able to step up to answer questions:

I was there for the follow-up discussion after the Youth Funding Youth Ideas interview. The boys apologized to her. She apparently did most of the talking in the interview. And the boys said some disrespectful stuff to her afterwards and she got really upset and shut down. I think it had been really hard for her. She had been the one who had been prepared and went there. And on her part, I think there was a little bit of "I have to do this because they're not going to." But I think with the guys, a lot of times what you have to do is step back and create space for them to step into it or they're not gonna just step up right away necessarily ... But whatever, they're in the big grant interview, she's probably freaked out about getting it, so she took up a lot of space. So that might be something that the girls, at times, might have worked on in terms of stepping back some. These two girls are young women who are articulate and communicate and are used to talking to different people: adults, youth, whatever. And I don't think the same is true for the boys, and that means they might need a little more space and support. And I think that's a dynamic that didn't totally get worked out.

Rashna reveals her thinking about how the adult instructor's role might entail intervening to provide more support for the boys in helping them learn how to represent the team's project in front of people outside of the project. Both young women benefited from their years of participation in Sister Space's leadership development programming for girls, in which they received training in how to articulate their project's needs to potential supporters.

However, Rashna acknowledges that the boys do not yet have equal communication skills in representing their team to outsiders and that this may be why they deferred to the girls. Instead of writing off the young men as irresponsible or lazy, Rashna reflects on possible reasons for their inadequate participation, such as insufficient training to improve their presentation skills. Rather than placing the onus solely on the young men, she then acknowledges that the instructors should take a role in intervening in a group dynamic where the girls are more skilled in representing the team to outsiders than the boys. Indeed, this tension between unequal presentation skill levels between the girls and boys may have contributed to the boys' hurtful remarks after the interview, in which they failed to meet their own expectations. Rashna acknowledges that the instructors can effectively intervene in this unequal dynamic by increasing their support to the boys, explicitly coaching them on how to better articulate the project's goals. This focused training in the area of communication skills has the potential to better prepare the young men for success in representing their team's project. Finally, Rashna acknowledges that even if the girls are more skilled in articulating their needs to strangers, the girls also have a role in supporting the young men's attempts to represent their project by stepping back to allow space for the young men to step up and represent their team.

In addition to the follow-up discussion about the YFYI interview, Jocelyn led a debriefing activity about the interview. The debriefing activity instructed that everyone verbally self-evaluate their own behavior during and after the grant interview, naming factors that were a "plus" (positives) and those that were a "delta" (elements that could be changed or improved) about their own behavior. During this activity, the boys took full accountability both for abandoning their assigned roles during the grant interview and for their name-calling afterwards, identifying aspects of their behavior that could have been improved. Finally, all three boys publicly apologized to Chenda for making her do all the talking during the interview and for being disrespectful to her afterwards through name-calling and put-downs. Chenda graciously accepted their apology and the team moved forward with the day's agenda with a team-builder and light-hearted laughter.

These two conflicts that arose between student researchers negatively impacted group dynamics. In both the conflict between Chenda and Alejandra and the conflict following the student researchers' participation in the YFYI grant interview, the instructors successfully intervened to distill what worked. The instructors' successful interventions included: (1) signaling by instructors that the conflict and ensuing dynamics it created were important, by addressing it immediately after learning of the conflict; (2) direct communication between an instructor and the student researcher involved; (3) convening parties experiencing conflict to discuss the issue with an instructor in the role of a mediator; and (4) a public apology or recommitment, where warranted, to rebalance the group dynamics.

Increasing Voice and Empowerment to Build Agency

The adult role in supporting youth voice and input is to intervene, encourage, and draw out young people's knowledge and expertise by building on what they already know. Adults scaffolding youth voice is an important factor in building youth empowerment and agency. As Ameera articulates:

> We are youth and we all have our opinions, but we need someone to gather us and collect all the youth and let us express ourselves and say what we want. We need an adult to get help, to get more ideas. Because some people think that youth don't have a voice, but together with the adults, they help us get that voice. And we can take it out all the way to City Hall.

As a result of the CYU presentation, the Central Youth Task Force invited the student researchers to present at another community forum, scheduled for the end of the summer, before presenting to City Hall. The adult role in youth–adult partnerships is to support young people's agency to use their voice in the service of transforming their communities. For example, Emelda, a member of the Central Youth Task Force, describes her vision for supporting the student researchers in achieving their project's recommendation that they build a Youth Center. She says:

> Our dream is really to have a space for youth in this neighborhood … And we really want a place that is specifically for young people. And a place that can kind of be a hub of services for young people and their families in Central. And one of the good things about Central is that it's one of the last neutral areas in the city. So a lot of kids from other neighborhoods feel safe coming down here just because they don't face the same kind of issues that they face in their own community. So we really see it as being a city-wide youth center. But especially for Central youth.

As a member of the Central Youth Task Force, Emelda is an adult supporter of the CYU's evidence-based recommendation to bring about the creation of a youth center in their neighborhood.

When there is sufficient time allocated to the process of supporting meaningful youth participation and leadership, the outcome may be a sense of empowerment. In this vein, Chenda describes feeling agency to use her power and voice. She expresses her feeling of empowerment, asserting:

> Youth can make a difference. We have a voice. Even though some adults may think it's foolish to hear from a youth—to listen to their opinion. But I think youth have good ideas about their community 'cause they know what's there and they know what's happening.

An intentional process to support meaningful youth involvement in program decisions and leadership may result in young people having a growing sense of agency and empowerment to use their power and their voice.

For example, the most significant example of youth voice in the project seems to be evidenced by Central Youth United's final presentation and how the student researchers experienced this culminating event. At this event, the youth research team present their PAR project's final report, with its findings and recommendations for meeting the needs of young people in Central. The Central Community Development Center (CCDC) convenes the Central Youth Task Force, which is composed of representatives from CCDC, Sister Space and Representing Ourselves. Janice, the Executive Director of CCDC, explains the role of the Central Youth United needs assessment as including youth voice in process to determine Central youth's needs for a youth center:

> The youth center is what the Central Youth Task Force is primarily working on at this time. We've been able to get monies from the mayor's

Office of Community Development to do the feasibility study, which they did this past fiscal year ... The only other component that we need to develop the youth center is the youth voice. And that always comes in. And so we would like to marry this [CYU] needs assessment group and the tools that they've learned and their methodology in order to help them to infuse their voice into that process as well. But we've intentionally left it in tandem because we don't want the needs assessment to be "You're trying to figure out the outcome before the need." No, you have to do "What is the need?" And start from nothing and then work from there.

The Central Youth Task Force is a decision-making body of adults who intend to be adult allies to Central young people by using their power as adults to develop a youth center, but who are waiting to hear from Central Youth United's recommendations to decide how the youth center, and its programming, should look.

About a week before the team's presentation, Victor clarifies the potential impact of youth voices for adults who take youth voice seriously.

DW: Do you think that adults will listen to young people in your final presentation?
V: They don't really have to listen. But maybe if they listen they'll think that we have good ideas to help the youth in Central.

Alejandra agrees with Victor that it is important for their PAR project to garner adult support to successfully implement their research recommendations. She remarks:

Adults could support youth by telling other adults they work with what we're doing and that we're trying to make a change. Having those adults come out and try to see what we're doing and telling other adults (and telling adults that work with youth), that could really put a word out there for us.

Central Youth United's final presentation entailed a PowerPoint presentation to an audience of over 60 adults who work in youth development organizations, service providers, city officials, other young people in Central, community leaders and media representatives. Alejandra recalls, "The presentation was way more people and way more scarier than I expected. I'm not used to speaking out. And everything that I learned, it's gonna help me in life. And all this is a good cause." Ameera reflects her sense of empowerment with her assessment of the team's presentation and its potential impact, commenting:

It's been seven months and this had to be done because Central is just becoming worse and worse every day. So hopefully this will make a limit to this. Saying, "Stop. We want this and that." So, hopefully, that makes it clear to the government that our needs should be taken care of … Hopefully, the Youth Task Force will take this into consideration and build a youth center.

In her interview shortly after the final presentation, Ameera conveys her sense of empowerment and enthusiasm in successfully presenting their findings and recommendations to an audience of over 60 people:

DW: So, check-in. You just did your final presentation. How are you feeling on a scale of one to ten?

A: Like twenty out of ten. Really. I feel really, really excited. And everybody says we did a really good job and that made me feel really relieved. So no more burden!

DW: That's great. How did it feel when the presentation first started?

A: I was really scared and I didn't have my glasses on so I didn't really see people. And so at the beginning I was really scared but then once we went on it was okay.

DW: Okay. What did you think about the audience?

A: They were really great 'cause they gave the support to us afterward. And after we presented, their questions were really cool. They really listened. After we did the presentation, when everybody said that we did a good job that made me just feel really good.

Ameera felt excited and empowered after she had experienced her team's successful presentation of their research in the public sphere. She also notes that she felt a great deal of responsibility to represent young people's needs in her community and that she felt relieved that the student researchers received a positive response from the audience. Ameera notices that the audience actually listened to the young people's findings and recommendations, as evidenced by their questions and positive evaluation of their presentation. She states that she feels really good that her team succeeded in their presentation and reached the project's goals. Similarly, Alejandra relates her sense of empowerment in the way she describes her team's agency in standing up for young people's needs in Central. She concludes:

I think our presentation is a big part of getting a youth center because to all of the people that come out and watch, it's showing how we youth are working for us. And we youth are showing what we need and not just letting the adults think of what we need. We're showing them what the youth need. And us presenting our project and our process on how we got there shows that we really put hard work into it … We're gonna really push on forward and try to get what youth really need in the community.

Alejandra's empowerment and sense of agency is based on her team's ability to act as self-advocates and convey their research-based recommendations to adult decision-makers and leaders. After experiencing the audience's reaction to their presentation, Chenda also describes her feeling of empowerment and agency. She asserts:

Having the opportunity to listen to our presentation and what we found, they were willing to make that happen. They really wanted change, wanted to make a difference in their community. Saying that they do want a youth center, they want all those things that we found out about to happen. We were really energized, like, "Yes, we are gonna do it. We're gonna make a change here."

The student researchers felt energized and a sense of agency through the process of advocating for young people's needs to an audience that was receptive to hearing about the team's research findings and recommendations. The process of using their voices and visions towards community development efforts promoted a sense of empowerment and agency.

The student researchers all describe experiencing their own power and agency to represent their own needs and those of young people in Central both to their own community of youth and adults and to other stakeholders such as public officials, the media and policymakers. Giving her perception of the ways in which Central Youth United's final presentation empowered the action researchers and their community, Rashna contends:

I think those young people feel empowered and I think other young people feel more empowered by seeing their peers stand up and represent them and say these things. I think also when you have a community that from the outside seems really depressed or seems really oppressed, it can feel really sad. And there's something important about it also looking really strong and looking really like, "We stand up for our rights. We stand up for what we believe in. This is our community." And so young people taking this on is a really big deal. And they have done all this work. They've done all these focus groups. I think it shows the city: Young people live in Central and young people care about Central. And you need to pay attention to that. You can't just keep redeveloping and redeveloping because this contractor wants to make a lot of money. There are actually young lives here and they have something to say.

When the student researchers presented their recommendations for community development, not only did the youth presenters gain a sense of power and agency, but also some members of the audience might have gained some sense of power and agency from witnessing Central youth advocate for themselves. For other team members, they envision the Central Youth United project as a possible place for young people and adults to disrupt the status quo of adultism and take action to impact their environment for the common good. Alejandra portrays a scenario of a cycle of self-interest that could be broken through a societal shift to a new cycle of intergenerational interdependence and generosity in which adults take action to help support younger people's interests. She comments:

> Because if you look at it: You're going to school and then when you go to college you're an adult. Then, as soon as you get it in your head that you're an adult, you'll be like, "Oh, I gotta work on *me*, I gotta worry about getting a job, I gotta worry about maintaining myself." And then, they just focus on themselves: me, me, me—an adult, an adult, an adult. Thinking of adults and what adults want. They don't think of kids and what *they* want. But sooner or later those kids are gonna be adults. And then those kids could be like, "Oh, these adults did it for us." And then, "Now we're adults, we can do it for these kids." And we could just be going in a cycle. But they don't think about that. They just think about: adults, adults, adults. And then when those adults die, the kids who are now adults are gonna be like: adults, adults, adults. That's *their* cycle. But we should change it up.

Alejandra believes that if adults genuinely wish to act in the interests of youth, and if young people represent themselves, they can disrupt what she describes as a cycle of self-interest. Perhaps breaking the cycle of adultism takes the commitment and partnership of both young people and adults in supporting youth voice and ideas. Jocelyn explained her perspective on the purpose of the CYU team's final presentation. She believes the purpose is to infuse youth voice into a larger community process:

> [The presentation is about] showing the community that this is important. That as young people, you are always saying like, "We don't have a voice." Here's your chance to voice your opinion, to voice what you've researched and then challenge people to help us. To say, "We've done this groundwork so now we need you as a community to take it from us and let it happen. And *make* it happen." And so I just really want them to challenge the community.

After the presentation, many stakeholders and policymakers committed to helping the youth team to realize its recommendations. For example, the

Central Youth Task Force convened an emergency meeting immediately after the presentation at the center of the room so that Alejandra could join the meeting in sharing recommendations for next steps. Rashna asserts that youth-led PAR projects should also secure commitments from adult decision-makers such as community organizers or city officials to be accountable for carrying out the PAR team's recommendations. She observes:

> A lot of times, even if [PAR projects] don't go into a full action phase together, action happens from those projects. Just like Alejandra sitting at the table [as a new member of the Youth Task Force], that was a huge step. Like how many all-adult committees have young people sit at the table and participate fully in planning a town hall meeting? It's really strategic and really important. That's a first step, and so I would say [that] integrating youth into what's already going on is actually really good. Especially in areas where there is a lot of organizing going on all already around something. It doesn't make sense for a four-person group to have its own separate action, when they could be working together with the people who have been doing this for a long time and feeding into their results. So I think that these young people shouldn't carry out all of their recommendations. Then where's the accountability of the rest of the community to do that work? So it is [incumbent] on everyone—from city officials to grassroots organizers—to also hear those recommendations and pick them up and make them part of campaigns, funding, materials, whatever it is.

It can be important for adult allies to commit to implementing the youth-led PAR research recommendations.

Impact of the PAR Presentation and Next Steps

The Central Youth Task Force was so impressed with the CYU team's presentation, and enthusiastic about their research-based recommendations from their PAR project, that within moments after the CYU presentation, the Task Force called an impromptu meeting on site. They gathered the student researchers and invited them to join the task force in order to participate on this decision-making body and contribute their ideas and vision for the next steps. Alejandra immediately accepted this invitation and joined the Task Force on the spot. This demonstrated that the Task Force was taking this youth-led PAR team's recommendations seriously.

Shortly after this emergency meeting in which Alejandra joined the Task Force, the CYU research team were invited to present their recommendations at an upcoming community forum. The Central Community Organizing Alliance representatives, who sit on the Task Force, had begun planning this community forum and rally at City Hall to demand that elected representatives fund and support a youth center. A grassroots community organizing nonprofit, the Central Community Organizing Alliance had successfully implemented an earlier 2001–2002 youth-led PAR project's recommendations to build a new elementary school campus, construct a new public park in the neighborhood and create a new middle school in Central. Executing these earlier youth-led PAR recommendations took time. It took two years to build the new elementary school campus, over two years to build the park and four years to create a new middle school. While the plan to build a youth center is a three- to five-year plan, with the support of adult allies from the Central Community Organizing Alliance and the Central Youth Task Force the prospects that the community will succeed in mobilizing to implement the CYU student researchers' recommendations are promising.

Discussion

A central tenet of Kreisberg's (1992) well-cited scholarship examining power is the notion of "power over" versus "power with." The concept of "power over" is synonymous with power as domination and control over others (De los Reyes, 2002; Kreisberg, 1992). The idea of "Power over" reflects the familiar way we conceptualize the misuse of authority in a given situation to benefit the more powerful at the expense of the less powerful. In contrast, the concept of "power with" is "characterized by collaboration, sharing, and mutuality" (Kreisberg, 1992, p. 61). Kreisberg raises the question: "Have empowerment theorists made a wise decision in avoiding power as a central concept in their work?" (p. 55). In alignment with Kreisberg's principles of power over and power with, in the Central Youth United case youth empowerment efforts are most successful when they directly engage discussions about power issues—both within the context of the project itself and in the wider society. In this case, it was important that diverse youth and adults discuss the ways in which they wield power with each other. In a similar vein, Delpit's (2006) seminal study of teachers' power within their teaching relationships with students provides an analysis of the potential dangers for adult instructors in avoiding their responsibility and accountability in wielding power over students.

Correspondingly, research finds that the most essential indicators of high-quality youth development programs exist when youth are fully engaged as partners in program development (Villarruel, Perkins, Borden & Keith, 2003). They conclude that youth engagement as partners in program development includes young people's participation in: (1) the structure and operation of the program; (2) identifying program needs; and (3) program implementation and evaluation. Further, other research indicates that effective program governance may entail a further step to embrace "youth infusion" within an institution (ICCYD, 2001). The concept of "youth infusion" is defined as existing after structures have been created to ensure that youth voices are represented in organizational planning and decision-making (ICCYD, 2001). With youth infusion, youth voice and representation in programmatic planning and decisions is institutionalized as part of the design, structure, agenda and mission of youth-serving organizations. For schools or youth organizations aiming to build youth decision-making and leadership skills, one viable approach to building civic leadership skills is participatory action research (PAR) (Atweh et al., 1998; Berg & Schensul, 2004; McIntyre, 2000; Sabo, 2003a).

A key principle of participatory action research projects is that the individuals who are closest to the problems they face have the most knowledge and expertise in understanding these problems and developing effective solutions (Fals-Borda & Rahman, 1991; Whyte, 1991). That is, in PAR projects with youth, student researchers' voices and funds of knowledge are valued and legitimized as sources of expertise in devising solutions to the problems they face (Atweh et al., 1998; Ginwright, 2008). Delpit (2006) finds that for marginalized students in particular, it is helpful for them to understand that in addition to the funds of knowledge they carry with them to learning environments, they are learning dominant "codes of power" (e.g. language, expectations, rules, tools) to enable them to successfully negotiate these settings. That is, Delpit (2006) finds that as marginalized students expand their understanding of power relationships between macro and micro levels, these students achieve a higher degree of control over their own learning experiences when they learn about the "codes of power" needed to be effective in navigating their sociopolitical landscapes. In a similar vein, Kenway and Modra (1992) conclude that understanding the sociopolitical and historical location of knowledge allows students to become "critically resistant readers and writers of their social, cultural, and educational environments" (p. 144).

Delpit's study (2006) concludes that it is important for instructors to be explicit about the useful function of learning dominant codes of power to successfully mediate school institutions, work environments or other social landscapes. Kenway and Modra (1992) also find that understanding politically dominant codes of power allows learners to examine the ways in which knowledge is "historically, culturally and economically located," and the role of knowledge in their participation in political action or other forms of civic participation (p. 143). In alignment with Delpit's (2006) findings as well as Kenway and Modra's (1992) findings, the two instructors, Rashna and Jocelyn, although unwittingly, were not explicit about the ways in which one member violated group expectations, and they neither explicitly taught him how to wield codes of power in the CYU project, nor effectively intervened when he failed to meet team expectations, which might have enabled him to stay on as a functional group member.

PAR projects that support young people as agents of community improvement (Morrell, 2006; Whyte, 1991) can potentially allow student researchers to use learned codes of power to navigate their environments. In PAR projects, codes of power may include research language, research methodologies and research products such as final reports and presentations of the recommendations regarding ways of improving the participants' communities. The PAR process emphasizes that the results of action research are meant to be research-based solutions or other actions serving to improve the problem studied, such as a final report and presentation to stakeholders with findings and recommendations advocating for community improvement (Hart, 1997; McIntyre, 2000).

8

TENSIONS AND DILEMMAS IN SUSTAINING COLLABORATIVE WORK

Introduction

This chapter centers an analysis of the barriers and tensions in maintaining partnerships between student researchers and instructors to support youth-led action in the public sphere. Instructors face dilemmas in attempting to share power with young people in order to maintain a collective leadership approach. Some of the pitfalls of youth–adult partnerships to support youth-led work include knowing when to step back to allow young people to practice their emerging leadership and when to intervene to address group dynamics. In learning settings in both school classrooms and community-based youth programs, maintaining healthy and functional group dynamics is key to successful group processes. In the Central Youth United (CYU) participatory action research project (PAR), the power relations between student researchers and instructors in the face of unanticipated, catalyzing events severely impacted group dynamics. In the midst of the wider societal culture that typically marginalizes youth voices and does not provide structured support for their contributions to policymaking in schools and communities, curriculum development and/or community improvement strategies, understanding the nuances of using empowering practices to teach youth leadership is no easy task. In analyzing the tenuous power balances in the delicate, nuanced nature of partnerships between instructors and student researchers to support youth-led projects, this chapter aims to contribute to understanding the emerging trend in practices striving for "youth-driven" and "youth-led" programming supported by youth–adult partnerships.

Instructors' roles, responsibilities and intervention strategies, and the ways in which they inhibit or support all student researchers' engagement and participation, are core to this discussion. In youth–adult partnerships to support youth-led work, adults are charged with supporting and guiding young people who design, plan, and implement an initiative (Zeldin, 2004). However, in the CYU case there were challenges and tensions in attempting to create and maintain youth–adult partnerships. Rather than place the blame or onus solely on student researchers or solely on instructors in CYU, this chapter aims to thoughtfully examine the tensions that exist in youth–adult partnerships aiming to share adults' power with young people. It provides an analysis of project design, structure and planning to identify strategies to effectively support youth-led initiatives. To this end, the chapter highlights the systemic issues of design, planning and assessment protocols of the project, which provided barriers to full youth participation for all student researchers at all points in the project's duration. There were significant elements of the design, planning and structure of the project that operated as barriers to the ongoing full participation of the four young men of color.

Catalyzing Events Impacting Group Dynamics

There were several catalyzing events that impacted the group dynamics over the seven-month period of this project. Three weeks into the program, Jason was shot and non-mortally wounded after leaving the CYU project. This catalyzing event caused ripple effects in the group dynamics of the team for four months afterwards. This chapter analyzes the instructors' roles, planning and strategies in handling the resulting group dynamics. Three weeks after Jason had been shot, he returned to the project. At the following CYU session, Jocelyn announced that she was throwing aside her planned curriculum and that the day's agenda was now for the student researchers to make "get well soon" cards out of colored construction paper and markers. In describing the research team's reaction to Jason's being shot, Jocelyn confides that she was aware of the probable impact that Jason's hospitalization due to street violence would have on the group dynamic. She notes:

> Three weeks into the project, Jason got shot and I did not expect that. I was like, "That's gonna throw the dynamic off." And I just remember the day that we met afterwards and everyone was just with long faces and they're just like, "What are we gonna do? Jason's not here."

Everyone on the team had been with Jason at CYU just before the incident and each expressed shock and disbelief that this had happened and that he was absent from the day's meeting. Terrence, Miguel and Victor, who were close friends of Jason, were quieter than usual and they focused on carefully cutting out symbols from construction paper to glue onto their colorful cards for Jason, writing encouraging messages and expressing hopes that he would get out of the hospital soon.

During this card-making activity, Terrence, Victor and Miguel told their stories of what they had witnessed. They had all witnessed Jason lying on the ground with a bullet hole in his back while they waited a full hour for an ambulance and the police to arrive. Eric, Chenda, Ameera and both instructors, Rashna and Jocelyn, quietly listened to these stories, shaking their heads at this disconcerting news while creating vividly colored cards with positive messages wishing that Jason would get well soon. Ameera describes how this situation impacted her. She recalls, "We had one co-worker who got shot, and that really affected the whole group ... He was like a brother in our team, so when somebody really close to you just gets shot, we all just felt it." Victor had heard from Jason's family that he was in a critical condition in the hospital, and Terrence and Miguel expressed their concern that Jason might not live through his injuries. Terrence mentioned that he had heard that because Jason's injury was near his spine, it was uncertain whether or not he would be able to walk again. Jocelyn had planned a team visit to the hospital for the next meeting, but was informed by the hospital that Jason could not receive visitors other than his family members until his medical condition stabilized.

After the card-making session, later that evening, another program that Jason participated in simultaneously, Representing Ourselves (RO), held a reflective circle for Jason's friends and family. Representing Ourselves is the youth development organization that referred Alejandra and all of the young men—Jason, Terrence, Victor, Eric and Miguel—to the Central Youth United project. Housed at the neighborhood's recreation center, RO is located one block away from the community center where CYU meets. Victor, Chenda, Terrence and Jocelyn from CYU all attended this evening reflective circle, as did his mother, his social worker, Representing Ourselves staff and about 20 of Jason's friends and fellow participants at RO. I also attended this reflective circle, facilitated by Kevin and Emelda from Representing Ourselves, because I was concerned for Jason's well-being and wanted to show my support to Jason's family, friends and youth workers. Emelda explains the theoretical principles underlying Representing Ourselves' decision to hold a reflective "grief circle" for Jason's condition:

> A lot of young people—a lot of people in general—have just lost that connection to each other as human beings ... One of the things that's been good for us [at Representing Ourselves] is just to be able to have kind of "grief circles" with young people, because a lot of times they just don't talk about what's going on in their lives. They don't have anyone to talk to. Other young people that they're talking to may not necessarily give them great advice ... They've got this trauma that they're been through. They've got different situations that they've gone through that their parents don't necessarily understand.

At this grief circle, Representing Ourselves staff facilitated a process in which everyone present went around the circle one by one to directly address Jason's tearful, worried mother with their good wishes for Jason's successful recovery from his injuries. When it was Terrence's turn to speak, he turned to face Jason's mother from his place in the circle and told her, "Jason is like a brother to me. I love him. Every night I pray that he has a good recovery." Jason's mother dabbed her eyes with a tissue and nodded at Terrence, thanking him.

Several other close friends of Jason echoed Terrence's feelings, and a couple of them confided that each night they lit candles on their family altars as part of their prayers that Jason would live. After everyone had had a chance to address Jason's mother, she said she wanted to say something. Jason's close friend from RO quickly volunteered to translate her words from Spanish to English as she spoke. Jason's mother expressed that over the past few days she had been extremely worried over her son's medical condition and safety. She then thanked everyone for coming out in the cold weather to give their support to his family. Someone passed around a hat and most people donated a few dollars to help defray the cost of Jason's medical expenses. Afterwards, Kevin, the director of RO, gave a brief talk to the circle in which he noted that people in a community always come together to say how much they will miss someone after they die or are killed, but that we rarely share how much people mean to us in our daily lives. He stressed that this was an opportunity for us to express how important people are to us while they are still alive. Then Kevin and Emelda invited everyone to share in the meal laid out on the long tables at the back of the room. Six weeks later, Jason had fully recovered and called Jocelyn's cell phone to say that although he realized he had missed over ten sessions during the last five weeks, he really hoped to have his job back and rejoin the team. Jocelyn responded to Jason's request by welcoming him back to the project.

Shortly after Jason recovered and returned to the project, Miguel left the project. Miguel was an active participant in CYU, and although he was one of the youngest members, he was highly engaged and acted as a coach to keep the other three young men on task when they slipped and lost focus. Unfortunately for the project, but fortunately for Miguel's personal safety, after the shooting in the streets that hit Jason, his parents decided that Central was an unsafe environment for their son. The shooting incident prompted them to arrange for Miguel to immediately move out of Central and go and live with his mother in a working-class suburban neighborhood that seemed safer so that he could begin at a new school there. His move meant that Miguel had to leave the program in late February. A couple of weeks later, in early March, Jocelyn fired Terrence for not showing up to the project on five occasions without an excuse. Two months later, in early May, Eric was fired for over four unexcused absences. Two weeks after that, Jason was fired from the project in mid-May. With Terrence, it seems as though his departure from the program was out of some loyalty to his close friend, Jason. After Jason got shot, the CYU project did not appear to be a priority for Terrence. Perhaps his withdrawal from the project was a response to this traumatizing event. Eric stopped coming to the program because of a combination of his growing family problems at home and problems in school, and in response to his being picked on by Jason during project meetings after Jason returned. The instructors did not manage to intervene effectively to stop Jason's harassment of Eric during CYU meetings or to change his behaviors, or address the underlying causes of them.

The Importance of Reflective Space in Group Processes

The CYU case reveals the importance of reflective processes as an intentional intervention by the instructors when a group process and group dynamic is ruptured. Towards the end of the project, Emelda reflects on the lessons learned regarding strategies instructors could use in future PAR projects to effectively respond to young people facing serious trauma. Emelda responds that the intermediary organization, Youth Voices, could develop a process to support Jocelyn, the primary instructor, in leading a reflective process. She advises:

> Maybe what Youth Voices could learn from this situation is just to understand that you may need that kind of reflective space to process and discuss these things. If something like this happens, take a couple meetings to process it, to have kids talk about it, to talk to each other about how they're feeling, to talk about their fears. Even though they won't always jump at the chance to do that. Usually, if you set it up and encourage them to participate, they'll take advantage of it. And sometimes the ones that don't say anything are the ones that need it most. And they will just kinda listen to other people and that can be helpful to them to know that other people are feeling the same way that they're feeling. So just that kind of therapy. And clinical therapy is expensive, and it's got a stigma attached to it, and it's not always culturally relevant or appropriate for our people, but I think that just talking and having adults that will listen is a good process.

As a youth worker with an organization that was able to successfully engage all of the young men in the PAR project, Emelda discusses the importance of creating a reflective space where adult instructors listen to young people's thoughts about events or circumstances in the project or in their lives that impact their participation in the project. One lesson learned is that it is important for the instructors to facilitate a reflective space to support the process.

Examining "communities of practice," Wenger (2003) discusses the importance of collective reflective spaces in improving group learning practices and the way we work with others. In addition to Jocelyn's card-making session, the instructors might have shepherded a process over several group meetings to allow the team members to process their feelings about Jason being shot. To be fair, it is easier to reflect on lessons learned afterwards and for outside actors on the sidelines, such as educational researchers, to draw these connections. Furthermore, it is understandable that both instructors were overwhelmed by the unexpected catalyzing event, Jason being shot and hospitalized, especially as they remarked that they were not trained in ways to respond to seriously traumatizing events young people may face. These two instructors were caught in the day-to-day expectations as well as their well-planned, tight timeline to train the team in research methods and in activities designed to address the social justice context of their community needs assessment. As Emelda acknowledges:

> I know it's hard when you have a timeline that you're trying to stick to, and there's a certain amount of time that you have to complete a project, and you're trying to accomplish certain things that youth need, to stop and take stock and spend a week or two doing something that's totally unrelated to accomplishing any of your goals.

It is understandable that the importance of throwing out the planned curriculum to intervene with either a few reflection circles or group discussions to deal with one team member's prolonged absence was not readily apparent during the project, but the need for these actions became more obvious in hindsight.

Instructors experienced tensions in knowing when they should step in to intervene within group dynamics that evolved which threatened the youth research team's functioning. Both instructors as well as all of the student researchers noticed a remarkable change in Jason's behavior after his return to the group following his five-week absence during his hospitalization. The instructors understood that Jason was understandably traumatized as a result of being shot in the street in his own neighborhood. Jason told the instructors that since the shooting, every time he left his home to walk down the street he felt incredibly anxious because he feared for his life. He shared that he felt so unsafe in his own neighborhood following the shooting that whenever he walked down the street he constantly glanced back over his shoulder every few minutes to ensure that no one wielding a gun was behind him. The instructors cared about Jason's well-being and wanted him to be successful. They thought that remaining in the CYU program might help him normalize as he worked through his trauma over time. After Jason's return, his behavior was completely different. In contrast with his enthusiasm for the process before the shooting, he began to constantly break group agreements by texting and taking phone calls during group sessions, and being generally disengaged in discussions. He then began to taunt and harass his fellow group members. Jason's actions began to seriously disrupt the group process and the two instructors attempted to support him by intervening to point out his unacceptable behaviors and encouraging him to honor his group commitments. When instructors worried that intervening might threaten Jason's emotional recovery, they hesitated to enforce consistent consequences when he did not adhere to group agreements. Ultimately, the instructors were unable to respond effectively to Jason's new set of disruptive behaviors and the ways these impacted the group dynamics. While Chapter 7 analyzed two instances where instructors successfully intervened in conflicts between student researchers that negatively impacted group dynamics to distill what worked, this chapter delineates the factors that led to some unhealthy group dynamics toward the end of the project.

The Importance of Critical Care Approaches in Teaching Students of Color

Analyzing pedagogical approaches and structures, research finds that some teachers' common notions of care conflict with those of Latino students and advocates for critical care approaches, which call for high expectations, reciprocal relationships between educators and students, and a strong commitment to the success of every student (Antrop-González & De Jesús, 2006; De Jesús, 2012; De Jesús & Antrop-González, 2006). Gay (2000) notes, "A most effective way to be uncaring and unconcerned is to tolerate and facilitate academic apathy, disengagement, and failure" (p. 48). Other research advocates for a "critical care praxis" that translates a historical and political understanding of students' racialized lives into pedagogical approaches that benefit Latino students, uses caring counternarratives to enable caring connections between teachers and students, and attends to caring at both the interpersonal and the institutional levels (Rolón-Dow, 2005). Gay (2000) examines dimensions of caring that honor the humanity of students of color, use strategies to fulfill high expectations for performance, teach students within a cultural context and use knowledge and strategic thinking to move from self-determination into social responsibility. Enacting critical care approaches is a culturally relevant strategy that can educate students of color effectively (Garza, 2009; Gay, 2000; Roberts, 2010). Scholars have found that relationships categorized by critical care can support increased student engagement and academic success (De Jesús, 2012; Gay, 2000). In the CYU case, the instructors would have benefited from understanding notions of critical care (De Jesús & Antrop-González, 2006) approaches in order to teach and work with Jason more effectively.

Tensions in Partnerships Between Student Researchers and Instructors

Reflecting on the ways in which Jason's traumatic experience altered the group dynamics, Jocelyn discusses the impact this had on her role as adult instructor:

I think that was one of my challenges: To see that their own co-worker got shot. You know, and how do they deal with that? How do I deal with that as an adult? You know, a youth getting shot on the street right after work, right after you just saw him. And I think that was one of my challenges. And then [my challenge was] to kind of recuperate with the group after that happened. And then Jason coming back and, you know, he changed a lot. He came in here like the leader and everyone listened to whatever Jason said. But after he got shot it just became a whole different dynamic.

After he had recovered from his hospitalization, Jason's changed behavior after returning to the group affected the group dynamics. For example, he began to disrupt the team's discussions and activities by texting on his cell phone during meetings, making frequent bathroom trips, claiming to have to take emergency phone calls several times during a meeting, and threatening the other team members. As Rashna summarizes the ways in which Jason's behavior changed dramatically:

It's been this constant fight over cell phones. And when I facilitate, I don't need young people to be sitting upright, in a classroom style, never having a side conversation. Have a side conversation, have a laugh once in a while, lay on the couch as long as you're with it for the most part. And that wasn't happening. It'd be like: Lay on the couch and take a nap. Or have a side conversation and be threatening each other. And that crosses a boundary and that isn't gonna work during a training. It's too much. So those were some of the challenges for sure.

Both Rashna and Jocelyn were challenged to mediate this different dynamic that occurred with the research team after Jason returned. Both instructors were unable to figure out how to meet this challenge and, as a result, Jason's participation suffered and this negatively impacted the entire group's participation. Rashna, the secondary instructor, articulated the ways in which this incident affected the whole group's dynamics. She noted, "I think the challenges stemmed from a young person being shot in week three and I think that [impact] was really pervasive throughout the project even though it was pretty unspoken after a while." Jason's new behavior after returning to the project was unmentioned and unaddressed by both instructors. When he crossed clear boundaries and broke group agreements, neither Jocelyn nor Rashna met his behavior with immediate feedback and consistent consequences. This was a consequence of both instructors' lack of professional preparation, and training in how to address serious trauma faced by young people. Further, although both instructors had been engaging in youth work for years, neither facilitator had the experience of having one of the young people fall victim to street violence in the youth programs they had facilitated, and they were unfamiliar with these issues and how to address them effectively. An alternative strategy would be to employ the critical care approach (De Jesús, 2012) outlined earlier, which calls for high expectations, reciprocal relationships and a commitment to the success of every student.

Impacts of Jason's Disengagement on Group Dynamics

While Jason followed the ground rules prior to the shooting, after his return to the project he began to break the group agreements with increasing frequency. Each time he was reprimanded for transgressing group norms and expectations, Jason would launch into persuasive rationales describing how the rule did not apply to him because of extenuating circumstances. He displayed a savvy analysis of exactly how far he could push the instructors and the extent to which Rashna and Jocelyn would allow him to get away with not meeting the group expectations. The questions began to arise, "Why does Jason come? What motivates him to return week after week?" When instructors queried student researchers about why they came to Central Youth United and returned twice a week, everyone, including Jason, always answered, "Because I want to help my community." Jason expressed that he was heavily invested in the purpose and goals of the project because they matched his vision and values for contributing to his neighborhood's improvement.

During a discussion on how to select a research sample, Jason is the only student researcher who is not actively participating, and seems bored and distracted. Early on, he raises his hand, asking "Can I go to the bathroom?" Rashna responds, "Sure" and everyone's eyes, including Rashna's, follow Jason's hand from his bag to his pocket as he slips his cell phone into it. After Jason returns, the discussion has become somewhat heated, with student researchers voicing strong opinions about whether their research sample should include only teenagers or should also include both elementary students aged 8–12 and adults from local nonprofits who work with youth. Eric and Miguel argue passionately that adults often stereotype young people, assuming youth can only be knowledgeable about other youth and not about overall neighborhood needs. Miguel voices his opinion, saying, "If we collect information from adults, other adults who make decisions, such as the mayor and city officials, will take our final report recommendations more seriously." As the team debates these topics, Jason drums his hand loudly against his chair. He then begins to text someone on his cell phone under the table. Rashna asks in an even tone, "Jason, can you put away your phone and participate? I want to hear your brilliant opinion on this." Jason responds, "Okay, okay," as he blatantly continues to text.

Five minutes later, Jocelyn intervenes: "Jason, please put away your phone, all cell phones are off during our meetings. Come on, participate in this discussion." Jason finally puts away his phone and offers his views on the research sample, asserting that it should be more representative of Central youth. He offers, "We should also interview kids in Central who don't go to school. Kids on the corner, kids in the streets. We should hear what they say about what Central needs." Jason then offers to be responsible for conducting outreach with this particular subgroup if the team decides to include them in their research sample. Both Rashna and Jocelyn reinforce the value of Jason's comment, and it is recorded on the flip-chart paper taped to the wall documenting the running list of subgroups to include in the research sample.

After his contribution, Jason begins to show signs of losing interest in the conversation again. He shifts his weight in the chair, drums on the table, sighs loudly when Ameera speaks, and looks out the window and around the room. He raises his hand again and directs a question at Jocelyn, "Can I go to the bathroom again? Got a cold. Gotta get a tissue." Jocelyn grants him this second bathroom trip within 20 minutes, while shaking her head. She follows this with a long sigh, seeming to indicate both annoyance and resignation. I note that Jason has claimed to have a cold and to need to leave the room to go and get tissues every week for the past two months. After Jason returns from the bathroom, he still appears restless. Two minutes later, Eric yells at him, "Stop it, man, I'm not playing." Jocelyn takes this up, inquiring, "What's going on?" Eric protests, "He keeps kicking me under the table, man." Jocelyn responds to this complaint, saying, "Jason, stop harassing Eric. I'm tired of monitoring you two—why can't you just leave him alone for once?" Jason denies Eric's accusation and Jocelyn does not respond with any consequence. After a few minutes, Jason and Eric disrupt the activity. This time, Jocelyn makes Jason go and sit between Ameera and Chenda. This seems to work for five minutes, but then Eric stops his contribution to the group discussion mid-sentence, saying in an aggravated tone, "Forget it. I don't remember what I was saying. Just forget it." Jocelyn looks back at Jason just in time to see the paper he has been holding up in Eric's line of vision with Jason's scrawled handwriting, which reads, "You're a snitch!" Evidently Jason is taunting Eric for telling the instructor a few moments previously that Jason was kicking him under the table.

Jocelyn seems to be exasperated at this point and finally raises her voice: "Jason, 'no put-downs' is one of our group agreements! Besides, you should be paying attention and participating instead of writing notes." Jason begins to deny that the note is intended for Eric, when his phone vibrates. "Oh, I gotta get this, I gotta get this. It's my PO!" Before Jocelyn can confirm that it is actually his probation officer, or even consent to Jason answering his phone during the meeting, Jason has the phone to his ear and is out of his seat and out through the door to talk in the hallway. This scenario describes the new dynamic between Jason and the instructors, which became a pattern in which Jason broke group agreements and the instructors allowed him to wriggle out of consequences. In this pattern, neither instructor responded to Jason's behavior with immediate feedback and consequences. The result was that the dynamic increased to a point at which both instructors felt drained and exasperated, and the healthy functioning of the group was threatened. As Rashna recalls, this dynamic prevented her from getting through her training material during a session's agenda. She describes how she experienced this new dynamic and its effect on her facilitation:

> Sure, young people disengage or they act out, or they do whatever, but I really couldn't get through the material. And couldn't find points of engagement a lot of times, which was really hard to work through. And I think it just wasn't sustainable then. It was just like month after month; by the end I couldn't wait for it to be done in some ways because it was just so draining always, you know. And it was just really demoralizing often to go and feel like, you really care about these young people, you care about what their experiences are and what they're gonna say, but you just can't somehow find that point of connection 'cause there's too much going on, you know. And there's one person who's really creating a lot of barriers because of his own stuff and you just don't know how to hold all of that.

Rashna expresses feeling drained and demoralized, and unable to get through her training material. She also expressed being overwhelmed by not knowing how to hold what had happened to Jason and his acting out as a result of his recent trauma. Rashna is honest about her struggle to engage the young people when the level of respect and safety in the room had diminished. In contrast, active participation and engagement was highest when the instructors ensured that no name-calling or disrespectful comments were tolerated during the "Three 'I's of Oppression" activities in the first half of the program. However, just as youth engagement was highest when the level of respect and safety rose, so too engagement fell when group members perceived that they were no longer safe to be vulnerable and engage in mutual risk-taking because they had noticed that the instructors had stopped intervening to correct Jason's behavior.

In another interview, Rashna describes how the group dynamic resulted in her not being present as an instructor and facilitator of the group project. She reflects:

> I think it was really hard on the whole team. I think people couldn't show up fully and be themselves because they'd be made fun of, or it was just like I became really not present as a facilitator. I mean, I would be walking to the training and feeling like, "Oh, my God. I don't wanna go. I don't wanna go." And if I'm like that, how would I be ready to train?... So I think it was just really hard to be present as a facilitator in that room. And then so how do you engage people if *you're scared to be engaged?*

Because I would be like, "I just spent four hours preparing—I came up with a game today to do this really boring thing, like data analysis. I just developed something new because I just want to make it work." And then it's like, "Really we can't play the game because I'm gonna spend time fighting with you about how you don't want to do it. And you have a really horrible attitude. And you wanna go to the bathroom ten times." And I would feel like, "Well, fine. Then I'm just gonna throw it together and hope it works. Cross my fingers." But it was like we couldn't get to the work because it was constantly, like, "Quiet. Please stop. Please stop. Please pay attention."

As the secondary instructor, Rashna was impacted by the diminishing level of respect in the room and was not able to be fully present and engaged as an instructor. She confides that she was scared to be engaged, owing to the growing lack of respect and safety in the room.

Lessons Learned About Instructors' Roles and Interventions

The two instructors, Jocelyn and Rashna, might have devised different interventions to support Jason's full participation after his return. They struggled to consistently hold Jason accountable to the "group agreements," or ground rules, that the student researchers had crafted for themselves to ensure that their meetings ran smoothly. For example, this list of group agreements that the student researchers compiled was written on a flip-chart paper in the first week:

Group Agreements
One Mic (No side conversations)
Step Up/Step Back (Participate! And remember to step back to let other people talk)
No Put-Downs
Respect: Everyone's Opinions and Experiences
No Freeloading (Don't steal someone else's ideas without acknowledging them)
Keep It Real—Keep It Professional
Be Willing to Try New Things
No Cell Phones, No Texting
Support Each Other
Be Open Minded: No Judging, No Stereotyping
Have Fun but Focus
Keep This a Safe Space

Jason was not consistently held accountable to these youth-created group agreements. Further, when he broke them, the two instructors were inconsistent in enforcing the consequences. After Jason's repeated breaking of the group agreements, Jocelyn called Emelda to seek support about how she should intervene to regulate Jason's participation.

Emelda advised Jocelyn that when they answered their phones, she should inform them that she would dock their stipend paycheck for 15 minutes for each infraction. Emelda emphasizes the importance of being consistent:

> When Jocelyn was telling me about the [young men's] issues with the phone and those little games, I was like, "Dock them every time they do it. Dock 'em 15 minutes. If you ask 'em once and they don't do it, dock 'em, 'cause they'll learn real quick if you do that."

Emelda's suggestion is to dock their modest stipend, which functioned to compensate for their time in participating in the PAR project. She suggests docking their pay in accordance with the time they wasted when engaged in off-task behavior. Although Emelda advised Jocelyn to apply immediate feedback and consistent consequences, there were countless examples of Jocelyn issuing empty threats to Jason that she would dock his paycheck for answering his phone. Emelda later explained that she did not intervene more directly because she was busy with increased work responsibilities at Representing Ourselves and also because she had just given birth to a baby and was not able to be as involved in the PAR project as she had planned. Jocelyn also sought support from Rashna and eventually Kevin, who also worked at Representing Ourselves. Jocelyn later confided that she did not seek further support because she felt that she had already tapped her professional support system and because she had always been successful in figuring out ways to manage new situations in her past experiences both as an instructor and as a youth worker. Jocelyn also had two other part-time jobs that entailed forms of facilitation and youth work, and she may have been too overextended to sufficiently address what initially appeared to be a temporary situation as Jason emotionally recovered from his recent trauma.

On many occasions, Jocelyn stated definitively, "Okay, Jason, your next paycheck will be docked 15 minutes for taking this call." However, Jocelyn later admitted that she never followed through and docked his paychecks because when she was turning in his timesheet, she felt concerned about him and decided not to penalize him but instead to go easy on him. This meant that when Jason received his stipend check every other week, he could see that his stipend was all there and that Jocelyn's threats to dock his pay were merely empty threats. Jocelyn felt concern for him because she surmised that he was acting out because of the trauma of being shot. However, her decision to "go easy on him" may have exacerbated the problem. Rashna shares her belief that these empty threats were no substitute for more direct interventions and consequences for off-task behavior. She says:

I think probably what we needed to do was pull him aside, one on one, the adult facilitators and him, and do a check-in. Way early, like when he came back from being shot. You know, "How's it going?" What are you gonna need?' It made me think that during the trainings, instead of giving him so much attention, I wish I had just said to him, "Why don't you take a walk for ten minutes? And then come back if you feel like you can be engaged, present." And just been really clear about it. Instead, I would operate from this place of feeling bad or feeling like I wanted to be compassionate towards him. But my compassion wasn't honest. I was annoyed and I couldn't facilitate. So everybody's getting hurt—all of us. And I think we should have figured out faster: Does he stay or does he go? Because I feel like there were lots of threats, but never any action.

Rashna reflects on her and Jocelyn's failure to intervene with a consequence and concludes that their inactions resulted in prolonging a dysfunctional dynamic. Rashna expresses that she wished she had intervened to ask Jason to leave when he could not function in the group, or to pull him aside for a one-on-one check-in with Jocelyn. Another empty threat was Jocelyn's familiar threat to call Kevin, the director of Representing Ourselves. She often threatened, "If you don't behave, I'll call Kevin tonight and tell him how you're acting." However, Jason would plead with Jocelyn not to tell Kevin, and she would concede. This may have been because Jocelyn believed Jason would keep his word to improve his behavior. She had witnessed his model behavior in the program prior to the shooting and may have believed his acting out was only temporary. Jocelyn also disclosed that she greatly desired to help Jason through this difficult period in his life and that she believed that putting up with his inappropriate behavior and keeping him in the program would help him cope and improve. She also confided that the idea of firing him sparked feelings of guilt and that these guilty feelings kept her from acting swiftly to uphold consequences aimed at improving his behavior. Finally, threatening to tell Kevin, who would address Jason's unacceptable behavior and enforce consequences, is a response that communicated that she had given up on handling this situation and had transferred her authority to Kevin. The message Jason may have received from this threat was that Kevin was the authority to respect and Jocelyn had relinquished her authority and responsibility in this situation.

After ostensibly being worn down, Rashna and Jocelyn ceased to hold Jason accountable to the group agreements when his disengagement did not disturb others. In teasing out the rationale behind her decision to not to fire Jason, Jocelyn notes that in spite of his behavior, she hoped to support him during this difficult time in his life. She remarks:

I know he was always scared walking down the street. I know he's vulnerable and there's all these things that he's going through mentally, physically. And I think we tried to support him. We tried to be there for him. We tried to understand what he's going through. We tried to keep him on so he can have a job in a positive space.

Jocelyn was earnestly hoping to support Jason by allowing him to continue to participate in the CYU project. This reasoning explains the otherwise puzzling decision to keep Jason involved in the project despite the ways in which he sabotaged the group process.

Both Rashna and Jocelyn hoped to support Jason and ensure that he was able to remain in a job in a positive environment. Both instructors also acknowledge that their well-meaning inconsistencies in upholding high expectations for Jason's conduct and not holding him accountable when he failed to meet these expectations resulted in a disservice to Jason. The two instructors tolerated Jason's unacceptable behavior and did not consistently enforce consequences because they felt concerned for him and wanted to support him. They did not know what to do to remedy the situation and had little support outside of the project to figure out a solution. While the instructors intended to support him, learning that there were no real consequences for his unacceptable behaviors did not prepare Jason to function successfully in other work or school environments.

From the perspective of a student research team member, Chenda believes that consequences would help all student researchers and support their participation. She suggests:

> If they don't do it [meet expectations], there's a consequence to it. It could be a funny consequence: They would have to go around saying one good thing about everyone. So if they don't pay attention, now you have to do five push-ups or something like that ... It gets them [to be] alert that what they're doing is wrong, especially if they have a consequence for it.

Chenda points out that it is important for instructors to issue consequences for unacceptable behaviors in order to communicate to young people that they have transgressed group expectations and are not fulfilling their responsibilities. From a student researcher's perspective, she expects instructors to respond to unacceptable behaviors with clear consequences to help young people become aware of their actions and their impact on others and the group process. Communicating clear boundaries and consequences for transgressing them would help student researchers learn to self-correct their behavior. Clear consequences for unacceptable behavior would also communicate to the student researchers that the instructors had high expectations for their behavior and so would not tolerate anything less than acceptable behavior. Consistent consequences would also communicate that the instructors cared about preparing the young people to meet future employers' or teachers' expectations and felt accountable for student researchers' long-term success—so much so that they were willing to be somewhat uncomfortable in the short term to ensure that the youth were prepared to meet society's expectations for performance in groups and professional settings.

From the perspective of an adult youth worker at Representing Ourselves affiliated with the CYU project, Emelda stated her belief that

> [i]n one respect, the good thing is that they [the fired student researchers] learn a lesson: If you don't do what you're supposed to do, you'll be fired. And I think it would've been more detrimental to them to keep them on and let them continue to participate if they weren't fully fulfilling their responsibilities or meeting the expectations of them in that group ... If they're not doing it, let 'em go.

In the larger world of other jobs and school, Jason would very likely face severe consequences for this same behavior: He would probably be fired, suspended or expelled. In a school, he might be pushed out or ejected to the other side of the school-to-prison pipeline. Therefore, insisting on clear expectations and boundaries, and consistently enforcing consequences when these expectations were unmet, might have been the most beneficial strategy the two instructors could have used to support Jason.

Teaching Codes of Power to Navigate Environments

It is important for young people to learn the expectations of the institutions and systems that they participate in, in order that they can successfully navigate them to meet expectations and successfully fulfill their responsibilities. Delpit's (2006) study finds that it is particularly helpful for marginalized young people to understand that to successfully navigate school or work contexts, they must learn and use dominant "codes of power," such as expectations, rules, norms and tools. The two instructors might have helped Jason understand the importance of learning these codes of power, such as work performance expectations, rules and consequences. Delpit (2006) finds that it is especially beneficial for students of color and working-class students when instructors are explicit about the function of learning the dominant codes of power to successfully navigate school and work environments. In a similar vein, Jocelyn acknowledges that over several months she hesitated to fire Jason because she hoped the program would be a supportive space for him to grow. She says:

> Jason had to be let go. I had support from other folks to let him go, but then it was like, "No, no, no. I gotta keep him." I kept him longer than I should of, you know. 'Cause I felt like maybe this is a space for him to

change. But then again, it takes more than one person to help him change. It's not just me. But afterwards I carried that with me and I felt guilty for a while.

Jocelyn felt that if she dismissed Jason from the program, she would be thwarting his potential growth. She confesses that she was operating from a sense of duty and guilt in allowing Jason to stay. She concludes that this sense of duty and guilt overrode her judgment and resulted in her refusal to dismiss Jason even though his behaviors were negatively impacting the student researchers and instructors. Jocelyn may have felt overly responsible for Jason's success because of her position of authority as the primary instructor and because she cared about his well-being and was invested in his success. Emelda concurs with Jocelyn's assessment that although it seemed like a supportive environment, perhaps it was unwise to place Jason back on the program. She reflects:

> I was kind of against putting him back on, but then everyone was saying that he was doing so great, and I really feel just even personally for Jason that was a pretty big turning point. And I was hoping that if we continued his involvement in the needs assessment, then he would kinda get back on that positive road that he had been headed up ... It might've been better on our part, too, to not have put him right back on after he was shot.

Over time, Jocelyn, Rashna and Emelda realized that while this was a critical juncture in his life and a potential turning point, their support would not be helpful until Jason decided he wanted to change his behavior.

Perhaps what was difficult for both instructors and Emelda was that they had witnessed Jason's earlier enthusiasm to improve Central and had seen how his leadership and popularity had inspired everyone else to participate in the PAR project. It is understandable that the instructors and other adults wanted to try to help Jason through his trauma by engaging him in a supportive space. Rashna articulates this hope:

> It's been one of the most challenging projects for me to facilitate and I've facilitated a fair amount of projects using this [PAR] process. And I think after Jason got shot, I don't know that this project met his needs. I know he was getting support in other ways. But I still don't know that this project was the most helpful thing for him or for the rest of the group. So I think we weren't totally prepared to face that head-on. I think we were surprised that he was so eager to get back into the project, so we were like, "Great. Let's just keep him engaged. Keeping him engaged is gonna help." But I don't think that is what happened.

Rashna confides that she was not prepared to face head-on the issues he was experiencing and support Jason after he had experienced such a serious trauma. It is understandable that the three adults reasoned that keeping Jason engaged in the project would be supportive for his growth. In hindsight, both facilitators and Emelda realize that although they had good intentions, their decision to keep him in the CYU program did not help. What would have helped would have been to enforce consistent boundaries to hold Jason accountable to his work responsibilities. If doing so had not worked, then perhaps after a handful of times when he did not meet work expectations, the instructors should have made the difficult decision to fire him so that he would learn that he could not get away with not being accountable for not fulfilling his responsibilities in a work environment. While the adults were faced with a difficult situation, they were obligated to uphold high expectations for Jason and to act accordingly if he did not meet them. In hindsight, the adults could have reached out for support from broader community resources earlier on, such as bringing in Kevin, the director of Representing Ourselves.

Sacrificing the Whole for One: The Need for Boundaries

Jason's unfocused behavior seemed to rupture the momentum and energy of the discussion or group activity. The other seven PAR team members would sigh, roll their eyes or otherwise show a visible sign of frustration over Jason's frequent disruptions. The student researchers shared that Jason's off-task behavior affected their own participation and the group dynamics. This became cyclical: Jason's unfocused behavior was followed by negative attention and fraught group dynamics. Several PAR team members indicated that their least favorite part of the day's activity was Jason's limited participation. For example, Chenda remarked that she experienced Jason's behavior as impacting fellow group members' participation and dragging down the group:

c: Jason was *off*—and [he was] *on* a couple [of] times when he shared his experiences—but then, there was a couple times when he started goofing off too much.
dw: Did his behavior impact anything?
c: When he was off, my participation lagged. It dragged the group down, and then it wasted time.

All of the student researchers reported in their interviews that Jason's off-task behavior affected their own participation and dissipated the momentum and energy of the entire group. In this way, one person's disengagement threatened to drain the whole group's enthusiasm and engagement. Rashna, the secondary instructor, also saw that Jason's behavior impacted other team members' participation and implies that she and Jocelyn could have responded differently:

> When Jason did come back as time went on and on, he took up a lot of space in ways that were pretty inappropriate: by acting out to get in trouble—to get attention from the facilitators. And he got that attention. I think what we weren't able to see beyond was that there's other student researchers here who are just gonna start acting out themselves—and who did—or who are just gonna shut down and just wait. What ended up happening is that during that time, they lost out on their own wanting to be there. Because they had to sit there and wait while someone gets disciplined and disciplined and disciplined.

Rashna expresses regret that when Jason broke group rules, she and Jocelyn paid attention to him at the expense of the other team members. They did not notice how Jason's disengagement either caused others to act out or shut them down, reducing their enthusiasm to participate. In a later interview, Rashna goes even further and very candidly admits that she became so "worn thin" from dealing with Jason that she realized that at times she became short with other student researchers:

> Sometimes because I felt so worn thin by Jason and then everyone that would follow [him], it would lower my capacity to work well with the people who were really engaged, like Chenda. She was really on top of it, so willing to always step up, and make [phone] calls that needed to be done, or to get grants, and I would find myself being really short with her a lot of times because I think I was just so fried on them, I would just get annoyed. But of course, I don't wanna be like that towards her. She was awesome, you know? But it was almost like I wanted to be like, if you're so good, why can't you use some of it to hold them accountable? But God—she's like 14. I don't know, I would say that kind of thing was hard.

The dysfunctional group dynamic influenced Rashna's behavior in ways that she regrets. Rashna says she was "worn thin" and burned out at times, to the point of being "fried," from her attempts and failures to manage Jason's acting out and the resulting slump in everyone's enthusiasm. She admits that being this "worn thin" at times led to her being snappy with Chenda and other engaged PAR team members. Holding unrealistically high expectations for Chenda to hold her fellow student researchers accountable and notably low expectations for Jason may have served to reproduce different expectations for both males and females, and negatively impacted both Chenda and Jason. It appears that the group dynamic evolved to become dysfunctional as a result of the instructors failing to hold Jason accountable when he acted out, disrespecting his fellow student researchers as well as both instructors. Both instructors observed that they made genuine efforts to reflect on the lessons they had learned about how they might have more effectively intervened to respond to Jason's acting out. These issues are far from uncommon and are reflected in the critical care literature, which calls for high expectations, reciprocal relationships and a commitment to the success of every student (Antrop-González & De Jesús, 2006).

In the CYU project, clear boundaries and consistent enforcement of high expectations might have helped scaffold Jason's successful participation as well as the whole group's participation. This finding aligns with research on the importance of explicitly teaching underrepresented students the boundaries, rules, norms and expectations they need to understand and abide by to be successful (Delpit, 2006; Kenway & Modra, 1992). Jocelyn confesses that she let Jason's disruptive behavior continue for so many months because she was hoping that the program was providing, or would provide, a safe, positive space for him. However, over time Jocelyn reflects on a lesson learned about the instructor's role in successfully supporting all student researchers, including Jason. She recalls that the impact on the other members becomes clear to Jocelyn when the rest of the team beg her to fire him:

> I don't know, I should have fired [Jason] a long time ago 'cause he missed so many days, but I didn't because I felt like maybe this could be a space for him that's positive. 'Cause I kept talking to him and he kept saying, "Okay, I'm sorry, I'm sorry, I'm sorry," and he was so apologetic and he was like, "Okay, I'll be better." And he was [better] for like two weeks. Then he'd fall back into it again. So it came to a point where all three of the other youth were like, "Can we let him go?" So I was like, "Is that what you guys want?" And they're like, "Yes, it's not fair." And they said, "Because he's missed this day and that day." They know the days that he's been missing. He didn't come to a [team-led] focus group. I said, "Okay, whatever you guys want, I'll do it. I'll do it next meeting." And so that's what I did.

After prompting from the rest of the team, Jocelyn realizes that she had unwittingly decided to sacrifice the participation of the group in order to try to support Jason.

Jason's behavior violated group agreements that the PAR team members created themselves to ensure that the team could succeed in working together. These group agreements functioned as ground rules and required that team members would respect each other to work together to share decisions, leadership and responsibility for the project. There may be situations both in classrooms and in non-school settings in which young people perceive instructor-created rules as masking instructors' concerns to wield their authority over student researchers. However, the student researchers brainstormed the list of group agreements with the premise that these were the necessary group guidelines and effort to enable their team to reach their goals. Jason's behavior during meetings not only failed to meet these group agreements, but also threatened to sabotage the group process. Emelda reiterates Jocelyn's conclusion that Jason was responsible for getting himself fired because of his behavior. She remarks:

> When Jason got fired, he was like, "You got me fired." I was like, "No, I didn't. You got yourself fired. I just told Jocelyn to do what she should've done a long time ago." And he didn't say anything after that 'cause he knew [it was true].

While it may have been too little too late, the instructors finally attempted to hold Jason accountable to high expectations for his behavior to communicate the message that instructors believe that he is capable of meeting such expectations.

Rashna elaborates her viewpoint that she and Jocelyn should not have sacrificed the whole group's participation in an effort to solely reach out to Jason. She reflects:

> One thing I learned was if a young person is disrupting the whole process, you have to make some tough calls about that young person's participation. 'Cause it's not just about them anymore, but it's about the other members—the other young people in the room. I feel like we had Eric, a young person who was great but then who started acting out and who left because he was being so impacted by what was going on. And we didn't reach out to Eric. We just kept reaching out to Jason … That was a huge lesson … I just got so flustered and frustrated after a while that I just I didn't know what my tools were anymore. I'd just be like, "I'm done."

Rashna became so impacted by the changing group dynamics that she was not prepared to address the fact that she was no longer able to access her facilitation tools or outside support to devise successful strategies to address Jason's behavior. She also admits that she became burned out after unsuccessfully engaging Jason over time and just gave up, feeling that she was done with even trying anymore. Neither Jocelyn nor Rashna pulled him aside after the meeting, enforced consequences or followed up on threatened consequences. The lesson is that holding young people accountable for their actions through consistent consequences is an important method of intervening in problematic behavior to change it.

For the first time, Terrence's attendance slacked considerably after Jason was hospitalized. Jocelyn remembers:

> Terrence, he just stopped showing up after Jason was shot. 'Cause it felt like he wasn't gonna be there if Jason wasn't gonna be there. So he just stopped showing up. He chose going to basketball games more than he chose going to the group. And you know, I would talk back and forth with Kevin [from RO]. Kevin's like, "If you want me to let him go, I'll let him go." I was like, "I need you to let him go." If he doesn't come today because he's at that basketball game, then let him go." So he saw him at the basketball game and he said, "You know what? You ain't at work. So, I'm gonna have to let you go." So Kevin let him go. And then Kevin calls again and he's like, "I have one more person if you want someone to join the group." And that was Eric.

Terrence, a close friend of Jason's, may well have stopped attending Central Youth United meetings because of Jason's absence. Emelda offers a similar explanation that also explains Terrence's new behavior. After the shooting incident, Terrence may have struggled to make the transition to meet the project expectations, but was unable to vocalize this. She remarks:

> For any of them, it's hard sometimes to make that transition. And so I think their way of saying it, you know, they just won't show up. I think some people would find it irresponsible. But I think sometimes young people just won't show up because they don't want to disappoint. And so if they know that they're not being true to what they're saying in the meeting or what they're expected to do in the project then they'll just kind of stop coming around. Instead of saying like, "I can't do that, so I'm not gonna come."

Terrence may not have known how to articulate his needs during a potentially uncomfortable conversation with the instructors. Ideally, one of the instructors or Emelda or Kevin would have checked in with Terrence to see why his attendance faltered and to determine how to best address his needs and concerns. This intervention may have worked to keep Terrence involved in the project.

Both instructors and one affiliated adult facilitator speculate that Eric's attendance petered out because Jason was constantly picking on him. Emelda concludes:

> I think for Eric it was kinda hard because Jason was picking on him. And we would have the conversation with him over here [at RO] like, "Dude, stop messing with them," or, "Get it together." So, I think that was one of the reasons why Eric started falling off ... He's been kinda going back and forth with family problems, with school problems.

In addition to Eric's school and family problems, the CYU space became another stressor for him. Remembering Eric's dramatic change in demeanor, Rashna recalls:

> There was a challenge in the tension between Jason and Eric. And Eric, who was really engaged and really amazing when we first started, started to fall off and he began to act out. And he joked in a training a couple weeks ago where he was like, "Oh yeah, I know you all thought I was this sweet, perfect angel and now look at me."

Being constantly harassed by Jason may have influenced Eric's changed behavior, since as a result of this harassment the program became an unsafe space for Eric. Jocelyn discusses the impact that the revolving door of student researchers had on the team. She notes:

> I think the different transitions that happened from having different people coming in, and coming out, it was hard … When folks would leave, they would be replaced by a different person. And so it's like, one: getting used to that person, getting to know that person. And two: trying to find different ways to help build a relationship with them.

The large number of transitions in the project—gaining new student researchers Eric and Alejandra, and losing four young men in a few months—impacted the project's ability to build team and build relationships.

The Construction of Four Context-Free "Bad Boys"

There are moments in which both instructors reflect on ways they could have better intervened to support all group members' participation in their role as instructors. Both instructors take some accountability for the ways their actions or inactions exacerbated the problem of Jason's increasing disengagement. However, the general consensus is that Jason could not function in a program at that point in his life, which is why he was fired. However, while Jason was steadily breaking ground rules at Central Youth United, he was simultaneously participating successfully in similar programming at Representing Ourselves. In his article on the "politics of representation," Hugh Mehan (1993) finds that for students who are labeled as bad, deviant or otherwise requiring special attention, the problem is often assumed to lie "between the ears" and "beneath the skin" of the labeled young person. That is, the problem is often identified as residing within the labeled young person. However, his study finds that oftentimes it is not the young person who is problematic, but rather that this young person is constructed as a problem over time. Mehan (1993) concludes that the labeled student in his case study is not, in fact, "context free" because evidence was presented to an academic committee indicating that the student was able to focus successfully at different points in time and in other contexts. Building upon Mehan's analytic framework, this case reveals that while Jason is labeled as incapable of meeting the research project's expectations, he is not context free. Jason did not break rules regarding cell phone use, texting, bathroom trips or taunting others during his simultaneous participation in youth programs and events organized by Representing Ourselves.

From the perspective of an adult program instructor, Emelda shares her knowledge of Jason's participation in RO programming. She reports that Jason obeys all the rules at all times in their programs during this same exact time period that he was acting out at Central Youth United. This includes RO's ground rules that student researchers cannot text or receive phone calls during meeting sessions unless it is a verified emergency and cannot disrupt program activities by talking, making bathroom trips or texting. Instead, they are held to the group agreement to actively participate in all exercises. Emelda remarks:

> [At RO] we have rules for all of our meetings or workshops or just for anything we do in our program. It's: "One mic," and that's when one person is talking, *only one person is talking*, and they have the mic. No side talking. And not to say that it doesn't happen, but we can say, "One mic," and they know what we're talking about and stop it … But it's "one mic, no freeloading, respect, and cell phones off." We'll go over it at the beginning of every meeting or workshop … If they're stepping out every five minutes to take a phone call, then that's not okay. [In Jocelyn's position] I would have let them know, "Look, I'm not gonna play this mess. You wanna do that, go somewhere else."

Emelda had different behavioral expectations for Jason at Representing Ourselves than Rashna and Jocelyn did at Central Youth United. When youth participants at RO break the group agreements, Emelda responds with immediate feedback and consequences. When there is side-talking, the adult staff at RO remind the youth participants of the group guidelines, and the behavior stops. If Emelda, Kevin and the other RO staff did not address the rule-breaking each time, it would likely snowball into more and more rule-breaking. It seems that if the RO staff only addressed rule-breaking behavior with empty threats, their interventions would begin to carry less force until these empty threats became unheeded. This information from Emelda reveals that Jason was indeed capable of following ground rules in other contexts. This prompts the question: What was it about the context of the CYU program that failed to support Jason? In addition to the roles, responsibilities and strategies that Jocelyn and Rashna used or did not use, as analyzed earlier in this chapter, what factors were amiss in the design, planning and structure of CYU? In other words, what were the barriers in the design, planning and structure of the program that prevented a successful intervention to support these four young men of color: Jason, Terrence, Eric and Miguel?

Discussion

Roles, Strategies and Approaches in Central Youth United

In considering the challenges that the Central Youth United project experienced with intervening to manage Jason's behaviors, Emelda discusses why the strategies and interventions that Representing Ourselves used with Jason were successful. She responds that it may be that RO uses a unique approach:

> Our approach is really that we work with the kids from just unconditional love. Our doors will never close on a young person. A young person may be at a place in their life where they're not really ready to totally be down with our philosophy of stopping the violence and all of that. And that's fine. We don't judge them. We don't tell young people that they're bad. But we do tell them that sometimes they make bad choices. And so we approach them with just unconditional love ... But in terms of discipline we don't have to do that. So we just definitely love the kids and let them know that we're there for them no matter what they need. And eventually the ones that are resistant respond to that. Because that's what a lot of them want is somebody that they feel like cares. That's what a lot of them are missing.

The approaches that the two organizations operate from may relate to the differences in outcomes in these two settings. RO has a reputation for consistency in communicating to its youth participants when they have not met group expectations. Its staff then discusses next steps with the young person to ensure that expectations are met in the future and to explain what the consequences will be if they violate expectations again. As was described earlier in the chapter, Emelda also had different expectations for behavior than Rashna and Jocelyn. Emelda expected Jason or any youth participant not to answer their phone during meeting sessions for any reason. When behaviors did not align with this expectation, Emelda responded with immediate feedback and consequences. Emelda's approach highlights honoring young people's humanity, clear, high expectations, consistent consequences for failing to meet these expectations and clear communication, which aligns with the principles of critical care (De Jesús, 2012; Antrop-González & De Jesús, 2006).

Yet instructors' roles, strategies and approaches are only some of the components that provided barriers to youth–adult partnerships to support full youth participation. There are components of the design, planning and structure of the project that operated as barriers to keeping the four young men of color as student researchers in the project. These four key structural barriers to full participation were: (1) an unfit match between the two instructors and recruited student researchers; (2) the lack of an activated, formal support network for the two instructors; (3) a lack of a process protocol for guidance in how to bring two widely different youth development organizations together; and (4) the lack of any connection between the macro- and micro-level social justice issues relevant to participation in the PAR project.

Design Issue: An Unfit Match?

One barrier in the design of the program is that it appears that neither instructor had experience in working with the demographic of low-income young men of color that Representing Ourselves (RO) serves, especially those living in neighborhoods impacted by structural disinvestment. Emelda noted that in planning the project, Youth Voices should have been aware of its organization's customary demographic, and self-assessed. She notes, "If you want us to work with RO boys, then we need to have the facilitator be someone who knows how to do that." Many of the young men from RO were experiencing difficulties either in school or at home. For example, during the program Jason was assigned a probation officer and a social worker in order to address some of the struggles he faced. Eric had to navigate both problems in school and family problems. Victor struggled to succeed in most of his classes in school except for math. Terrance and his family had faced a vulnerable housing situation and now lived in sliding-scale housing that was subsidized by the community development center and located in the center complex above where the PAR team meetings were held. The two instructors also may not have had experience or training in how to approach a situation like Jason's, where he had experienced a high degree of trauma that impacted his participation in the project. Therefore, the two instructors are unprepared for events and behaviors that educators and youth workers with more relevant experience very likely would have known how to successfully intervene to address such situations of unhealthy group functioning.

In addition, the two instructors were both women assigned to work with four young men from RO in addition to the other team members. In their interviews, both Linh from Sister Space and Emelda point out that it might have been better to have had a man as one of the instructors, so that the four young men could respond to someone of their own gender. Emelda observed:

> Especially with teenagers, they gravitate towards an adult of their same gender. Or they'll listen to the authority of an adult of their same gender. They may still respond to an adult of a different gender, but I would've pulled in a man. I'll be really hard on 'em sometimes because I don't want them to feel like they can disrespect women or behave disrespectfully towards women. So, I would've been tougher on them.

It is interesting that Emelda provides two contradictory opinions at once. On the one hand, she muses that perhaps a man might have been a stronger guide.

On the other hand, she discusses how she would have successfully handled the situation by providing strong guidance, which demonstrates that a woman would have been equally successful through employing a critical care approach that includes clear consequences for disrespectful speech or behaviors. Therefore, it seems that while the gender of the instructors is a relevant issue to consider, an instructor of any gender who embodies a critical care approach that includes clear boundaries and immediate consequences for transgressing them would have been successful. These tensions in working with young people are common in both school classrooms and non-school learning settings, therefore, the importance of employing a critical care approach are instructive for educators in both learning settings.

Design and Planning Issue: A Lack of Support for Instructors

In the project design, both instructors were isolated from wider support networks that could have provided regular recommendations for effective interventions. Additionally, the two instructors were isolated from each other. In the design of the project, there was no schedule for regular meetings for the instructors to check in with each other about their "problems of practice" (Wenger, 2003). Reflecting on how she would have improved her communication with Jocelyn to develop intervention strategies more effectively, Rashna states:

> I would change how we worked with the more challenging participants earlier on. I wouldn't have let it drag on for months. I would have worked with Jocelyn more closely to figure out what we need to do … And instead of figuring out ways to reel [Jocelyn] back in and not let her be burned out, it was more like, "I'll overcompensate and I'll show up every week."

Both instructors were too overworked to consider designing a communication plan that provided adequate time to assess the project's progress and devise solutions to meet growing needs. In a later interview, Rashna realizes how this design setup impacted her ability to support Jocelyn:

> I kind of felt like I wasn't doing what I felt the site facilitator [Jocelyn] needed, but then I didn't know how to answer that need. That's where I think the communication breakdown was: The need wasn't clearly stated. And so then I would just feel bad that I wasn't fulfilling this not-clearly-stated need. I think that Jocelyn was needing something and couldn't say it and then I would sort of talk all around it to try and get at it, but not just say, "Hey, what is going on? Clearly something's happening."

Rashna regrets that in her role as both an instructor and a PAR trainer tasked with providing capacity-building support to Jocelyn, she did not adequately meet Jocelyn's needs. In the program design, there was no planning for meetings between instructors to communicate their needs and provide suggestions at regular intervals in the project. Both instructors had full work schedules, which likely prevented them from considering a communication plan that entailed regular check-ins to assess the project's success and strategize solutions. As the PAR curriculum developer from the intermediary organization, Rashna's role was to provide research training, technical assistance and capacity-building support to two other PAR projects, each meeting bimonthly. Jocelyn was hired as an independent contractor and held two other significant jobs: one as part-time staff at a youth development organization for girls and one as a teacher of a Filipino Studies class at an urban public school. As outlined in the project contract, part of Rashna's capacity-building role was to provide training and curriculum to build Jocelyn's capacity to partner with student researchers and institutionalize youth voice. Therefore, Rashna's organization, Youth Voices, ideally should have supported Rashna in providing capacity-building support to Jocelyn. Rashna did have access to Youth Voices' staff meetings, which occasionally used a "communities of practice" tool to allow staff members to provide feedback and suggestions about staff members' "problems of practice." But although in theory Rashna did have access to a support network at her organization, she did not access this network to gain support for how to provide capacity-building support to Jocelyn and the project. Perhaps this was because Rashna felt too embarrassed to ask for help when she has a reputation as a master PAR trainer and usually experienced success in providing training and consulting to PAR projects with young people. This sense of embarrassment and vulnerability in asking for help due to seeing oneself as holding expertise and a reputation as a successful educator may translate to school settings as a barrier to asking for assistance from available colleagues and networks or accessing other resources to successfully address behavior issues and group dynamics.

Additionally, Jocelyn and Rashna did not have access to a formal, activated support network of other instructors or adult advocates of youth voice. Wenger (2003) discusses the importance of collective reflective spaces in improving our practices and the way we work with others. Participation in such a professional support network could have served a function similar to that of a reflection circle for both instructors. Rashna expresses how isolated she felt without having others to help her work through her problem of practice:

> I will not miss feeling really tense and how I kicked into control mode—or total defeat mode—versus having some balance of presence. I won't miss that feeling of constantly feeling in crisis. Definitely. I got really tense sometimes. I remember a couple [of] times I cried before I had to go [to facilitate]. I'd have a moment where I would just totally break down and be like, "This is so hard." [Because] it was just non-stop.

> I felt really isolated in it. And I think that's the worst, you know? It's like you don't even feel like you're in connection with other people to work through it. You're just on your own and supposed to figure it out.

Rashna and Jocelyn were isolated from a wider support network of other youth development practitioners that could have helped provide feedback and suggestions for intervention strategies and practices. For example, Jocelyn was not housed at either Sister Space or Representing Ourselves, and in fact was not housed at any youth organization. Therefore, she did not benefit from staff meetings, communities of practice with other youth workers, or other structured reflective spaces in which to receive support and advice about her problem of practice.

The Central Youth Task Force and Youth Voices were involved in the initial planning meetings for the Central Youth United (CYU) project. Active organizational members of the Central Youth Task Force were Sister Space and Representing Ourselves, the two organizations that referred student researchers to CYU. The Central Youth Task Force had a general plan for Emelda from Representing Ourselves and Linh from Sister Space to attend some project meetings. Sister Space sent Linh to attend some CYU sessions in an effort to support the two Sister Space girls' participation. Emelda expressed regret that she had not been able to attend any CYU meetings, as she had planned. She mentions:

> I totally intended to be a bigger part of it, but we've been so busy, and then, with the baby, too, it was really hard to come to participate. I really expected to participate a whole lot more, but it was just impossible. But I think it would've helped a lot if I had been there 'cause Jason wouldn't have done that mess if I was there.

On top of being swamped with work at RO, she and her partner, Kevin, had a baby at the outset of the CYU project, which meant that she was not able to support the two adults as she had expected. Perhaps under different circumstances, Emelda could have been one of the adults affiliated with the CYU project to support Rashna and Jocelyn in navigating this crisis of dysfunctional group dynamics. RO could have lent its youth development expertise and advice to the CYU project. Therefore, one key challenge in this project was the lack of support for the instructors who were challenged by Jason's behavior.

Design Issue: Bridging Two Youth Organizations

This was the first time that Youth Voices had brought two separate youth development organizations together to converge within a single PAR project. Therefore, one issue in the project design that presented a barrier to all team members' full participation is that there was no protocol in place to provide guidance in how to bring two different nonprofit organizations together. Both Sister Space and Representing Ourselves both serve primarily low-income, urban youth of color. However, these two organizations serve very different populations within these categories. Sister Space works mostly with low-income girls and young women of color who might face academic struggles or who might not be civically engaged. In contrast, as its website says, Representing Ourselves conducts street outreach and outreach in community centers, juvenile justice centers and schools, to work with "youth who have been involved in the juvenile justice system." Emelda observes that Sister Space and Representing Ourselves serve remarkably different demographics:

> Sister Space and us deal with different populations. Not the fact that they're girls, and we have boys, but if it had been another group of girls—like from the Girls for Justice project [a pseudonym]—that were gutter [street-savvy] and a group of boys that were gutter, I think they would've connected a little better. But I think it was just two totally different populations, and so it was hard for them to make that connection. Or even if we had sent some more "square" boys instead of some of the worst ones, that would've been easier.

Using the term "gutter," which is popular slang for "street-savvy," Emelda notes that the young men who her organization referred to Central Youth United were far from the most "square" boys they could have referred to the PAR project. Importantly, she points out that the project design might have been more successful if the two organizations that referred young people to the research team served more similar populations of young people. For example, Representing Ourselves young people might have shared more in common with a referring girls organization such as Girls for Justice that served girls who had personally experienced incarceration or involvement in the juvenile justice system and its accompanying social injustices. This would have ensured that the PAR team had had experiences that were familiar to a large number of young people from RO. This difference between the two referring organizations was apparent in discussions about police surveillance and harassment that the RO boys experienced personally and frequently, and which the Sister Space girls learned more about through these conversations. This design issue presented a challenge in building connections across such diverse experiences and backgrounds. Presumably, working with young people from Representing Ourselves required facilitators who were experienced not only with PAR but also with training in how to address trauma, anger and behavioral challenges related to responses to police profiling and harassment, street violence and involvement in the juvenile justice system.

RO boys and Sister Space girls had different experiences with some of the inequities that their research project aimed to address, which might have been an asset to the Central Youth United project because team members learned to value different perspectives and experiences across widely different backgrounds. Continuing to analyze the barriers in the design and planning of the project, Emelda points out that selecting student researchers who were not at such polar opposites of the spectrum might have posed less of a barrier in the project design. She notes that the lack of attention to this issue in project planning and design may stem from the fact that Youth Voices might not be experienced in bringing two organizations together for a project and may not have a protocol for how to successfully do this. Indeed, Youth Voices had not brought together such immensely different organizations and had rarely engaged in any organizational collaborations for a single PAR project. Emelda observes that the CYU project could have benefited from some guidance or a protocol for how to bring together two organizations, especially such different organizations:

> Not to say that you need to pick a group of kids that are similar, but I feel like our kids were like, "boom": At the opposite end of the spectrum. Maybe find kids that are more middle-ground. Kids that are a little more similar. But I don't know if this is the first time that Youth Voices has had two organizations [work together]. Maybe it's usually one organization that's doing this kind of process, so maybe having some guidance around the process we're choosing to use if it's multiple organizations participating in an assessment or a project.

Emelda speculates that Youth Voices was inexperienced in collaborations across widely different organizations and demographics of young people, which indicates a great deal of trust in Youth Voices given her decision to send the young men who struggled the most from Representing Ourselves to participate in the Central Youth United project. In hindsight, Emelda and Kevin's decision did not carefully consider these factors and dynamics before referring these young people to participate in the PAR project. As the intermediary organization supporting the project's process, Youth Voices did not provide any guidance, protocol or direction for a process that bridged two youth organizations serving very different demographics. Further, Youth Voices did not offer any technical assistance or capacity-building support to Rashna or to the project in terms of guiding a process that involved two distinct youth development organizations. It is important to note that according to its project history documents, in its 15-year history Youth Voices has only rarely participated in a process that brings two different youth development organizations together. It seems that Youth Voices was unfamiliar with how to provide capacity-building guidance in a project design that brought two organizations together. This is an unmet challenge in the project's design and ongoing planning that could not have been easily predicted or resolved. This design and planning issue became especially apparent when Jocelyn needed support in how to intervene when Jason's acting out threatened the healthy functioning of the group. Jocelyn concludes, "The whole Jason incident was pretty challenging. The whole process was. I'm not gonna say this was easy. It was very challenging to work with a diverse group of people from different backgrounds."

Ideally, Rashna might have received support from Youth Voices in how to bring together into one project two organizations that serve different populations. However, Youth Voices might not have been positioned to draw upon its limited experience in this area. Therefore, it seems that this project design, which brought together two different affiliated organizations, presented a challenge to both instructors and the many affiliated organizations: Representing Ourselves, Sister Space, Youth Voices and the Central Community Development Center. It was difficult to bridge two organizations serving distinct groups of young people without adequate training, resources and support to serve their needs. It is crucial that PAR project coordinators pay careful attention to the types of organizations and range of demographics involved in planning collaborations across organizations to execute PAR projects.

Design Issue: Connecting Macro- and Micro-Level Violence

It is well known that many schools also serve student bodies where a significant number of students have witnessed gun violence or know family members, friends or neighbors who are victims of gun violence. However, it is rare for the classroom curriculum to address the systemic nature of gun violence and the causes of violence through discussions, activities or class projects. The Central Youth United case reveals that it is important for educators to engage these issues and their causes. The PAR project did not make connections between the neighborhood safety and the interpersonal violence Jason experienced and the structural violence resulting from the impact of poverty, gentrification, displacement and structural disinvestment in their neighborhood. To be fair, violence and its impacts on emotional and psychological well being of young people is a difficult topic to address, more so because it impacts everyone in the group. However, it is important for young people who have witnessed or experienced violence to make explicit connections between the personal and political in order to arm them with an understanding of the root causes of violence and possible root cause solutions for collaborative action aiming to reduce or ultimately eliminate street violence. It is clear that the two instructors needed more support to figure out how to address Jason's shooting in reference to the team's community needs assessment that centered safety and violence as one of its main foci.

Perhaps if these connections had been made more explicitly for team members, the student researchers would have understood more deeply the relevance of their neighborhood needs assessment in improving safety on the streets to meet youth needs in Central. There were some connections between the neighborhood violence Jason suffered from and their PAR project. For example, Ameera describes the impact that Jason being shot had on her person-ally and as it related to the research topic they were exploring:

> It's evidence of what we were seeing in Central. We're seeing that it's dangerous, and now there's proof to us because it happened to one of our co-workers. It's a really big, strong evidence that will be with us ... If he got shot then others will also be. So he's just one of all these other youth in Central. So why is that? We have to change this. Is it something wrong with them or something wrong with the police? What is the real problem?

As her remark attests, Ameera connects the micro-level neighborhood shooting with larger, macro-level political issues such as neighborhood violence and criminal justice systems, including the police force. Ameera's comments allude to the perspectives that she and her peers shared during the team's earlier socio-political analysis activities designed to connect micro-level experiences to macro-level political issues (as described in Chapter 5). However, the instructors did not draw explicit connections between the neighborhood shooting and the goals of the youth-led needs assessment, especially in light of the needs assess-ment's research question: "What do youth really need in Central?" It would seem that the instructors would draw on some of their previous sociopolitical analysis skill-building workshops to make connections between Central youth needs, safety and violence, and forms of structural violence in Central that the team identified, such as gentrification and police profiling. These issues reflect the topics that were not adequately addressed in the Central Youth United cur-riculum. In building youth and adult partnerships to engage in PAR projects, these issues signify some of the complexities involved such as some young people possibly participating in and being survivors of violence while participat-ing in a program that attempts to engage issues of violence without narrowly blaming or shaming young people in their community. In this case, more explicit connections between micro-level and macro-level violence would have benefited the PAR curriculum and overall project.

In discussing pedagogical approaches to build critical thinking skills, Bartolomé (1994) describes the process in which students develop an aware-ness of the connections between macro-level socioeconomic and political forces and their micro-level lives and learning environment, as developing "political clarity." If the instructors had made such connections between macro- and micro-spheres more tangible for the student researchers, increas-ing their political clarity, perhaps this would have bolstered participation, enthusiasm and motivation to participate in the community needs assessment. During political education activities, such as the "Three 'I's of Oppression" activity discussed in Chapter 6, Jocelyn facilitated a process and discussion that supported young people in making connections between Central youth needs, violence and institutional oppressions. However, the two instructors did not engage in a process to help team members draw out these connections more fully.

Representing Ourselves referred five young people, the four young men and Alejandra, to the PAR project. Central Youth United was designed to develop youth activism and agency to improve their communities. Emelda believes her organization may have referred a few young people who were not yet at a place to think about the connections between macro-level social justice issues and implications for their own lives, decisions and neighborhood in the context of the needs assessment.

Conclusion: Implications for Youth–Adult Partnerships

There are real and difficult pitfalls for instructors in attempting to support youth-driven and youth-led work while still maintaining appropriate intervention and guidance when young people fail to meet group expectations and group needs for the group to be functional. While it is understandable that instructors may shrink away from being too authoritative in their efforts to embrace and support youth-led work, there are dangers for group dynamics, safety and group functioning when adults shirk from using their authority and fail to intervene to correct group processes. Given both instructors' active awareness of conceptions of adultism, in which youth are subordinated in relation to adults, the two instructors had an understandable concern about how to wield their power as adult allies. Their faltering around how to responsibly exercise adult power yet still support youth leadership reflects a common tension in youth–adult partnerships (Atweh et al., 1998; Zeldin et al., 2005).

The instructors in the CYU project faced challenging situations that exemplify the tensions, barriers and dilemmas for adult advocates of youth learning and growth when adults attempt to create and maintain equalizing partnerships with young people within youth-led projects. One lesson this case reveals is that adult-supported youth-led work requires that instructors attempt to take on the onerous and tricky task of offering support and guidance, while still stepping in to intervene to re-route behavior. Instructors even had to fire some student researchers because their behavior threatened to dismantle the PAR team's dynamics and existence. Adults wield significantly more power in youth–adult relationships. Therefore, adults are charged with the difficult and nuanced task of learning when to step back to allow young people to make mistakes and learn from them, and when to step up to intervene when young people's actions and behaviors threaten the well-being of the group. In this case, the project instructors understood the ways in which their power as adults gave them a responsibility to maintain the group's dynamics. However, in trying to support a troubled student researcher there were times that the instructors struggled to determine when and how to step up and intervene when one group member's misbehavior threatened the group's functioning.

This situation presented an understandable dilemma, as demonstrated by the fact that even seasoned and capable instructors faced difficulties in determining how to address unanticipated group dynamics. Upon reflection, both instructors saw that the lesson to be learned here was that sometimes an instructor may have to address a struggling young person in different ways. The instructors also learned that if these tactics remain unsuccessful owing to extenuating external circumstances, it may be necessary to ask one member to leave for the well-being of the group.

The two instructors' roles, responsibilities and intervention strategies presented barriers to full participation of all student researchers in a participatory, youth-led activist project aiming to establish a strong youth–adult partnership. This chapter delineates the lessons learned regarding strategies and practices instructors can use to successfully intervene when one student researcher faces serious trauma and begins to act out and disengage. Beyond implicating the adult responsibility to devise and implement more effective intervention tactics, there are areas for improvement in the project's structure and design. That is, there are structural issues of design and planning that presented barriers to the full participation of all youth members of this youth–adult partnership project. In conclusion, there were four key project design barriers to full participation: First, both instructors lacked experience in successfully working with low-income young men of color. Second, there was no activated, formal support network for the two instructors. Third, the intermediary organization did not provide a process protocol for guidance in how to convene two widely different youth development organizations in a single project. Fourth, the PAR curriculum was not designed to deeply connect the macro- and micro-level social justice issues relevant to participation in the PAR project.

Yet in spite of these barriers in the areas of instructor roles, responsibilities, strategies, design and planning, there were project successes in the areas of youth–adult partnerships. For example, Jocelyn successfully executed intervention strategies to resolve interpersonal conflicts between various team members, as discussed earlier. Further, Chapter 5 discusses the adult role in successfully supporting youth participation, voice and agency.

Adults' Support of Participatory Action Research Projects With Youth

Adults can be allies in youth-led projects through sharing power with young people. Sharing power with student researchers sometimes includes significant adult intervention to address conflicts and restore group functioning. Maintaining youth–adult partnerships to support youth-led work entails that adults engage in regular cycles of reflection about youth and adult roles and responsibilities. Instructors should engage in this reflective practice with other adults outside of the project and with youth and adult team members. Participation in regular assessment of project process and reflection about roles for student researchers and instructors will support adult allies in determining when to step back and when to intervene to support youth leadership.

Instructors can experience dilemmas in navigating youth–adult partnerships as to how to responsibly use their power to intervene in the group process to respond to changing group needs. Instructors in Central Youth United largely used their authority effectively to step back to allow young people to make decisions and learn from their mistakes. This case revealed that successful adult support of youth-led PAR projects also entails that instructors act to intervene and proactively respond to breaches of group expectations with immediate feedback and consequences. During phases where group safety and trust faltered, correspondingly, healthy group functioning and individual participation and engagement also faltered. Further, instructors may need additional support from other instructors or adult staff to discuss how to navigate the uncertainties of how to use their power and authority to support student leadership. In particular, instructors need outside support to determine when to step back to allow student researchers to take leadership and when to intervene in group processes to meet group needs and support healthy group dynamics and functioning. Finally, instructors can best support student leadership through regular reflection about how to navigate the challenges of balancing student researcher and instructor roles.

9

CONCLUSION

Summary of Key Points

Young people were highly engaged in a *pedagogy of praxis*, in which young people develop their critical analysis about the nature of the problems they aim to address and then engage in leading a research-based action plan to address them. Second, student researchers engaged their *sociopolitical analysis development* skills, in which they built their analytical skills by connecting their personal, micro-level experiences of sociopolitical inequities to larger, macro-level sociopolitical forces. Third, youth leadership development has a strong relational component that centers the sharing of ideas through a collaborative process to make project decisions, which can be termed *relational leadership*. Fourth, adults can best support youth-led work by employing a reflective approach in which they share power with young people and intervene to support their goals to build their leadership capacities.

A Pedagogy of Praxis

As an interactive, experiential teaching strategy that uses a problem-posing method to elicit learners' expertise, a pedagogy of praxis is effective in engaging young people. Through a pedagogy of praxis, learning was situated in young people's lived experience, which built their confidence to use and develop their existing expertise to develop solutions to community problems. Through this pedagogy of praxis, student researchers were encouraged to analyze the sources of community problems and take action on research-based solutions to solve these problems.

In order to facilitate such interactive, participatory learning approaches, it is important for learning environment conditions to be characterized by trusting relationships, safety and respect between peers and between youth and adults. These learning-setting conditions elicited vulnerability and risk-taking to learn, and developed skill sets. This point aligns with research that finds that settings characterized by trust and safety are important in promoting youth leadership development (Pittman & Wright, 1991; Wheeler, 2000; 2002; Zeldin, Larson & Camino, 2005). For example, McLaughlin (2000) finds that young people in urban areas rate safety as a highly important component of community-based youth organizations and that they feel safer in these programs than they do at school. Further, when the level of respect in the learning space diminishes and there is no intervention to address this, over time student researchers disengage from the learning process and youth engagement decreases. Thus, respectful relationships and interactions between student researchers and between the student researchers and the two instructors bolstered participation and engagement. There may be an incongruity between the traditional school curricula and the developmental, interpersonal and intellectual needs of teenagers. Students are highly engaged in a pedagogy of praxis, in which young people analyze their communities and implement a research-based action plan to improve their settings. This conclusion is supported by other studies that find that young people's developmental outcomes are better when they engage in action to improve institutions in their environments. Positive youth development research has found that for healthy development, young people need to experience situations in which they are not just acted upon by their settings, but also have agency to act upon their settings to transform institutions and systems for the common good (Lerner et al., 2002). Lerner et al.'s (2002) research finds that young people thrive when they are able to transform not only themselves, but also the institutions and systems in their environment across multiple domains, including their institutions, communities and the larger civil society. This investigation builds on Lerner et al.'s (2002) study to consider that student disengagement may stem from a lack of teaching and learning approaches that aim to support students in improving their schools, other community institutions and civil society. Greater engagement on the part of students may occur when classroom learning is connected to a larger purpose that seeks to improve their school and community environments.

Significance of a Pedagogy of Praxis

Scholarship on participatory action research (PAR) with young people aims to reconceptualize young people as resources capable of contributing to solutions that address the sociopolitical problems that societies face. Cammarota and Fine (2008) insist that PAR as a praxis connects theory with action to develop agency to promote social justice:

> [PAR] represents a systematic approach for engaging young people in transformational resistance, educational praxis, and critical epistemologies.

By attaining knowledge for resistance and transformation, young people create their own sense of efficacy in the world and address the social conditions that impede liberation and positive, healthy development. Learning to act upon and address oppressive social conditions leads to the acknowledgment of one's ability to reshape the context of one's life and thus determine a proactive and empowered sense of self. The intended consequence of [PAR] is praxis and thus changes of consciousness that allow the young person to perceive him/herself as capable of struggling for and promoting social justice within his or her community.

(pp. 9–10)

As researchers and scholars on PAR projects with young people, Cammarota and Fine (2008) emphasize that as a pedagogical approach, PAR provides young people with the tools to develop critical epistemologies, act to address social injustices and build agency to transform their community contexts. McIntyre (2000) contends that PAR with youth seeks to dismantle the positivist monopoly of knowledge production that exists in traditional research designs and researcher–researched relationships. She insists, "PAR is counterhegemonic and attempts to create new spaces in social science research for investigating how people examine their realities in order to transform them" (p. 20).

Freire (1970/2000), a foundational PAR theorist, has described young people's schooling as overwhelmingly using a "banking approach" to education, in which educators, as subjects, deposit decontextualized knowledge into the heads of students, as vessels and passive objects. In the process of losing subjectivity through such a pedagogical approach, Freire asserts that students become "lifeless and petrified" because the only action available to them in this process is to receive, store and repeat the knowledge they passively receive (p. 52). In contrast to such a traditional, disengaging process, Freire says, "knowledge emerges only through invention and re-invention, through the restless, impatient, continuing, hopeful inquiry human beings pursue in the world, with the world and with each other" (p. 53). As a process of collective inquiry, the youth-led PAR framework and pedagogical approach offers an opportunity for young people's subjectivity to shift from being the passive consumers of knowledge to becoming the active producers of knowledge.

Researcher and scholar of PAR projects with youth Ernest Morrell (2008) points out that

youth, especially youth from low-income communities, are seldom engaged as potential knowledge producers … if we are to understand how to eradicate the social conditions that contribute to [social] issues, then we must listen to the young people who are most affected by them.

(p. 158)

Participatory action research is a framework that intends to support those closest to the research issue studied in examining their own realities in order to change them (Fals-Borda & Rahman, 1991; McIntyre, 2000). PAR projects with young people enable educators and learners to engage in learning as knowledge producers who can contribute to the process of creating the conditions for social justice. As knowledge producers, young people are the active subjects of creating knowledge rather than the passive subjects that receive knowledge. Cammarota and Fine (2008) find that in PAR projects with youth, "education is something that students do—instead of something being done to them—to address the injustices that limit possibilities for them, their families, and communities" (p. 10). In the PAR model and approach with young people, education is an engaged, participatory, active process.

Research and scholarship on PAR projects with youth stress that as a pedagogical approach, PAR provides young people with the tools to develop critical epistemologies, take action to address social injustices and build agency to transform their community contexts (Cammarota & Fine, 2008). This examination builds upon studies of PAR with youth (Cannella, 2008; Ginwright, 2008; Irizarry, 2009; Kirshner, 2010; Kirshner, Possoboni & Jones, 2011; Morrell, 2008; Romero et al., 2008) to find that youth engagement is high in learning projects when young people are given the opportunity and support to connect their analysis of social injustices with action to improve their communities. Engaging young people as knowledge producers requires empowering pedagogical approaches. More traditional pedagogical approaches help students develop their analysis and epistemological frameworks through reading about published theorists and listening to lectures by instructors and guest experts, which are highly acceptable and effective teaching approaches. These are perfectly sound, viable pedagogical approaches to help students build their theoretical frameworks. However, relying solely on traditional teaching methods in which students build their analytical capacities through listening to lectures and reading texts, and taking part in discussions based on reading these texts, may not always work with middle and high school students who have low literacy levels and who are disengaged from this pedagogical process in school. Further, after-school programs that work with students who just spent an entire day at school may need to incorporate more interactive, participatory pedagogies to engage student researchers.

Finally, pedagogical approaches that center structured, interactive, experiential activities grounded in students' knowledge and experiences may be more empowering than traditional top-down ways of transferring knowledge and skills, and building theory and analytical skills. Empowering young people through PAR projects may require not only curriculum content that is empowering and intends to build youth agency to address social injustices, but also a pedagogical process that is empowering. As is discussed more in detail in Chapter 4, a pedagogical process in which young people are knowledge producers through using their prior knowledge and lived experiences as text to build upon and generate new knowledge is an empowering pedagogy.

Critical youth studies theory asserts that within the youth discourses, there is a dual notion to protect more privileged youth and to control less privileged youth (Griffin, 1993; Lesko, 2012; Wyn & White, 1997). These dual notions to protect wealthy youth enrolled in well-resourced school districts and those tracked in honors classes within schools and control low-income youth, enrolled in poorer, under-resourced school districts and regular and remedial education tracks within schools impact pedagogical practices and approaches. This idea of protecting those young people who systemically benefit from educational resources rationalizes an avoidance of difficult discussions about current social injustices in the curriculum as a protective measure "for their own good." Similarly, this notion of controlling those young people who are systemically denied access to educational resources rationalizes a pedagogical approach that avoids students learning about current social injustices, owing to a fear that doing might threaten the current social order and status quo.

Yet, upon closer examination, such unspoken assumptions embedded within the youth discourse, and within the related, dominant educational discourse, seem unfounded as threats to democracy. In fact, a curriculum that incorporates an analysis of power and social justice issues aligns with the history and ideals of a democracy in which its members agitate to strengthen institutions and advance systems to become more democratic. Broader conceptions of democratic learning as a process of collaborative inquiry about the world we live in allow for an approach that engages all students in the difficult intellectual work of examining current complex social issues in order to contribute their ideas about a variety of solutions to social problems and strengthen democratic institutions and civil society (Kinloch, 2012). Ideally, democratic classroom learning should foster independent thought, sound understanding of concepts, and collaboration throughout the inquiry process. To undertake this work, it is also important for educational researchers, policymakers and practitioners to rethink our assumptions about marginalized youth (Patel, 2013).

The Development of Sociopolitical Analysis

In building relationships characterized by trust and safety, youth–adult partnerships are able to team-build and scaffold the development of sociopolitical analysis. The development of sociopolitical analysis entails drawing analytical connections between micro-level personal experiences of social injustices and macro-level social and political systems. Once the young people and adults in the project examined in this book felt safe enough to take risks and be vulnerable, they were able to share personal experiences of racism, classism, sexism, adultism and xenophobia that they faced. The same could be said for ableism or heterosexism or any other system of discrimination in society. Their vulnerable sharing of these painful and humiliating accounts encouraged them to delve deeply into discussions of these sensitive issues to analyze the social and political forces that act on their experiences. As a result of learning and developing critical thinking about issues of power that play out in the larger society and in their own lives, young people build confidence about their analytical abilities. The PAR process is useful in promoting student researchers' own analysis of the social and political forces impacting their neighborhood and their lives.

Scholarship distills several core principles for teaching critical thinking: encourage students' input and opinions, listen attentively, value their contributions, reflect their ideas and actions, demonstrate support for their efforts to think critically, participate in egalitarian relationships, affirm critical thinkers' positive self-regard, model critical thinking, help them create networks and explore mistakes without judgment, and evaluate progress (Brookfield, 1987). The active learning approach enacted in the Central Youth United project used a curriculum and pedagogy that enacts many of these principles. As a result of the adults' approaches and processes aiming to empower team members, the student researchers began to speak their truths about their experiences and name these injustices. This process increased their confidence to use their voices to speak out about social injustices they experienced. Further, they increased their sense of agency: the belief that they were able to make an impact on other people and circumstances. There was a relationship between developing one's voice through analyzing issues of power and becoming empowered. This echoes something Ameera said about the link between the group discussions about power and her growing sense of agency to change social injustices in spite of them. In her interview, Ameera remarked:

> [In the activity] [w]e had to put [down] all the hate slurs, the bad stuff, about that community or group. It was kind of sad to hear and see all this bad stuff said about that group. But I liked about it that we are actually mentioning it. Some people never mention this stuff ... And we always hear it and we listen, so now we get to talk about it, and hopefully we can change it.

Discussions of power between youth and adults are central to an effective strategy to build youth agency and empowerment. This aligns with the findings of educational theorists and researchers on the relevance of discussing social justice in a curriculum for young people (Bartolomé, 1994; De los Reyes, 2002; Ellsworth, 1989; Gore, 2003; Kenway & Modra, 1992; Ladson-Billings & Tate, 2006; Shor, 1992; 1996).

Young people are constantly grappling with issues of injustice in their lives and they deeply appreciate a forum in which to discuss these issues with adult guidance and support. For example, Alejandra reveals that she is personally committed to stopping the violence in Central because five people she knows personally have already been shot and she does not want this to happen to any more of her friends. While this fact may not have come up in group discussions, Alejandra's articulated and demonstrated commitment to addressing issues of violence and safety in Central show that she participated actively in a forum to discuss violence. The student researchers noted that their teachers and adult staff at other out-of-school-time youth programs were reluctant to engage with issues of power and discrimination with young people. Perhaps their teachers were concerned that students were not yet ready to be exposed to issues of injustice beyond abstract discussions.

However, young people voiced their need to discuss difficult issues of discrimination and injustice, issues that they are already confronting on a personal level, in a supportive learning environment. Research reminds us that conducting PAR with youth calls for youth from marginalized communities to share their expertise about issues of social injustice with adult researchers to jointly build an analysis and produce knowledge about how we can all act to solve social justice problems (Morrell, 2008; Torre et al., 2008). As McIntyre (2000) asserts, she expected youth in PAR projects to critique what seems natural and to be "researchers about their daily lives, to pose questions that arose from their life experiences, and to find strategic responses to their concerns as adolescents" (p. 21).

These findings build on studies on youth-led PAR projects that find that student researchers benefit from an analysis of the social and political forces that shape their contexts (Cahill et al., 2008; Morrell, 2008; Torre et al., 2008). In the Central Youth United PAR project, young people benefited in specific ways from developing their sociopolitical analysis skills, namely through: (1) feeling affirmed through sharing their experiences of injustice; (2) channeling their feelings of alienation and frustration regarding injustice into positive, proactive steps towards community improvement and social justice; and (3) expanding their self-conceptions to see themselves as leaders in community development efforts. Increasing student researchers' voices and empowerment are key factors in expanding young people's self-efficacy and self-conceptions as agents of community change.

The youth-led PAR process develops critical thinking skills as a method to develop youth agency. Cammarota and Fine (2008) find that PAR "teaches young people that conditions of injustice are produced, not natural; are designed to privilege and oppress; but are ultimately challengeable and thus changeable" (p. 2). Building on these findings, the Central Youth United case closely examines the necessary conditions and teaching strategies in PAR projects that empower young people to expand their analysis of social justice issues. Namely, an interactive *pedagogy of praxis* approach allows students to draw on their expertise to research the root causes of social justice issues and develop and implement a research-based plan of action to meet community challenges. Such a teaching and learning approach that builds critical thinking and sociopolitical analysis skills about social justice issues calls for the learning setting to be characterized by safety, trust and respect.

Relational Leadership and Agency

In the Central Youth United (CYU) project, the collective component was central to leadership development. The young people in the CYU project placed great importance on voicing their ideas with one another as a part of collaborative decision-making. This finding extends the positive youth development literature by highlighting a relational element of building leadership with others. Through observing student researchers brainstorm their ideas together in group discussions, it became clear that young people related to each other to challenge assumptions, build from their peers' analysis, pose suggestions and agree on decisions and next steps. *Relational leadership* entailed collaborative decision-making, group accountability, peer mentorship and ownership over the project process and direction. Through participating in leadership roles, student researchers developed ownership over the research process and product. Young researchers developed a sense of ownership over the research process that stemmed from assuming increasing responsibilities to plan, assess and lead the project tasks and direct the project trajectory.

Group dynamics and the group process gave them a space in which to team-build, resolve conflicts, balance dynamics and reflect on their own participation. In this way, the team meetings served as a sphere in which they could try on different leadership roles and reflect on the ways in which their own participation impacted other members and group dynamics. An example is the "step up/ step back" team agreement, which draws members' attention to times in the discussion or exercise when they may need to step up to participate more, or step back to participate less to allow others a chance to contribute. This rule encourages student researchers to consider the impact of their behavior on others. These are skills that are often expected of college freshmen in seminar courses; however, they are learned skills that are often not explicitly taught in classrooms serving low-income, urban youth of color, except in honors courses. Educational scholar Lisa Delpit would call these participation and teamwork skills (expected in settings such as college seminars, committees or staff meetings) "codes of power" that are crucial for marginalized people in understanding how to navigate school and work institutions (2006). Further, in her book on pedagogical approaches to benefit marginalized, urban students, Delpit (2006) concludes that it is important that adults explicitly teach these codes of power to students. Group dynamics and meetings are a space in which student researchers learn and practice small-group participation skills grounded in mutual accountability to each other and the process. This set of interpersonal skills may possibly bolster youth participation and communications in school, work and volunteer settings.

Relational leadership can promote a sense of accountability regarding the research project's goal. When student researchers share in project leadership, this leadership role spawns their accountability to their neighborhood community to use the research productively to improve their setting. For example, I discovered that as a result of the student researchers' direct interactions with their neighbors during the youth-led focus groups, residents challenged them to use their final research report in the service of meeting their community's needs. Direct interactions with residents in their own neighborhood during the team's eight local focus group sessions led the student researchers to develop a sense of accountability to align their action research goals with improving identified community needs. Further, as a result of this growing awareness that community members were highly invested in the research outcomes because of their project's potential to meaningfully impact their neighborhood, student researchers became highly motivated to excel in their roles and reach community expectations.

High levels of decision-making power, youth leadership, ownership, accountability and agency lead to greater youth engagement. There is a connection between youth ownership, power and agency and their motivation and engagement. Recent research on youth development has also found that when young people sense that they do not have control, ownership or agency, their intrinsic motivation can become blocked, leading to disengagement (Larson, 2006). However, young people are motivated to tackle challenges when they perceive themselves as having ownership, control and agency over their actions (Larson, 2006). Thus, when educators use a pedagogical approach that values student input, perspectives and decisions, and uses these to shape their learning direction and outcomes, this builds ownership and agency and is much more likely to result in high student engagement. Therefore, it may be that schools are struggling to engage students because they have rarely used pedagogical approaches that build ownership and agency by sharing decision-making power with students regarding the content, direction and purpose of their learning. Schools will have more relevance to all students if students have input on what they learn and the purpose and direction of their learning projects.

Youth–Adult Partnerships: "Power With"

Adult instructors hold particular roles and responsibilities in supporting young people's empowerment and agency in youth-led learning projects. Guiding and supporting student researchers requires that the instructors refrain from dominating the group process yet intervene to support it. Both instructors in the Central Youth United project faced dilemmas about how to successfully share power with young people in youth–adult partnerships in a PAR project. Sharing power with youth does not require a type of principled abandonment of authority. Rather, part of adults' responsibility in sharing power with youth to guide and support their work is to intervene when group safety is threatened, to restore respectful relationships in accordance with group needs. To set up young people for success, it is crucial for adult leaders to set up a process by which the team can articulate group expectations, and to provide immediate feedback and consequences when youth members cross these boundaries. The group's functioning is compromised when adult staff do not succeed in providing immediate feedback to alert the student researcher that they have crossed a threshold that threatens healthy team dynamics and group safety.

For example, when one student researcher responded to his life trauma by acting out and failing to meet team expectations over the course of several months, and his behavior went unaddressed, the other members felt uncomfortable participating, as they deduced that no consequence would follow if this student researcher disrespected them. Such interventions would have ensured that Jason understood that there were high expectations for his participation and would have assured other team members that adults would uphold group agreements regarding respect of others at all times. It became evident that the adults needed support from outside adults to discuss how best to address his disruptions to support Jason and the other members. One way that the adults could have received support about how to support the four young men of color who eventually left the program is through regular communication with adults affiliated with the project. Another way in which adults might be supported in navigating the nuances of youth–adult partnerships might be through careful program planning, design, and ongoing cycles of reflection and assessment about program setbacks and progress.

Dilemmas and Challenges the PAR Project Faced

There were several dilemmas and challenges in this PAR project. One dilemma that the project faced was that with the exception of one or two team-building activities, young people did not facilitate activities, workshops or meeting sessions. Although this was a youth-led process, young people did not receive training and support to learn how to facilitate project activities or parts of the biweekly meeting session agenda. One challenge the project faced is that there was no planning to determine a way to support youth in facilitating a project meeting activity.

Another challenge was that while the PAR project curriculum was designed to encourage youth input, there were challenges in supporting young people's voices at all times. It was challenging for the instructors to ensure that all group members, including the quieter ones or those in the minority on the research team, were supported to enable them to contribute their input. One lesson learned is that the two instructors could have paid closer attention to the group dynamics and intervened to ensure that all voices were heard by calling on the quieter group members.

Finally, the PAR project faced a challenge in figuring out how to bring together student researchers referred by two youth organizations—Sister Space and Representing Ourselves—which each serve different populations. As Representing Ourselves' website describes, this organization works with young people who have been involved in the juvenile justice system (or are likely to become involved in this system). In contrast, Sister Space works with young women who have largely not been involved in the juvenile justice system. The fact that the team was composed of team members from the neighborhood with such different backgrounds and experiences in many ways strengthened the project, especially since the team's data analysis benefited from multiple Central youth perspectives and experiences. Bringing together youth research team members from two very different organizations also presented challenges in group dynamics, and the two instructors had to invest a great deal of effort into team-building across researchers with such diverse experiences. The PAR project faced a challenge in receiving guidance and support about how to bring together student researchers from two very different organizations into the same needs assessment.

Transferability of Study Findings

Though this examination was focused on one neighborhood in a West Coast city, this neighborhood shares many similarities with other urban neighborhoods that house low-income families and residents. The Central neighborhood faces systemic issues that many urban neighborhoods face nationwide. Some of these factors are described in more detail in Chapter 3, including systemic issues the Central Youth United research project uncovered. Some of the similar structural issues facing urban neighborhoods and their low-income residents are a disparity of resources between high-income and low-income families; gentrification and displacement; police hyper-surveillance and harassment of young men of color; limited access to good schools and other public institutions; economic and structural abandonment by city services, resources and institutions; issues of safety, crime and violence; and lack of adequate public spaces or maintained public facilities. The systemic inequities facing urban neighborhoods like Central are issues that the residents of these neighborhoods face, particularly low-income families, elderly residents and young people. Therefore, these study findings are transferable to other urban neighborhoods nationwide.

Recommendations for Teaching and Schools: PAR as Pedagogy

It is commonly recognized that high schools and middle schools are struggling to engage all students in the learning process. However, in many out-of-school-time and community-based learning settings, such as theatre or writing programs, or other community-based youth development organizations, school-aged teenagers are actively engaged in learning and developing skills transferable to classroom learning that have implications for teaching in school classrooms (Jocson, 2008; Kinloch, 2011; McLaughlin, 2000; Winn, 2007; 2011). Indeed, research has shown that many non-school learning environments successfully engage students who are underperforming academically in their schools (Irby, Ferber, Pittman, Tolman & Yohalem, 2001). Therefore, it seems that it would benefit classroom-based pedagogical practices if schools incorporated best teaching practices from non-school settings. As researchers on pedagogical approaches assert:

> As standardized testing and other high-stakes accountability measures increasingly organize education inside schools, non-school experiments are, for some young people—especially those enrolled in poor, isolated districts—among the few places they can go for rigorous, sustained learning experiences culminating in products that promote youth development and social action.
>
> (Chávez & Soep, 2005, p. 417)

It may be likely that some young people enrolled in under-resourced schools regularly participate more in "rigorous, sustained learning" in non-school settings than they do in school. This investigation revealed several components of pedagogical approaches that were successful in engaging and developing research skills with students who were struggling academically in school. There are several implications for pedagogy, as set out in what follows.

1. *Teachers should center an analysis of power in classroom discussions.* Students would benefit from structured support to discuss issues of power, oppression and injustice that they face in their lives. Students feel increased empowerment if they discuss and analyze issues of power, and connect their micro-level experiences of discrimination and social injustices with macro-level social injustices. Doing so allows students to understand the patterns connecting their experiences with larger social, economic and political systems. This connection allows students to feel validated about their experiences of injustice, channel their frustrations about these injustices into proactive steps towards civic engagement to improve their institutions and promote social justice, and expand their self-conceptions to see themselves as leaders and agents of community improvement. Further, through analyzing the impact of socioeconomic and political forces on their lives and social locations, students are able to understand that, while inequities exist, they can be challenged and transformed. Through group inquiry about socioeconomic and political forces, students consider that these systems have changed over time and have been improved through civic engagement that holds these systems accountable to becoming more democratic. Analyzing systemic issues of power that play out in their lives, students build their agency

to understand that they can act with others to further strengthen social systems and institutions, and make them more democratic. Such analysis will support intellectual growth and help develop students' critical thinking and analysis skills, particularly their sociopolitical analysis skills.

If students were supported in providing input in their learning content, they would likely elect for that content to address current social and political forces impacting their everyday lives. One first step in shifting teachers and schools to securing student input on their curriculum content is to start by addressing issues of power and privilege in classrooms. Students' input on their curriculum content would likely include their interest in discussing current events as they relate to issues they face because of who they are in society. Discussing the ways in which power functions and operates in the United States' social systems builds student interest and agency in working with others towards social justice to democratize institutions and settings.

2. *Teachers should receive training on maintaining respectful group dynamics.* When students experience a learning environment characterized by trust and safety, this learning setting is more conducive to being vulnerable and taking risks by contributing to group discussions on difficult topics, such as an analysis of power. A classroom culture that supports respectful disagreement with other perspectives in discussions promotes learning from different perspectives. In order for students and teachers to feel safe and comfortable to participate in group inquiry about social and political issues that elicit strong opinions and emotions, it is essential that the learning environment is one in which there are clear group expectations to respect others' opinions. Such an environment will allow students to feel safe to participate in classroom discussions and freely share their viewpoints, experiences and analyses.

When adults take accountability for maintaining group dynamics based on respect and supportive relationships between students, and between teachers and students, student participation will likely increase. This means that teachers, as the facilitators of group activities and discussions, must be accountable to the group process when group expectations are not met by intervening with immediate feedback and consequences, to ensure a climate of respect in pursuit of intellectual growth. Teachers should demonstrate that they take young people's conflicts that erupt in classrooms seriously by intervening to rebalance the safety level of the learning space for all students. With such adult support, young people will likely respond with a greater commitment to resolving conflicts and taking each other's ideas and views seriously.

3. *Students should have a role in designing and directing their learning curriculum.* Students have buy-in and are engaged in learning enterprises when the purpose and goals are relevant to their own learning goals and visions. Positive youth development literature finds that young people are intrinsically motivated and

engaged when they perceive themselves as having ownership control, and agency, in their settings. Student engagement will likely improve when students are responsible for curriculum design, direction and outcomes. Students will more meaningfully participate as the producers of knowledge than as the consumers of knowledge. Learning environments should support classroom teachers and facilitators in non-school settings to receive input from learners in designing their curriculum units, lesson plans or workshops. Administrations could support teachers in surveying students to determine their visions for learning goals at the beginning of the school year or at several intervals throughout the year. Moreover, administrations could support teachers in developing lesson plans that factor in regular student input and feedback about learning goals for project-based learning.

4. *Teachers and school staff should receive training to develop their capacity to support and guide students in directing their learning curriculum.* Often, adultism results in young people being ignored or not being consulted when decisions are made that directly impact them. Such decisions that directly impact students include decisions concerning the school curriculum, textbooks, teacher hires, school reform and improvement policies and initiatives, and community development initiatives. However, when teachers receive training and support to learn strategies to develop young people's leadership, empowerment and agency, they can be successful in supporting youth-led projects. When teachers support and guide youth in directing their own learning curriculum, young people are willing to exert greater effort in their contributions. That is, when young people's input is taken seriously, they respond with high levels of participation and engagement to collaborate with others to make decisions that direct the scope and nature of their group project. Teachers need support in shifting to an asset-based lens in order to interact with all students as if they have valuable expertise to contribute to directing learning goals and curriculum.

5. *School administration hiring policies should prioritize the hiring of teachers interested in supporting young people in designing, planning and directing their curriculum.* Administrators and teachers are capable of considering the ways in which they wield power and authority in schools. Administrators and teachers need support, training, resources and coaching from outside intermediary organizations to learn how to build their capacities to institutionalize youth voice in their curriculum planning. Outside training organizations can provide schools with organizational learning tools that support institutions as learning organizations that reflect on their practice to improve organizational structure, cultures and norms.

6. *Participatory action research with youth should be embraced as a pedagogical approach to meet young people's values and visions to improve their communities.* Students thrive on learning approaches in which they have a chance to make a meaningful

difference in improving their communities through project-based learning. When the goals and purpose of participatory action research match with young people's values and visions for community improvement, once they become engaged they are highly enthusiastic and motivated to learn and contribute to the research project. Current positive youth development research finds that healthy youth development requires that young people transform themselves to adjust to current institutions and sociopolitical systems, and that they act to transform these institutions and systems to strengthen civil society for the common good. Thus, in order for students to develop positively and experience psychological health, they need to experience situations in which they act to transform and improve their institutions and systems in their communities.

As a pedagogical approach, participatory action research with youth enables adult educators to support and guide students in the process of working collaboratively to improve their institutions and communities. When young people are treated with respect and relied upon as experts regarding the problems they face in their neighborhoods and communities, they are highly engaged and committed to the process of group inquiry and action to improve their communities.

7. PAR projects with youth should use a structured, participatory, experiential curriculum and pedagogical approach to promote youth input to design, plan, evaluate and direct the project. When instructors employ a well-prepared, experiential curriculum that uses interactive, experiential workshop activities, this provides structured support for skill development. A participatory model in which knowledge is built from the text of researchers' lived experiences is more engaging than a top-down pedagogical model in which instructors solely rely on handouts or lectures to transfer research skills to student researchers. Experiential, participatory activities in which young people learn new skills through the process of experiencing these skills are more effective in training student researchers to take leadership. For example, student researchers best learn about research design and the pros and cons of using surveys as a research method through participating in both conducting and taking a survey and brainstorming the pros and cons they experienced. A curriculum and pedagogy in which knowledge production is situated in students' lived experiences and perspectives supports youth in developing their confidence about their expertise. Practitioners of this interactive, experiential facilitated process commonly call this process a "popular education" approach. This empowering pedagogical approach enables them to increase the quality and frequency of their contributions to group activities and group discussions.

PAR projects with youth require young people's analysis of the issues that their communities face in order to develop a relevant research question. Youth-led PAR projects also require young people to analyze their collected data in order to draw research findings and recommendations. Given the heavy reliance on student researchers' analytical abilities in PAR projects with youth, a participatory, empowering pedagogy that promotes young people's critical thinking and analysis will strengthen the goals and outcomes of PAR projects.

8. *Schools, organizations, universities and networks conducting PAR projects with youth should receive training and capacity-building to support both student researchers and their instructors in building their skills.* Youth-led PAR projects should use a structured, participatory, experiential approach to promote youth input to design, plan, evaluate and direct the project. PAR can be strengthened when outside intermediary organizations provide training and capacity-building support to instructors to build their capacities to support participatory action research projects with young people. Intermediary organizations with knowledge, tools and resources can provide technical assistance and capacity-building support to facilitators of these projects. Supporting youth-led PAR projects is a nuanced process and can present challenges that instructors have to navigate for successful project results. One such challenge for instructors entails how to refrain from dominating PAR projects with youth yet still guide and support young people's leadership in making decisions at key points in the research project, including decisions about the research topic, research question, methods, data analysis and findings. Instructors can resolve such challenges by using a facilitated process to ensure that all student researchers' voices are considered and that they experience a fair, collaborative process of group decision-making, discussion and negotiation to reach consensus about key research project decisions.

Another challenge for instructors of PAR projects with youth concerns how to support student researchers in developing their skills in research design and research methods, developing research instruments, collecting data, analyzing data to draw findings, and creating a final product compiling their research recommendations. The instructors, affiliated organizations and staff members that conduct PAR projects can benefit from the experience and expertise of outside intermediary organizations that have a participatory training curriculum designed to promote student researchers' input in the research process and build their research skills. For example, student researchers show high levels of participation when skill-building training involves them in learning how to facilitate focus groups through role-playing—being focus group facilitators and focus group participants—and then brainstorming a list of facilitation tips and pitfalls based on their role-playing experience.

An interactive, experiential, skill-building training curriculum, conducted by experienced PAR trainers, can provide a strong infrastructure to PAR projects by providing structured, participatory activities to support student researchers who are learning new research skills. This process takes much longer than a top-down process in which adults transfer knowledge and skills to student researchers using solely the traditional methods of lectures, readings and handouts. However, when instructors of PAR projects use interactive activities to develop research skills, student researchers are engaged and actively participate in learning new skills by building upon their prior knowledge, experience and skills.

9. *Instructors who facilitate PAR projects with young people should receive training and capacity-building in order that they can give optimal support to these student-driven learning projects.* Outside intermediary organizations can provide capacity-building support to adult instructors in ways in which they can partner with student researchers to guide and support student-driven PAR projects. Instructors need support and guidance to know when to step back and allow young people to make key decisions about the research project's direction. Sometimes, sharing decision-making power with young people might mean student researchers make mistakes, though they can learn from these, and at other times, what adults fear might be mistakes turn out to be innovative approaches that adults were initially unable to envision. Sometimes instructors need coaching from outside trainers to understand when to let go of control and allow student researchers to take leadership over the project direction and outcomes.

On the other hand, instructors can benefit from coaching to know when to intervene in the group process by providing immediate feedback and consequences when research team members do not meet group expectations, in order to ensure healthy group functioning. Instructors need support from experienced PAR trainers to coach them in how to step in and intervene to rebalance group dynamics and restore a safe, respectful working environment conducive to learning and collaboration. Outside intermediary organizations can draw upon their experience in conducting PAR projects so that common pitfalls in facilitating these projects can be avoided. The current trend for philanthropic foundations to provide capacity-building grants to nonprofits, alliances and networks might enable outside intermediary organizations—with knowledge and a training curriculum to support PAR projects with youth—to be funded to strengthen PAR projects conducted by young people.

10. *Instructors of PAR projects with young people should facilitate a collaborative decision-making process in which leadership is shared between student researchers.* Participatory action research projects with young people benefit from high levels of youth engagement and participation when instructors use a collaborative decision-making approach that promotes shared leadership throughout the research project process. When youth are encouraged to share ideas through a collaborative decision-making process, they show strong commitment to contributing their input. Young people respond with a sense of accountability to the project and increased ownership when they are expected to have a role in contributing their input to influence the direction and scope of the project. Young people's participation as planners and leaders in the group process can result in their taking greater ownership over the PAR process and outcomes.

Student researchers thrive in leadership positions in which they can develop their leadership in relation to others, and this relational leadership will likely result in high levels of youth engagement.

11. *Instructors should support young people's analysis of power and sociopolitical forces shaping the research topic and research context.* PAR projects with youth will be strengthened in their process and outcomes when instructors use an interactive, participatory process that builds upon student researchers' existing analysis and situates learning about sociopolitical forces in student researchers' experience and perspectives. Young people experience discrimination and effects of social injustices in their daily lives, and have a great interest in discussing these issues with other youth and with adults in a supportive, structured environment. Young people benefit from analyzing how their individual problems reflect larger social and political patterns. Through analyzing how their micro-level circumstances are impacted by macro-level socioeconomic and political systems, student researchers develop their sociopolitical analysis skills. Such analytic skills are needed in the youth-led PAR process, as student researchers are expected to contribute their analysis to determine the research topic and research question and to analyze their collected data to draw findings and recommendations. The PAR process with youth requires that student researchers build upon their analysis of the root causes for inequities they aim to address in order to implement a sustainable plan of action to address these inequities. Therefore, PAR projects should support student researchers in building upon their existing sociopolitical analysis skills in order to further build their analytic capacities and consider the impact of social and political forces on their research topic.

PAR projects with young people also require student researchers to analyze their research context—and the sociopolitical forces that act on this context—to create a viable plan to take action towards implementing their recommendations. For example, young people whose action phase of their research project is to hold an accountability session with policymakers (such as school administrators or elected government representatives) need to understand how their recommendations for action will likely be perceived and responded to by these stakeholders. If the research team is recommending that resources be invested in a program to improve their educational or developmental outcomes, they need to understand the limitations that policymakers face, the stated and unstated reasons that this change has not yet happened, and the perceptions or misperceptions that may be barriers to implementation of their action research recommendations. Therefore, successful PAR projects with youth require that student researchers build their analysis skills to understand the nuances of the research contexts that their selected research issue is nested within.

Recommendations for Practice: Participatory Action Research

Participatory action research (PAR) with youth is an emergent field. Recent research shows that it is a successful framework and approach to enhancing young people's engagement, particularly for those enrolled in under-resourced school districts. There are several implications for ways that instructors inside and outside of schools can support high levels of youth involvement in participatory action research projects with youth, as set out in what follows.

1. *Community partners and funders of PAR projects should understand that it takes time to implement the action phase of the research project.* The action phase can be difficult to complete within the time frame of a single academic year. In a project that lasts for only seven to nine months, oftentimes the action phase entails that the PAR project's participants present their research findings and recommendations to an accountability session with policymakers, administrators, elected officials and other decision-makers. In such a community forum, accountability session or town hall meeting, the research team might present their research recommendations in order to secure commitment from adults to implement these recommendations. In this case, the research team might deliberately build a coalition with a network of adult supporters—an alliance of youth advocates, a community organizing group or a task force—who are willing to hold such decision-makers accountable for implementing this decision over the next year or several years.

Community partners, funders and other supporters might need to expect that long-term action research recommendations, such as recommendations for substantial school or institutional improvements, or community development projects, may need two or more years for the results of a fully implemented action research phase to be seen. For example, it might take several years to build a new neighborhood park, plan and build a teen center, create a professional development curriculum for teachers aiming to engage struggling students, or create and implement a school-wide bilingual program. Foundation funders, community partners and other supporters of PAR projects should understand that it is important to continue to support PAR projects with young people for at least a second year (and perhaps multiple years) to see long-term community development changes. The fact that foundations are already shifting towards multiple-year grant-making cycles to fund nonprofit organizations for three to five years may enable them to better support PAR projects.

2. *Youth-led PAR project community partners and funders should understand that a small number of student researchers are able to impact large systems to scale.* While there has been a funding trend to expect that youth programs and projects reach the greatest number of young people, it is important for funders to understand that small numbers of student researchers, say 4–12, in PAR projects with youth are capable of effecting large-scale change. Community partners, funders,

researchers, universities and other supporters of PAR projects should not necessarily expect the PAR model to be used to scale by anticipating that large
numbers of young people will join the research team. Rather, a small youth-led
PAR team can impact large systems to scale by evaluating these systems and
making system-wide recommendations for implementation. These large systems
might be a school district, a department of children and family services, or a
school-, organization- or city-wide policy.

Youth organizing, in which young people identify issues of concern and
mobilize other young people to create campaigns to take action to achieve their
goals, has not only contributed to youth and community development, but also
emerged as a useful strategy for school reform (Warren, Mira & Nikundiwe,
2008). Similarly, PAR with youth may prove useful as a youth development
strategy, a community development strategy and a school reform strategy. While
PAR projects often aim to improve institutions and communities, in the PAR
model such large-scale improvements generally occur when only a small
number of research team members are involved. Researchers, universities,
funders and other PAR project partners should expect that PAR projects can
effect systemic change provided that the projects are investigating research questions relevant to large systems or are collaborating with alliances, coalitions,
groups or networks (or other PAR groups) in ways that can result in large-scale
changes.

3. *Participatory action research with youth should be embraced as a positive youth development approach to build youth leadership, voice, skills and agency.* Given the positive
youth development field's emphasis on supporting youth voice and young
people as assets in contributing to community development, the PAR model is
uniquely positioned to be used as an approach in positive youth development
practice. Youth-led PAR projects offer a framework and approach to reach positive youth development outcomes such as building youth leadership, voice,
skills and agency. Youth development organizations have already hosted PAR
projects at their organizations. Youth development practitioners, organizers,
researchers, educators and other advocates of young people's healthy development may have a role in making more explicit connections between the emergent field of PAR with youth and the established positive youth development
field—both in research and in practice.

Implications for Policy and Planning

Critical youth studies scholarship (Griffin, 1993, Lesko, 2012; Wyn & White,
1997) and positive youth development research (Damon, 2004; Wheeler, 2002;
Zeldin, 2004) discuss the ways in which the voice of youth is often delegitimized both in U.S. society at large and in youth development approaches and
practices. Both these literatures discuss the ways in which youth are not seen as

experts. However, youth, including underserved and marginalized youth, are closest to the problems they face, and we need their input and expertise in order to find solutions to these problems (Irizarry, 2011). Policies designed to address these problems that do not incorporate youth input and perspectives are at risk of not working. When policymakers are able to have young people sit at the table, it is more likely that they will be able to create viable, relevant policies that work in local contexts. Participatory action research with young people is well positioned as a community-based method that can infuse youth input and recommendations into the policy-making process.

It is important to include young people, particularly marginalized youth, as decision-makers in curriculum, planning and policies that directly impact them. When the intended beneficiaries of policies are involved in policymaking and planning, the policies are more likely to be relevant to local contexts and succeed in meeting identified needs. In addition, participatory planning and policymaking processes can lead to greater community buy-in and support. When young people are involved in designing and planning community development efforts that aim to benefit youth, this involvement often generates enthusiasm and excitement in both youth and adult residents. Local policy can be informed by youth-led research, but these projects have to be supported with resources and funding. The youth participatory action process needs time before the long-term results, such as the building of a youth center, are seen. The results might only become visible in the second or third year of a project. Funders and other stakeholders need to understand that the results take time.

The youth-led PAR project model works with a small number of young people and aims to greatly impact them. Funders and policymakers need to understand that these projects can be highly successful when projects work with a small number of young people and projects do not necessarily need to take the model to a larger scale. The PAR process can be taken to scale when project goals, such as building a youth center, aim to influence many young people and adults over time. In addition, a youth research team of 4–12 members can influence whole systems by evaluating systems through their action research project. For example, there are PAR projects in the United States in which student researchers evaluate their own school districts, their social work agencies, and their city's low-income housing services to assess how these systems succeed in meeting their goals of benefiting youth. PAR with youth can be a model that goes to scale if a small group of student researchers build coalitions with other PAR projects and with adult allies and alliances (such as a youth task force) so as to impact communities on a larger scale. PAR projects might need to build coalitions with other groups, such as grassroots community organizing groups, to develop the infrastructure of neglected communities that are not democratically represented. These alliances and coalitions to ensure that institutions democratically represent the interests of all their constituents can both strengthen civil society and support an active, participatory democracy.

Implications for Future Research

More research is needed to investigate and further distill other specific strategies youth-led PAR uses to achieve positive developmental outcomes of youth participation, leadership and agency. Additional research is needed to examine the questions: What would policymakers gain by involving young people? And how does the PAR process facilitate or impede student researchers' analysis of their neighborhood? Given the student researchers' personal development during their research-based efforts to develop their neighborhood, more research is needed to understand the question: What is the relationship between individual development and community development? Research that examines the role of coalitions between youth-led PAR projects and local community organizing groups would be valuable in understanding community development processes. While not the focus of this examination, this case suggests that PAR goals such as building a teen center were more likely to succeed in collaboration with community organizers, who employed the power of numbers to challenge decision-makers to develop community infrastructure in communities that are not democratically represented.

Further, more research is needed to investigate how young people compare and contrast positive youth development approaches, youth organizing and participatory action research with youth and school learning. Academic research contrasting different approaches to youth leadership development may provide inside views on the nuances of youth–adult partnerships and the ways in which adults can act as allies to support and guide youth-led initiatives.

While gender differences between student researchers and instructors did not emerge as one of the salient themes in this investigation in comparison to other themes, future research may focus on examining the significance of adult staff in reflecting the genders of the student researchers or in being trained to work with a range of genders to successfully instruct youth-led inquiry projects. More research on the connection between individual and community development would be instrumental to understanding the experiences of young people in both positive youth development and PAR strategies aiming to increase leadership. Though not a focus of this examination, there was a connection between individual development and community development. Finally, longitudinal studies would be valuable in measuring the longer-term impacts on young people of a pedagogy of praxis and its components of sociopolitical analysis development, relational learning, and the experiencing adults using a *power with* approach to youth–adult partnerships.

Discussion

Owing to the inequality gaps between high- and low-income communities, to bridge the achievement gap within schools a combination of both in-school and out-of-school-time approaches are needed to decrease the inequality gaps between high- and low-income students and to help all students to excel in schools. It is important to support young people's healthy development using youth development approaches both in school and out of school, beginning in middle school and continuing through high school. For example, a staff member from Representing Ourselves, Emelda, explains why she referred Victor to the Central Youth United project and why his participation in it might have been important for Victor:

> We first referred Victor [to the CYU project] because in the work that we've done we've seen that by high school a lot of kids have made a decision about what they're gonna do. And I really feel like middle school is an important age for young people to try different things, get involved in different projects, activities, whatever—to find something that they like. And middle school is a really critical age for young people to make a decision about what they want—not what they want to do with their lives, like, "What am I gonna be when I grow up?" But whether or not they want to live or die. And that's the real situation right now. That's a decision that they have to make: if they want to live or die. And I was pushing to have Victor on there and I know Jocelyn kind of wanted older kids—only high school. But I was like, "Well, what if he's 13?" So I'm glad that Victor has stayed on this whole time. Because just back to our model, "It takes the hood to save the hood ... So I thought it would be really good for Victor since he's so young to be introduced to this work and just to increase his awareness about community involvement at a young age. So that he can kind of continue that and take it into his high school years.

Young people's growth and development may be bolstered by their experiences with community involvement at a young age. For healthy youth development, research has found that it is important that young people experience a sense of agency to transform institutions and systems in their environment for the greater good of society (Lerner et al., 2002). Therefore, for healthy youth development it is important that there are structured opportunities for young people's community involvement aiming to improve their communities. Positive youth development approaches may be needed both within schools and beyond school walls to holistically support all students' healthy development. Both in schools and in community-based organizations, nonprofit staff members and educators might create a synergy in their collective efforts to effectively help all young people to thrive and succeed in reaching their visions for themselves.

As schools and educators face difficulties in engaging young people, it may be necessary to look beyond school walls to investigate active practices in non-school settings that are successfully engaging these same young people. It may be that reconceptualizing young people as assets in working together to solve community problems will lead to an increase in student engagement. Indeed, when young people's experience and expertise are valued through pedagogical approaches, motivation and active participation increase. When educational projects align with young people's values and visions to improve their institutions and communities, learners become highly engaged and committed to learning goals.

Finally, student engagement may be significantly bolstered when adult educators—both within and beyond schools—share power with students and support and guide students in directing their own learning and curriculum. It is this framework and approach that participatory action research with young people offers schools and community-based settings. PAR projects with youth are an approach that can not only engage young people, but also include young people's input and knowledge in the policies designed to benefit them. Policies aiming to address these problems without incorporating youth input and perspectives are at risk of being ineffective, irrelevant and not suited to local contexts. Young people are the ones closest to these problems they face and we need their input and perspectives to find solutions to these problems. In including the input of the people the policies aim to reach, it is more likely that these policies will be relevant, successful and sustainable in local contexts. Participatory action research with youth is well positioned as a community-based method that can infuse youth input and recommendations in the policy-making process both in school-wide policies and in community development policies.

REFERENCES

Abrams, L. M., Pedulla, J. J., & Madaus, G. F. (2003). Views from the classroom: Teachers' opinions of statewide testing programs. *Theory into Practice, 42*(1), 18–29.

Adams, M., Blumenfeld, W. J., Castañeda, C., Hackman, H. W., Peters, M. L., & Zúñiga, C. (2013). *Readings for diversity and social justice* (3rd ed.). New York: Routledge.

Antrop-González, R., & De Jesús, A. (2006). Toward a theory of critical care in urban small school reform: Examining structures and pedagogies of caring in two Latino community-based schools. *International Journal of Qualitative Studies in Education, 19*(4), 409–433.

Atweh, B., & Burton, L. (1995). Students as researchers: Rationale and critique. *British Educational Research Journal, 21*(5), 561–575.

Atweh, B., Christensen, C., & Dornan, L. (1998). Students as action researchers: Partnerships for social justice. In B. Atweh, S. Kemmis & P. Weeks (Eds.), *Action research in practice: Partnerships for social justice in education* (pp. 114–138). London: Routledge.

Baizernian, M., & Magnuson, D. (1996). Do we still need youth as a social stage? *Young: Nordic Journal of Youth Research, 4*(3), 32–42.

Baldridge, J. V., Curtis, D. V., Ecker, G. P., & Riley, G. L. (1977). Alternative models of governance in higher education. In G. C. Riley & J. V. Baldridge (Eds.), *Governing academic organizations: New problems, new perspectives* (pp. 2–25). Berkeley, CA: McCutchan.

Bartolomé, L. I. (1994). Beyond the methods fetish: Toward a humanizing pedagogy. *Harvard Educational Review, 58*(3), 280–298.

Bautista, M. A., Bertrand, M., Morrell, E., Scorza, D. A., & Matthews, C. (2013). Participatory action research and city youth: Methodological insights from the Council of Youth Research. *Teachers College Record, 115*(10), 1–23.

Berg, M., & Schensul, J. (2004). Youth-led participatory action research for social change. *Practicing Anthropology, 26*(2) (special issue), 2–5.

Borda, O. F. (1979). Investigating reality in order to transform it: The Colombian experience. *Dialectical Anthropology, 4*(1), 33–55.

Boykin, A. W., & Noguera, P. (2011). *Creating the opportunity to learn: Moving from research to practice to close the achievement gap*. Alexandria, VA: ASCD.

Brookfield, S. (1987). *Developing critical thinkers*. Milton Keynes, UK: Open University Press.

Brown-Jeffy, S., & Cooper, J. E. (2011). Toward a conceptual framework of culturally relevant pedagogy: An overview of the conceptual and theoretical literature. *Teacher Education Quarterly, 38*(1), 65–84.

Brydon-Miller, M., Davids, I., Jaitli, N., Lykes, M. B., Schensul, J., & Williams, S. (2009). Popular education and action research. In S. Noffke & B. Somekh (Eds.), *The Sage handbook of educational action research* (pp. 495–507). Thousand Oaks, CA: Sage.

Bundick, M. J., Quaglia, R. J., Corso, M. J., & Haywood, D. E. (2014). Promoting student engagement in the classroom. *Teachers College Record, 116*.

Cahill, C., Rios-Moore, I., & Threatts, T. (2008). Different eyes/open eyes: Community-based participatory action research. In J. Cammarota & M. Fine (Eds.), *Revolutionizing education: Youth participatory action research* (pp. 89–124). New York: Routledge.

Camino, L., & Zeldin, S. (2002). Making the transition to community youth development: Emerging roles and competencies for youth-serving organizations and youth workers. *Community Youth Development Journal, 3*, 70–78.

Cammarota, J., & Fine, M. (Eds.). (2008). *Revolutionizing education: Youth participatory action research*. New York: Routledge.

Cammarota, J., & Romero, A. F. (2009). A social justice epistemology and pedagogy for Latina/o students: Transforming public education with participatory action research. *New Directions for Youth Development, 2009*(123), 53–65.

Cannella, C. M. (2008). Faith in process, faith in people: Confronting policies of social disinvestment with PAR as pedagogy for expansion. In J. Cammarota & M. Fine (Eds.), *Revolutionizing education: Youth participatory action research* (pp. 189–212). New York: Routledge.

Carter, P. L., & Welner, K. G. (2013). *Closing the opportunity gap: What America must do to give every child an even chance*. New York: Oxford University Press.

Ceaser, D. (2014). Unlearning adultism at Green Shoots: A reflexive ethnographic analysis of age inequality within an environmental education programme. *Ethnography and Education, 9*(2), 167–181.

Chávez, V., & Soep, E. (2005). Youth radio and the pedagogy of collegiality. *Harvard Educational Review, 75*(4), 409–434.

Checkoway, B. (2011). What is youth participation? *Children and Youth Services Review, 33*(2), 340–345.

Chow, E. N. (1999). Exploring critical feminist pedagogy: The dialogic, experiential and participatory (DEP) approach in teaching and learning. Paper presented at the Annual Meeting of the American Sociological Association, Chicago.

Connell, J. P., Gambone, M. A., & Smith, T. (2001). Youth development in community settings: Challenges to our field and our approach. In P. L. Benson & K. J. Pittman (Eds.), *Trends in youth development: Visions, realities and challenges* (pp. 291–308). Norwell, MA: Kluwer Academic Publishers.

Cooper, C., & Cromey, A. (2000). Teachers and students as action researchers: Using data daily. *NCREL's Learning Point, 2*(2), 8–12.

Cothran, D. J., & Ennis, C. D. (2000). Building bridges to student engagement: Communicating respect and care for students in urban high schools. *Journal of Research and Development in Education, 33*(2), 106–117.

Damon, W. (2004). What is positive youth development? *Annals of the American Academy of Political and Social Science, 591*, 13–24.

Darling-Hammond, L. (2010). *The flat world and education: How America's commitment to equity will determine our future*. New York: Teachers College Press.

Deci, E. L., & Ryan, R. M. (2000). The "what" and "why" of goal pursuits: Human needs and the self-determination of behavior. *Psychological Inquiry, 11*(4), 227–268.

De Jesús, A. (2012). Authentic caring and community driven school reform: The case of El Puente Academy for Peace and Justice. In M. Hantzopoulos & A. R. Tyner-Mullings (Eds.), *Critical small schools: Beyond privatization in New York City urban educational reform* (pp. 63–78). Charlotte, NC: Information Age Publishing.

De Jesús, A., & Antrop-González, R. (2006). Instrumental relationships and high expectations: Exploring critical care in two Latino community-based schools. *Intercultural Education, 17*(3), 281–299.

De los Reyes, E. (2002). *Pockets of hope: How students and teachers change the world*. Westport, CT: Greenwood.

Delpit, L. (2006). *Other people's children: Cultural conflict in the classroom* (rev. ed.). New York: New Press.

Eccles, J., & Gootman, J. A. (Eds.). (2002). *Community programs to support youth development*. National Research Council and Institute of Medicine: Committee on Community-Level Programs for Youth, Division of Behavioral and Social Sciences and Education. Washington, DC: National Academy of Sciences.

Eccles, J. S., & Wigfield, A. (2002). Motivational beliefs, values, and goals. *Annual Review of Psychology, 53*(1), 109–132.

Elden, M., & Levin, M. (1991). Cogenerative learning: Bringing participation into action research. In W. F. Whyte (Ed.), *Participatory action research* (pp. 127–142). London: Sage.

Ellsworth, E. (1989). Why doesn't this feel empowering? Working through the repressive myths of critical pedagogy. *Harvard Educational Review, 59*(3), 297–324.

Espiritu, Y. L. (2003). *Home bound: Filipino lives across cultures, communities and countries*. Berkeley: University of California Press.

Fairclough, N. (2013). *Critical discourse analysis: The critical study of language*. London: Routledge.

Fals-Borda, O., & Rahman, M. A. (Eds.). (1991). *Action and knowledge: Breaking the monopoly with participatory action research*. New York: Apex Press.

Fauske, H. (1996). Changing youth: Transition to adulthood in Norway. *Young: Nordic Journal of Youth Research, 1*(1), 35–51.

Fine, M. (2012). Youth participatory action research. In N. Lesko & S. Talburt (Eds.), *Keywords in youth studies: Tracing affects, movements, knowledges* (pp. 318–324). New York: Routledge.

Fine, M., Torre, M. E., Boudin, K., Bowen, I., Clark, J., Hylton, D., Martinez, M., Rivera, M., Roberts, R. A., Smart, P., & Upegui, D. (2003). Participatory action research: From within and behind bars. In P. Camic, J. E. Rhodes & L. Yardley (Eds.), *Qualitative research in psychology: Expanding perspectives in methodology and design* (pp. 173–198). Washington, DC: American Psychological Association.

Fine, M., Torre, M. E., Burns, A., & Payne, Y. A. (2007). Youth research/participatory methods for reform. In D. Thiessen & A. Cook-Sather (Eds.), *International handbook of student experience in elementary and secondary school* (pp. 805–828). Dordrecht: Springer.

Finn, J. (2003). Text and turbulence: Representing adolescence as pathology in the human services. *Childhood, 8*(2), 167–191.

Fisher, M. T. (2007). *Writing in rhythm: Spoken word poetry in urban classrooms*. New York: Teachers College Press.

Freire, P. (1970/2000). *Pedagogy of the oppressed* (30th anniversary ed.). New York: Continuum.

Freire, P. (1982). Creating alternative research methods: Learning to do it by doing it. In B. Hall, A. Gillette & R. Tandon (Eds.) *Creating knowledge: A monopoly* (pp. 29–37). Toronto: Participatory Research Network.

Freire, P. (1998). *Pedagogy of freedom: Ethics, democracy, and civic courage*. Lanham, MD: Rowman & Littlefield.

Freire, P. (2001). Education for critical consciousness. In P. Freire, *The Paulo Freire reader* (2nd ed.) (A. M. A. Freire & D. Macedo, Eds.) (pp. 80–110). New York: Continuum.

Gadotti, M. (1996). *Pedagogy of praxis: A dialectical philosophy of education*. Albany, NY: SUNY Press.

Garza, R. (2009). Latino and White high school students' perceptions of caring behaviors: Are we culturally responsive to our students? *Urban Education, 44*(3), 297–321.

Gay, G. (2000). *Culturally responsive teaching: Theory, research, and practice*. New York: Teachers College Press.

Gay, G. (2010). *Culturally responsive teaching: Theory, research and practice* (2nd ed.). New York: Teachers College Press.

Gee, J. P. (2014a). *Social linguistics and literacies: Ideology in discourses*. London: Routledge.

Gee, J. P. (2014b). Discourse analysis: What makes it critical? In R. Rogers (Ed.), *An introduction to critical discourse analysis in education* (pp. 23–45). New York: Routledge.

Gibson, C. (2001). *From inspiration to participation: A review of perspectives on youth civic engagement*. New York: Grantmaker Forum on Community and National Service.

Gillis, J. (1993). Vanishing youth: The uncertain place of the young in a global age. *Young: Nordic Journal of Youth Research, 1*(1), 3–17.

Ginwright, S. (2008). Collective radical imagination: Youth participatory action research and the art of emancipatory knowledge. In J. Cammarota & M. Fine (Eds.), *Revolutionizing education: Youth participatory action research* (pp. 13–22). New York: Routledge.

Ginwright, S., & Cammarota, J. (2002). New terrain in youth development: The promise of a social justice approach. *Social Justice, 29*(4), 82–95.

Ginwright, S., & James, T. (2002). From assets to agents of change. *New Directions for Youth Development, 2002*(96), 27–46.

Giroux, H. (1983). Ideology and agency in the process of schooling. *Journal of Education, 165*(1), 12–34.

GLSEN (2004). *Jump-start #7: Creating youth–adult partnerships*. New York: GLSEN-Student Organizing.

González, N., Moll, L. C., & Amanti, C. (Eds.). (2013). *Funds of knowledge: Theorizing practices in households, communities, and classrooms*. New York: Routledge.

Gore, J. (2003). What we can do for you! What *can* "we" do for "you"? Struggling over empowerment in critical and feminist pedagogy. In A. Darder, M. Baltodano & R. D. Torres (Eds.), *The critical pedagogy reader* (pp. 331–350). New York: RoutledgeFalmer.

Greene, M. (2008). Response to chapter 3. In J. Cammarota & M. Fine (Eds.), *Revolutionizing education: Youth participatory action research* (pp. 45–48). New York: Routledge.

Griffin, C. (1993). *Representations of youth: The study of youth and adolescence in Britain and America*. Cambridge: Polity Press.

Guishard, M., Fine, M., Doyle, C., Jackson, J., Staten, T., & Webb, A. (2005). The Bronx on the move: Participatory consultation with mothers and youth. *Journal of Educational and Psychological Consultation, 16*(1–2), 35–54.

Hall, B. (1981). Participatory research, popular knowledge, and power: A personal reflection. *Convergence, 44*(2), 6–17.

Hart, R. A. (1992). *Children's participation: From tokenism to citizenship.* Florence: UNICEF Innocenti Research Centre.

Hart, R. A. (1997). Action research with children. In *Children's participation: The theory and practice of involving young citizens in community development and environmental care* (pp. 91–107). New York: UNICEF International Child Development Center.

Heath, S. B. (1983). *Ways with words: Language, life, and work in communities and classrooms.* Cambridge: Cambridge University Press.

Heggen, K. (2000). Marginalisation: On the fringe of the periphery—Youth as a risky life stage? *Young: Nordic Journal of Youth Research, 8*(2), 52–83.

Howard, A. (2008). *Learning privilege: Lessons of power and identity in affluent schooling.* New York: Routledge.

Howard, T. C. (2003). Culturally relevant pedagogy: Ingredients for critical teacher reflection. *Theory Into Practice, 42*(3), 195–202.

Huber, M. S. Q., Frommeyer, J., Weisenbach, A., & Sazama, J. (2003). Giving youth a voice in their own community and personal development: Strategies and impacts of bringing youth to the table. In F. A. Villarruel, D. F. Perkins, L. M. Borden & J. G. Keith (Eds.), *Community youth development: Programs, policies, and practices* (pp. 394–404). Thousand Oaks, CA: Sage.

Innovation Center for Community and Youth Development (ICCYD). (2001). Rejecting the isolation of youth: Adults and organizations dramatically benefit. *Nonprofit Quarterly, 8*(4), 6–11. Boston: Third Sector New England.

Irby, M., Ferber, T., Pittman, K., Tolman, J., & Yohalem, N. (2001). *Youth action: Youth contributing to communities, communities contributing to youth.* Takoma Park, MD: Forum for Youth Investment, International Youth Foundation.

Irizarry, J. G. (2009). Reinvigorating multicultural education through participatory action research. *Multicultural Perspectives, 11*(4), 194–199.

Irizarry, J. G. (2011). *The Latinization of U.S. schools: Successful teaching and learning in shifting cultural contexts.* Boulder, CO: Paradigm.

Jocson, K. (2008). *Youth poets: Empowering literacies in and out of schools.* New York: Peter Lang.

Kenway, J., & Modra, H. (1992). Feminist pedagogy and emancipatory possibilities. In C. Luke & J. Gore (Eds.), *Feminisms and critical pedagogy* (pp. 137–166). London: Routledge.

Kinloch, V. (2011). *Urban literacies: Critical perspectives on language, learning, and community.* New York: Teachers College Press.

Kinloch, V. (2012). *Crossing boundaries: Teaching and learning with urban youth.* New York: Teachers College Press.

Kirshner, B. (2007). Introduction: Youth activism as a context for learning and development. *American Behavioral Scientist, 51*(3), 367–379.

Kirshner, B. (2010). Productive tensions in youth participatory action research. *Yearbook of the National Society for the Study of Education, 109*(1), 238–251.

Kirshner, B., Possoboni, K., & Jones, H. (2011). Learning how to manage bias: A case study of youth participatory action research. *Applied Developmental Science, 15*(3), 140–155.

Klem, A. M., & Connell, J. P. (2004). Relationships matter: Linking teacher support to student engagement and achievement. *Journal of School Health, 74*(7), 262–273.

Kreisberg, S. (1992). *Transforming power: Domination, empowerment and education.* Albany, NY: SUNY Press.

Ladson-Billings, G. (1995). Toward a theory of culturally relevant pedagogy. *American Educational Research Journal, 32*(3), 465–491.

Ladson-Billings, G. (2014). Culturally relevant pedagogy 2.0: a.k.a. the remix. *Harvard Educational Review, 84*(1), 74–84.

Ladson-Billings, G., & Tate, W. F. (2006). *Education research in the public interest: Social justice, action, and policy.* New York: Teachers College Press.

Larson, R. (2006). Positive youth development, willful adolescents, and mentoring. *Journal of Community Psychology, 34*(6), 677–689.

Larson, R. W. (2000). Toward a psychology of positive youth development. *American Psychologist, 55*, 170–183.

Larson, R. W., & Angus, R. M. (2011). Adolescents' development of skills for agency in youth programs: Learning to think strategically. *Child Development, 82*(1), 277–294.

Larson, R., Walker, K., & Pearce, N. (2005). A comparison of youth-driven and adult-driven programs: Balancing inputs from youth and adults. *Journal of Community Psychology, 33*(1), 57–74.

Lave, J., & Wenger, E. (2003). *Situated learning: Legitimate peripheral participation* (12th ed.). Cambridge: Cambridge University Press.

LeFrançois, B. A. (2014). Adultism. In T. Teo (Ed.), *Encyclopedia of critical psychology* (pp. 47–49). New York: Springer.

Lerner, R. M., Brentano, C., Dowling, E. M., & Anderson, P. M. (2002). Positive youth development: Thriving as the basis of personhood and civil society. *New Directions for Youth Development, 2002*(95), 11–33.

Lesko, N. (2012). *Act your age! A cultural construction of adolescence* (2nd ed.). New York: Routledge.

Lesko, N., & Talburt, S. (Eds.). (2012). *Keywords in youth studies: Tracing affects, movements, knowledges.* New York: Routledge.

Luttrell, W. (2003). *Pregnant bodies, fertile minds: Gender, race, and the schooling of pregnant teens.* New York: Routledge.

Mahoney, J. L., Eccles, J. S., & Larson, R. W. (2004). Processes of adjustment in organized out-of-school activities: Opportunities and risks. *New Directions for Youth Development, 2004*(101), 115–144.

Mahoney, J. L., Larson, R. W., & Eccles, J. S. (Eds.). (2005). *Organized activities as contexts of development: Extracurricular activities, after-school and community programs.* Hillsdale, NJ: Lawrence Erlbaum.

McIntyre, A. (2000). Participatory action research. In *Inner-city kids: Adolescents confront life and violence in an urban community* (pp. 13–33). New York: New York University Press.

McLaughlin, M. (2000). *Community counts: How youth organizations matter for community development.* Washington, DC: Public Education Network.

McLaughlin, M., Irby, M., & Langman, J. (1994). *Urban sanctuaries: Neighborhood organizations in the lives and futures of inner-city youth.* San Francisco: Jossey-Bass.

Mehan, H. (1993). Beneath the skin and between the ears: A case study in the politics of representation. In S. Chaiklin & J. Lave (Eds.), *Understanding practice: Perspectives on activity and context* (pp. 241–268). Cambridge: Cambridge University Press.

Milner, H. R. IV. (2010). *Start where you are, but don't stay there: Understanding diversity, opportunity gaps, and teaching in today's classrooms.* Cambridge, MA: Harvard Education Press.

Milner, H. R. IV. (2011). Culturally relevant pedagogy in a diverse urban classroom. *Urban Review, 43*(1), 66–89.

Mitra, D. L. (2004). The significance of students: Can increasing "student voice" in schools lead to gains in youth development? *Teachers College Record, 106*(4), 651–688.

Mitra, D. L. (2009). Student voice and student roles in education policy and policy reform. In G. Sykes, B. Schneider & D. N. Plank (Eds.), *Handbook of education policy research* (pp. 819–830). New York: Routledge, for the American Educational Research Association.

Moll, L. C. (1992). Literacy research in community and classrooms: A sociocultural approach. In R. Beach, J. L. Green, M. L. Kamil & T. Shanahan (Eds.), *Multidisciplinary perspectives in literacy research* (pp. 211–244). Urbana, IL: National Conference on Research in English and National Council of Teachers of English.

Moll, L. C., Armanti, C., Neff, D., & González, N. (1992). Funds of knowledge for teaching: Using a qualitative approach to connect homes and classrooms. *Theory Into Practice, 31*(2), 132–141.

Moll, L. C., & Greenberg, J. (1990). Creating zones of possibilities: Combining social contexts for instruction. In L. C. Moll (Ed.), *Vygotsky and education* (pp. 319–348). Cambridge: Cambridge University Press.

Morrell, E. (2004). Bakhtin's dialogic pedagogy: Implications for critical pedagogy, literacy education, and teacher research in the United States. *Journal of Russian and East European Psychology, 42*(6), 89–94.

Morrell, E. (2006). Youth-initiated research as a tool for advocacy and change in urban schools. In S. Ginwright, P. Noguera & J. Cammarota (Eds.), *Beyond resistance: Youth activism and community change: New democratic possibilities for practice and policy for America's youth* (pp. 111–128). New York: Routledge.

Morrell, E. (2008). Six summers of YPAR: Learning, action, and change in urban education. In J. Cammarota & M. Fine (Eds.), *Revolutionizing education: Youth participatory action research* (pp. 155–184). New York: Routledge.

Newman, R. S., & Schwager, M. T. (1992). Student perceptions and academic help-seeking. In D. H. Schunk & J. L. Meece (Eds.), *Student perceptions in the classroom* (pp. 123–146). Mahwah, NJ: Lawrence Erlbaum.

Noguera, P. A. (2003). The trouble with Black boys: The role and influence of environmental and cultural factors on the academic performance of African American males. *Urban Education, 38*(4), 431–459.

Noguera, P. A. (2014). Urban schools and the Black male "challenge." In H. R. Milner IV and K. Lomotey (Eds.), *Handbook of urban education* (pp. 114–128). New York: Routledge.

Noguera, P., & Wing, J. Y. (2006). *Unfinished business: Closing the racial achievement gap in our schools.* San Francisco: Jossey-Bass.

Paris, D. (2012). Culturally sustaining pedagogy: A needed change in stance, terminology, and practice. *Educational Researcher, 41*(3), 93–97.

Paris, D., & Alim, H. S. (2014). What are we seeking to sustain through culturally sustaining pedagogy? A loving critique forward. *Harvard Educational Review, 84*(1), 85–100.

Patel, L. (2012). Contact zones, problem posing and critical consciousness. *Pedagogies: An International Journal, 7*(4), 333–346.

Patel, L. (2013). *Youth held at the border: Immigration, education and the politics of inclusion.* New York: Teachers College Press.

Payne, Y. A., Starks, B. C., & Gibson, L. R. (2009). Contextualizing black boys' use of a street identity in high school. *New Directions for Youth Development, 2009*(123), 35–51.

Penuel, W., & Freeman, T. (1997). Participatory action research in youth programming: A theory in use. *Child and Youth Care Forum, 26*(3), 175–185.

Perkins, D. F., & Borden, L. M. (2003). Key elements of community youth development programs. In F. A. Villarruel, D. F. Perkins, L. M. Borden & J. G. Keith (Eds.), *Community youth development: Programs, policies, and practices* (pp. 327–340). Thousand Oaks, CA: Sage.

Perkins, D. F., Borden, L. M., Keith, J. G., Hoppe-Rooney, T. L., & Villarruel, F. A. (2003). Community youth development: Partnership creating a positive world. In F. A. Villarruel, D. F. Perkins, L. M. Borden & J. G. Keith (Eds.), *Community youth development: Programs, policies, and practices* (pp. 1–23). Thousand Oaks, CA: Sage.

Pittman, K. (1996). Community, youth, development: Three goals in search of a connection. *New Designs for Youth Development, 12*(1), 4–8.

Pittman, K. (2000). Balancing the equation: Communities supporting youth, youth supporting communities. *Community Youth Development Journal, 1*(1), 19–24.

Pittman, K., & Wright, M. (1991). *Bridging the gap: A rationale for enhancing the role of community organizations in promoting youth development.* New York: Carnegie Corporation.

Roberts, M. A. (2010). Toward a theory of culturally relevant critical teacher care: African American teachers' definitions and perceptions of care for African American students. *Journal of Moral Education, 39*(4), 449–467.

Rodríguez, L. F., & Brown, T. M. (2009). From voice to agency: Guiding principles for participatory action research with youth. *New Directions for Youth Development, 2009*(123), 19–34.

Rogers, R. (Ed.). (2011). Critical approaches to discourse analysis in educational research. In R. Rogers (Ed.), *An introduction to critical discourse analysis in education* (pp. 1–20). New York: Routledge.

Rolón-Dow, C. (2005). Critical care: A color(full) analysis of care narratives in the schooling experiences of Puerto Rican girls. *American Educational Research Journal, 42*, 77–111.

Romero, A., Cammarota, J., Dominguez, K., Valdez, L., Ramirez, G., & Hernandez, L. (2008). "The opportunity if not the right to see": The social justice education project. In J. Cammarota & M. Fine (Eds.), *Revolutionizing Education: Youth Participatory Action Research* (pp. 131–151). New York: Routledge.

Rothstein, R. (2004). *Class and schools: Using social, economic, and educational reform to close the achievement gap.* Washington, DC: Economic Policy Institute.

Ryan, R., & Deci, E. L. (2000). Self-determination theory and the facilitation of intrinsic motivation, social development, and well-being. *American Psychologist, 55*(1), 68–78.

Sabo, K. (2003a). A Vygotskian perspective on youth participatory evaluation. *New Directions for Evaluation, 2003*(98), 13–24.

Sabo, K. (2003b). Editor's notes: Youth participatory evaluation: A field in the making. *New Directions for Evaluation, 2003*(98), 1–11.

Salomon, L. R. (2003). *Roots of justice: Stories of organizing in communities of color.* San Francisco: Jossey-Bass.

Sazama, J., & Young, K. (2001). *Get the word out!* Somerville, MA: Youth on Board and the Resource Center for Youth and Their Allies.

Scales, P. C., & Leffert, N. (1999). *Developmental assets: A synthesis of scientific research on adolescent development.* Minneapolis: Search Institute.

Shor, I. (1992). *Empowering education: Critical teaching for social change.* Chicago: University of Chicago Press.

Shor, I. (1996). *When students have power: Negotiating authority in a critical pedagogy.* Chicago: University of Chicago Press.

Sleeter, C. E. (2012). Confronting the marginalization of culturally responsive pedagogy. *Urban Education, 47*(3), 562–584.

Spatig, L., Grimes, C., Farrar, J., Gaines, S., Terry, E., Vance, V., & Sadler, C. (2001). Teen girls take on community problems: Lessons learned from the field. Paper presented at the Annual Conference of the Women of Appalachia: Their Heritage and Accomplishments. Zanesville, OH, October.

Stovall, D., & Delgado, N. (2009). "Knowing the ledge": Participatory action research as legal studies for urban high school youth. *New Directions for Youth Development, 2009*(123), 67–81.

Strobel, K., Kirshner, B., O'Donoghue, J., & Wallin McLaughlin, M. (2008). Qualities that attract urban youth to after-school settings and promote continued participation. *Teachers College Record, 110*(8), 1677–1705.

Talburt, S., & Lesko, N. (2012). A history of the present of youth studies. In N. Lesko & S. Talburt (Eds.), *Keywords in youth studies: Tracing affects, movements, knowledges* (pp. 11–23). New York: Routledge.

Torre, M. E., Fine, M., Alexander, N., Billups, A. B., Blanding, Y., Genao, E., Marboe, E., Salah, T., & Urdang, K. (2008). Participatory action research in the contact zone. In J. Cammarota & M. Fine (Eds.), *Revolutionizing education: Youth participatory action research.* New York: Routledge.

Torres, C. A. (1992). Participatory action research and popular education in Latin America. *Qualitative Studies in Education, 5*(1), 51–62.

Tuck, E. (2012). *Urban youth and school pushout: Gateways, get-aways, and the GED.* New York: Routledge.

Tuck, E., Allen, J., Bacha, M., Morales, A., Quinter, S., Thompson, J., & Tuck, M. (2008). PAR praxes for now and future change: The collective of researchers on educational disappointment and desire. In J. Cammarota & M. Fine (Eds.), *Revolutionizing education: Youth participatory action research* (pp. 49–83). New York: Routledge.

Tyack, D. B. (1974). *The one best system: A history of American urban education.* Cambridge, MA: Harvard University Press.

U.S. Department of Education. (2014). *Public high school four-year on-time graduation rates and event drop-out rates: School years 2010–11 and 2011–12.* Washington, DC: National Center for Education Statistics.

Villarruel, F. A., Perkins, D. F. F., Borden, L. M., & Keith, J. G. (2003). Community youth development: Youth voice and activism. In F. A. Villarruel, D. F. F. Perkins, L. M. Borden & J. G. Keith (Eds.), *Community youth development: Programs, policies, and practices* (pp. 394–404). Thousand Oaks, CA: Sage Publications.

Villegas, A. M., & Lucas, T. (2002). *Educating culturally responsive teachers: A coherent approach.* Albany, NY: SUNY Press.

Walton, R. E., & Gaffney, M. E. (1991). Research, action, and participation: The merchant shipping case. In W. F. Whyte (Ed.), *Participatory action research* (pp. 99–126). Newbury Park, CA: Sage.

Warren, M. R. (2005). Communities and schools: A new view of urban education reform. *Harvard Educational Review, 75*(2), 133–173.

Warren, M. R., & Mapp, K. L. (2011). *A match on dry grass: Community organizing as a catalyst for school reform.* New York: Oxford University Press.

Warren, M. R., Mira, M., & Nikundiwe, T. (2008). Youth organizing: From youth development to school reform. *New Directions for Youth Development, 2008*(117), 27–42.

Wasonga, T., Christman, D. E., & Kilmer, L. (2003). Ethnicity, gender and age: Predicting resilience and academic achievement among urban high school students. *American Secondary Education, 32*(1), 62–74.

Watkins, N. D., Larson, R. W., & Sullivan, P. J. (2007). Bridging intergroup difference in a community youth program. *American Behavioral Scientist, 51*(3), 380–402.

Watts, R. J., & Guessous, O. (2006). Sociopolitical development: The missing link in research and policy on adolescents. In S. Ginwright, P. Noguera & J. Cammarota (Eds.), *Beyond resistance: Youth activism and community change: New democratic possibilities for practice and policy for America's youth* (pp. 59–80). New York: Routledge.

Watts, R. J., Williams, N. C., & Jagers, R. J. (2003). Sociopolitical development. *American Journal of Community Psychology, 31*, 185–194.

Wenger, E. (1998). *Communities of practice: Learning, meaning, and identity*. Cambridge: Cambridge University Press.

Wenger, E. (2000). Communities of practice and social learning systems. *Organization, 7*(2), 225–246.

Wenger, E. (2003). *Communities of practice: Learning, meaning, and identity* (8th ed.). Cambridge: Cambridge University Press.

Wheeler, W. (2000). Emerging organizational theory and the youth development organization. *Applied Developmental Science, 4*(1), 47–54.

Wheeler, W. (2002). Youth leadership for development: Civic activism as a component of youth development programming and a strategy for strengthening civil society. In R. Lerner, F. Jacobs & D. Wertlieb (Eds.), *Handbook of applied developmental science: Promoting positive child, adolescent and family development through research, policies and programs. Vol. 2, Enhancing the life chances of youth and families: Contributions of programs, policies, and service systems* (pp. 491–506). Thousand Oaks, CA: Sage.

Whyte, W. F. (Ed.). (1991). *Participatory action research*. Newbury Park, CA: Sage.

Winn, M. (2007). *Writing in rhythm: Spoken word poetry in urban classrooms*. New York: Teachers College Press.

Winn, M. (2011). *Girl time: Literacy, justice, and the school-to-prison pipeline*. New York: Teachers College Press.

Wyn, J. (2000). Negotiating social change: The paradox of youth. *Youth and Society, 32*(2), 165–183.

Wyn, J. (2001). Rethinking youth: Perceptions of young people shape public agenda. *Nonprofit Quarterly, 8*(4), 12–15. Boston: Third Sector New England.

Wyn, J., & White, R. (1997). *Rethinking youth*. Thousand Oaks, CA: Sage.

Zeldin, S. (2004). Youth as agents of community development: Mapping the process and outcomes of youth engaged in organizational governance. *Applied Developmental Science, 8*(2), 75–90.

Zeldin, S., Christens, B. D., & Powers, J. L. (2013). The psychology and practice of youth–adult partnership: Bridging generations for youth development and community change. *American Journal of Community Psychology, 51*(3–4), 385–397.

Zeldin, R., Larson, R., & Camino, L. (Eds.). (2005). Intergenerational relationships and partnerships in community programs: Purpose, practice, and directions for research (Special Issue). *Journal of Community Psychology, 33*(1).

INDEX

Page numbers in *italics* denote tables.